W9-AWP-966

THE SKY'S NO LIMIT

RAYMOND Z. MUNRO

CM, OStJ, OP NN, GCLJ, CL

WITHDRAWN

A TOTEM BOOK
Toronto

First published 1985
by Key Porter Books
This edition published 1986
by TOTEM BOOKS
a division of Collins Publishers
100 Lesmill Road, Don Mills, Ontario

© 1985 by Raymond Z. Munro

All rights reserved. No part of this publication may be reproduced, stored in a retrieval system, or transmitted in any form or by any means, electronic, mechanical, photocopying, recording or otherwise, without the prior written permission of the publishers.

Canadian Cataloguing in Publication Data

    Munro, Raymond Z., 1921–
      The sky's no limit

    Includes index.
    ISBN 0-00-217743-9

    1. Munro, Raymond Z., 1921– . 2. Journalists –
    Canada – Biography. 3. Air pilots – Canada –
    Biography. 4. Adventure and adventurers – Canada –
    Biography.   I. Title.

    PN4913.M75A3   1986   070'.92'4   C86-094227-9

Printed and bound in Canada

CONTENTS

FOREWORD

by Richard Rohmer

RAYMOND MUNRO'S LIFE clearly demonstrates the old saying that truth is stranger than fiction. Surely, no one in Canada has survived more crashes—in aircraft, motor vehicles, and balloons—than Munro. Like his grit and determination, his body has been battered many times, but never destroyed.

Raymond Munro is a consummate aviator. His skills as a pilot, his lust for the unique experience, and his insatiable taste for high adventure have placed him in the centre of countless hair-raising episodes. In this book, he recounts some of these events, many of which are so incredible that one is tempted to ask, "Is this true or the product of a fertile imagination?" Don't worry. His stories are true. His many medals, newspaper clippings, citations, and photographs attest to that.

Now silver-haired, and still strikingly handsome, Munro is filled with the same driving energy. He has combined all his impressive journalistic talents to do what few people can—tell the story of his own life. In doing so he has produced an action-packed record of his experiences during childhood, through his experiences in war and peace as a pilot, as a fearless investigative reporter, as a highly respected newspaper photographer, and as a man never afraid to take a valid risk in any area of endeavour. He is truly a remarkable Canadian, upon whom honours and awards have been heaped from all parts of the world, making him by far the most honoured man in his own country—and an Irish baron to boot.

Canadians drab and colourless, you say? Not Colonel Raymond Munro.

O. Henry once said, "Fortune is the prize to be won, adventure the road to it, and chance is what may lurk in the shadows." It was to those views that I held in all my endeavours. And when my opinion on death was sought, I merely asked how anyone who had fulfilled his adventurous earthly quest could fear it, since death itself is the ultimate adventure.

PROLOGUE

THE FIRST and only time I ever prayed for the safe return of my body to the sanctuary of the good earth I was flying low over the English Channel on the Brest side. A cannon shell had just exploded in the wing of my Spitfire, shredding the aluminium wrapping. The airplane was corkscrewing through the shrinking airspace towards the green and greedy sea.

"Oh Lord! Get me out of this one and I'll be your servant forever," I prayed — the Jesus factor.

There was little chance I'd survive. I was too close to the sea for the parachute to open in time. Besides, my Mae West life-jacket was riddled with holes that had been punched through its dual bladders and painted roundels during a beer-sodden dart tournament the night before. If I had jumped, I'd have drowned.

I had just attacked a German U-boat that threatened the convoy I was supposed to protect. On my first pass over the disappearing wave-washed conning tower, my cannon shells had exploded in the water along side of it and I'd hauled the Spitfire up with gut-wrenching force into the grey clouds. With my eyes glued to the gauges, I'd pulled into a tight loop. Powering off on the way down, I'd steadied the plane, caught the target in the gun sight, and pressed the firing button.

Suddenly, there'd been one hell of an explosion. An older, wiser man, someone with a surfeit of intelligence and a paucity of fear, might have known instinctively that a high-explosive shell had detonated in the breech of his wing-mounted cannon. But I thought I'd been hit from astern and was breaking up.

It was then the Spitfire rolled uncontrollably onto its back and angled, nose down, towards the swelling sea.

It was July 1941. I was nineteen.

DANGEROUS JOURNEY

AS I STOOD in the desert on the outskirts of Phoenix, Arizona, I was charged with emotion. Two weeks earlier I had run away from my family in Toronto. In that time, I had covered 2,500 miles, hitch-hiked in cars and trucks, and spent eleven nights in police cells where I sought refuge from the perils of the street. I was just sixteen years old.

It was the summer of 1937, and the face of America was gaunt from the crippling financial depression that stripped many people of their incomes, privileges, and pride, and made having a job a prize above all others.

Just ahead on the highway, I saw some cars turning onto a dirt road past a gaudy, painted sign stuck in the desert sand. It fairly screamed at passing vehicles: AIR SHOW! ACROBATICS! DOGFIGHT! RIBBON CUTTING! ACCURACY BOMBING! PARACHUTE JUMP! PASSENGER RIDES! HOT DOGS! COLD POP! $1.00 A CARLOAD.

I walked up the road to the one-room shack the cars had to pass. Beyond it was a small airstrip on which two biplanes were parked. "It'll cost you a quarter, kid," the skinny man said, as he collected a dollar from each driver. I didn't answer. I just walked back along the road until I saw a car with two elderly people in it. I politely explained to them that I had no money and that it would cost them nothing to let me ride in with them.

In minutes, I was within stroking distance of the two airplanes. A portly, vested man wearing a bowler hat and smoking a cigar stood in front of them, his eyes flicking this way and that to catch any kids who tried to duck under the rope barrier.

"I'll guard both the planes for a dollar," I offered. "I like airplanes and I won't hurt them or let anyone else touch them."

"What's a kid like you know about airplanes?" he asked past the cigar clamped in his teeth.

"The blue one's a Model 10 Waco about eight years old, with a 250-horsepower Wright Whirlwind R-760 engine. It carries two passengers in the front seat and a pilot in the rear and has a top speed of 160 miles an hour at sea level with a 14,000 foot ceiling." As I watched the man in the bowler hat, I read the production figures from the blackboard of my memory, where I'd written them while reading in the library.

As a young boy, I had spent as much of my time as possible in the College Street Public Library in Toronto. I used to hide the shame of my ill-fitting clothes in the back recesses of the book-lined rooms, devouring every line I could find on the bush pilots of the Canadian North and the airmail pilots of the northeastern United States. These men were my heroes, and they had imbued me with a sense of adventure and daring. I wanted to be like them. Making and flying rubber-band-powered models had not been enough to quench my thirst. I wanted to follow in the footsteps of my heroes: Zebulon Lewis "Lewie" Leigh, Clennel Haggerston "Punch" Dickins, and Wilfred Reid "Wop" May. These were but a few of the giants whose adventures I had relived a thousand times, many of whom I would know as friends in later years when I was elected to the charmed circle of membership in Canada's Aviation Hall of Fame. But there, in the Arizona desert, I did not see the future. I knew only that I wanted to fly.

"What's the range and the G-loading, kid?" the man asked as he flicked the ash off his cigar.

"That wasn't in the book," I told him, "but I'm saying it's 450 miles and six Gs positive and two negative."

"Close," he said, "but close don't count where gas is concerned and when you're doing acrobatics. What's the book on the red Waco A?"

"It's not a Waco A and you know it. That's a Waco F with any one of maybe six different engines in it, from a 100-horsepower Kinner to a 250 Wright. From here I'd say that's the big engine. It's a lot slower than the A and seats only one passenger and the pilot." I let him know he wasn't fooling me at all.

"You're all right, kid. You're all right. How much time you got?"

I knew he was asking me how many hours I'd flown. There was

no need to lie big to him, so I lied small and told him I'd only had a few trips in planes, but that I wanted to learn and take up flying for a living.

"Ever see a parachute jump?" he asked.

"Sure," I answered right back, as a force within me pushed out another lie. "I've made two of them, pull-offs from the wing of a Waco 10."

"You didn't say how old you were, kid."

"You didn't ask and there's no sign at the gate saying you have to be this or that to get in." I stood my ground.

"No offence." He dropped his eyes. "But I got me a problem, and maybe you're the solution." He told me that his mechanic, who doubled as the show's jumper, had gone drinking in Phoenix the night before and couldn't be found. A check with the police an hour earlier had brought no results. Just before I came, it was discovered that one of the air show's parachutes was missing as well.

"What was the name of the chute you used?" he asked me suddenly.

"Irving, 28-foot flat circular." I remembered every detail of the equipment used by a jumper I'd seen the year before.

"And at what height did you pull?" He tore the soggy end of his cigar off with his fingers.

"I climbed out on the lower right wing and hung onto the strut. When the pilot nodded at 1,500 feet over the field I just yanked the rip-cord and was pulled off the wing when the chute opened." I remembered the drill.

"Damnit boy, you *have* jumped with a parachute. Will you do it today, from the Ten?" He pointed with his thumb to the blue three-seater.

"I'm hungry. I need some money and I want a training ride in the Ten," I said, trying to hold down my fear.

"Nothing to eat before the jump, but we'll move it ahead to right after the low-level flying. Three dollars cash and a half-hour instruction from one hell of a pilot." He stuck out his hand.

"Nothing to eat, five dollars cash, and one hour of dual," I countered, getting sicker all the time.

"Nope. A couple of hot dogs and pop after the jump, three dollars cash and one hour's flying. Otherwise, I'll just tell everybody that the jump's off."

"I'll take it," I heard myself saying in a voice that sounded hollow.

"Done," he agreed, and we shook on it.

Drago, the pilot of the Waco 10, was a short, barrel-chested man, the spitting image of Hollywood actor Brian Donlevy. I felt sure he could see right through me.

"Did Artie tell you about the chute you're usin'?" he asked.

When I shook my head, he spelled it out for me. The spare equipment consisted of an ancient Russell Lobe parachute with no sleeve or pilot chute. It had been used by the show's jumper only if he had to make two descents in a row. The jumper had packed it a week ago. The pilot assured me it would work all right.

I knew the difference between jumping out of an airplane wearing a parachute, pulling the rip-cord to let the back of the pack open up and the parachute fill with air during the fall, and being pulled off the wing as you hung from a strut while the canopy filled with air behind you. Common sense told me that if the parachute opened behind me, I'd be safe hanging under it, and that I wouldn't hit hard because I was light compared to adult men. And I guessed that if the parachute didn't open, I'd still be on the wing. All I'd have to do was climb back into the cockpit. I felt much better after I'd reasoned that out.

The harness was made of flat webbing and was too large for me even cinched up tight. The rip-cord handle was made from a bent piece of water-pipe. The pilot went over everything very carefully with me. He assured me he'd jump himself if he hadn't taken a bullet in the leg from a German pilot during the Great War. We cinched up the harness with electrical tape and then went to the Waco 10 so I could practise getting out of the cockpit and to the end of the wing with the parachute on. Holding onto the crossed stainless-steel flying wires and edging to the outside strut was scary, even while the airplane was on the ground, but I managed all right, even though I almost told Drago the truth right then.

"You stay in the cockpit until I whack you on the head," he explained. "Then climb out slowly and turn and wait for the signal to pull the rip-cord. If you're not snatched off the wing, I'll wave you back into the cockpit and we'll land."

I practised jumping off the wing backwards after that, and my nerve started to come back a bit.

"How much money's Artie paying you for the jump?" Drago asked as he checked over the airplane.

I told him and he asked if I'd got the three dollars. When I told him I hadn't, he reached into an inside pocket of his leather coat and took out a small envelope, from which he counted out three one-dollar bills.

"This is for luck, kid. I'll get the money back from Artie after the jump, then we'll have a couple of hot dogs and a pop, and when the show's over you and me'll do some real flying." He put his arm around my shoulder. He smelled of gasoline, leather, and sweat.

I watched the two airplanes take off in close formation, while Artie used a megaphone to tell the crowd something about Drago and the other pilot, and the low passes they were going to make.

As the planes landed, I picked up the parachute and walked to Drago's airplane. I could hear snatches of Artie's spiel ripping through the megaphone: "'Daring ... death-defying ... parachute." Then I was into the harness, sitting in the front cockpit and smothering my fear as Drago lifted us in lazy circles above the crowd, which seemed a pitifully small gathering to watch a boy die.

When I felt the rap on my head from behind I wanted nothing more than to sink out of sight and stay there until my feet were firmly on the ground, but a second more forceful smack urged me to stand up slowly, heave my right leg and then my left out of the cockpit and onto the wing root, as I clung to the centre section struts for dear life.

I had just made it to the edge of the aileron, then looked sideways at the pilot for his sign to pull the rip-cord, when the right shoulder strap slipped off. I unclutched my left hand from the death grip I had on the strut in order to pull the webbing back into position, when the wind tore me loose and I fell off backwards.

I heard someone screaming, high and wild. I knew it was me yet I couldn't stop. I could hear the wind rushing by, tearing more horrible sounds from my throat. And as in a dream, I saw the plane revolving and growing small as I spun first on my back, then on my stomach, until suddenly I saw how big the cars looked.

Instinctively, I grabbed the rip-cord with both hands, pulled it loose with animal strength, and threw it away. By this time I was head down, and I watched the canopy pass between my legs, a long streamer of yellow silk. Suddenly I heard a report like a shotgun blast. I was slammed down into the harness. The metal chest connector smashed into my chin.

Half in and half out of the harness, I hit the edge of the clay runway and folded up like an accordion.

"Help me!" The words foamed out of my mouth in red spittle. I tried to sit up. When I saw Artie running towards me, I lay back. But instead of kneeling and saving me from the sea of pain in which I was drowning, he slid to a stop, and planted one foot on my chest.

"Jesus, kid," he shouted excitedly, "what an act! You made some woman faint!" He was looking at the distant crowd and waving his derby at them. When I tried to push his foot away, he put more weight on it. "Stay there, kid, and thrash around like you're all busted up. It's great for business!"

In a little while, Artie and Drago brought out an old army cot from the hut, put me on the bare springs, and carried me inside and left me. I vomited a lot, and then slept for awhile. When I woke up, it was dark and everyone had gone. I guessed later that they did that to a lot of kids like me.

I knew I couldn't stay in the shack because the desert cools to near freezing at night and I had no blanket, food, or water. I wasn't spitting up blood any more, but I felt sick to my stomach and ached all over. My knees were swollen and hard to bend. I figured they'd taken most of the shock when I'd slammed into the ground. I had no way of knowing how close to earth I had been when I heard the crack of the canopy deploying, but thirty years later, during my 526th parachute descent, I worked out by comparison that I had been not more than 200 feet above the ground when the parachute opened.

My first concern was for the money the pilot had given me. I'd wrapped it in my handkerchief and folded it inside the crotch of my underwear. The bills were still there, but someone had gone through my pockets and taken my penknife. What I couldn't see was how I looked. My shirt and pants were covered with dried blood. The deep cut on my chin no longer bled, but the bone was exposed and I could barely open my mouth.

I hobbled back to the highway along the road I'd so happily travelled only hours earlier. I resolved to head home to Toronto, knowing I had lived through a great adventure. More than anything else I now wanted a reunion with my family, however brief and unfriendly.

After three cars and a truck heading towards Phoenix flashed right by, I crossed the road and stuck out my thumb. A large truck was approaching. It picked me up in its lights and slowed down, finally stopping only a few yards past where I was standing. The driver leaned across the seat and opened the passenger door.

"Git on in. I got me some vegetables that'll rot if you don't hurry." The big cheerful voice came from a heavy-set man in a chequered shirt and a beat-up fedora. I climbed in.

"Where ya headed?" he asked.

"Mesa," I told him. "I'm on my way back home to Canada, and I'm staying there tonight."

"Canada?" He seemed surprised. "And what's a young fella like you doin' out near midnight hookin' a ride?"

I explained what had happened that afternoon. When I mentioned the pain in my legs, he put his right hand on my left knee and commented on the fact that it felt swollen.

We were a good five miles from Mesa when he started talking about sex, about boys and girls, and about girls and girls. When he began talking about boys and boys fooling around with each other, he grabbed my left hand and forced it through his already opened fly.

"Let go of me!" I shouted at him, and tried to pull my hand away. With my other hand I grabbed for the door handle. It wasn't there! There was no handle. Suddenly I was terrified. The thought of being killed began to paralyse me.

As I struggled to free my left hand, which he pressed against his hardness, he steered the truck onto the shoulder and began braking. With my right hand I grabbed the window crank and started to wind. When I felt the handle stop turning, I lashed out across the gearshift with my right foot, which hit him high on the chest. Then I got my right arm out the window and around the bracket of the side mirror. With one great screaming heave I broke free of his grasp, just as the truck came to a jolting stop.

I was half out the window, almost sitting on the sill, when he grabbed one flailing leg and started shouting like a crazy man about how he liked to screw girls and boys. I broke free and fell backwards, bouncing off the running board and into the ditch. Then I bounded to my feet, and was up and away into the darkness.

"Boy or girl I'm gonna fuck ya anyway!" he hurled his voice in a wild scream as he stumbled into the ditch after me.

I kept running through the tearing mesquite and sage until I couldn't run any farther. Then I lay in the sand and cried silently into the darkness, heaving the terror and pain from my empty stomach into my cupped hands so the sound wouldn't give me away.

I stayed there a long time, until thoughts of the scorpions and tarantulas spurred me to my hands and knees and then to my feet. When I got back to the highway, the truck was gone. The driver must have given up looking for me and driven off.

I walked all the way to Mesa in spite of my aching knees. At a truck stop, I cleaned up and bought some food.

Two weeks later I was back in Toronto. My mother was all tears and my older brother, Roy, was glad I was back. My father wasn't home. I didn't see him until the next day because he stayed out late that night.

My parents had never bothered much with hugging and kissing my brother and me. My father had never told me he loved me, and my mother was reserved in her physical caresses, letting her manner and tone of voice transmit her affection for me. And while I confided my adventures in broad detail to my mother and Roy, less the horror story of the truck driver's attempt on my life, I gave only a casual account of my travels to my father, who expressed little interest in my return. The feeling of not being really loved by my parents went back as far as I could remember, to my earliest memories.

CHILDHOOD YEARS

I WAS BORN at 10:02 on the morning of July 14, 1921, on the sidewalk outside Women's Hospital in Montreal, midway between a taxi-cab and the entrance to the emergency ward. My mother claimed later not to have had the slightest indication that I was due to arrive until she was suddenly drenched in amniotic fluid. My father was not present; he was at work aboard a railway express car somewhere in the Laurentian Mountains, north of the city.

My birth was a harbinger of my future. Before I reached the age of sixteen, I had crossed North America three times, lived in twenty-one cities from Saint John, New Brunswick, to Costa Mesa, California, and gone to school in three Canadian provinces and seven American states.

My father, Donald Washington Munro, was born in a narrow, three-storey house in Saint John, New Brunswick, in 1894. Father was slight and muscular, endowed with an athlete's body which refused, along with his mind, to accept the ravages of time.

My mother, Dorothy Violet Baker, was born in 1895 at Enfield, England, a suburb of London. Any goodness within me was undoubtedly transmitted from my mother and her family, as was an orderliness of living she tried to attain daily under seemingly impossible circumstances, while privately suffering pains of both body and mind. My favourite picture of her, a small snapshot taken when I was ten and lost these many years, showed her wearing a casually belted camel's-hair coat, her soft auburn hair flicked by a vagrant wind and her strength of character loosed in a laugh.

My parents-to-be met in England during the Great War while my father was hospitalized with wounds. My mother was a nurse. After she married my father, she sailed to Saint John, New Brunswick, and the house where my brother Roy was born in 1919. My father refused to remain with his parents and take over the small, family construction business. Instead, he, my mother, and brother moved to Montreal, where I was born and lived until my fifth year, when we returned to stay with my grandparents.

Early one Sunday morning, my parents packed my brother and me into an old sedan. After a tearful farewell from my grandmother, who saw us off, we drove through a snowstorm to Farmington, Maine, the first of many towns we would live in.

Following our stay in Maine, we moved to Lorain, Ohio, then to Pleasantville, New Jersey, where I happily entered the second grade. I was allowed to enjoy the heady atmosphere of school life and of my friendship with others of my own age for a short time. Soon we moved again, this time to Wilmington, Delaware, and once more I suffered the torment of separation, followed almost immediately by a wholly unexpected departure from the Atlantic seaboard.

Crammed into the back seat of a 1924 Dodge touring car, with all our worldly possessions, Mother, Roy, and I were driven in an often frightening manner across the United States. My father chose California because he knew someone from the Great War who had a house in the hamlet of Costa Mesa, where we could stay for a few weeks while he saw "some old school pals" in Hollywood.

My father's two childhood friends were Lou Meyer and Wally Pidgeon. They had attended Winter Street Public School in Saint John together. Wally was then in Hollywood under contract to the Metro-Goldwyn-Mayer Studios as Walter Pidgeon, and Lou Meyer was none other than Louis B. Mayer, partner of Samuel Goldwyn in the enormous enterprise that bore their names. As a result of the reunion, MGM gave my father a contract to erect a number of clapboard theatres in lesser communities in Arizona.

Our first stop was the tiny western Arizona hamlet of Baltz. It was in that community of about 400 souls that I set my all-time personal record for the shortest stay in an educational institution. At 8:45 in the morning, Roy was assigned a seat in the fifth row and I a seat in the third row, next to the door. It was one of the brightest moments of my young life. Ten minutes later, and before the national anthem had been sung, the door opened quietly, and my father's head and shoulders appeared. Conspiratorially he whispered, "Bring Roy to the door with you. We're leaving." I started to dislike him then for the selfishness he was continually visiting upon my mother, my brother, and me. I didn't stop sobbing until I fell asleep that night.

Roy and I were next enrolled in a public school at Gila Bend, a small town in Maricopa County, southwest of Phoenix. There was one Indian boy of twelve who arrived at school on a small horse, dressed like a story-book Indian, with buckskin trousers, a leather vest, moccasins, and a bright bandana wrapped around his kerosened black hair. Every morning he'd lope along until he was near the school, then boot his mount into a frenzied gallop, reining in in front of the rear schoolhouse window, which was opened each morning by a selected student. In one fluid motion, he would launch himself from the back of the trotting horse and vault through the open window, landing on the run near his third-row desk.

On my second morning, he arrived at full gallop, launched himself into space, and went completely through the large pane of glass. The teacher had forgotten to select a student to open it. He bled profusely and frightened us all until the sheriff took him away in a car with a flashing red light. I didn't see him again because I left a week later.

We went to Buckeye, then we moved again, bringing us a breath closer to the state capital of Phoenix.

Goodyear Public School students were drawn from about fifty families. The children were Negro, Indian, Mexican, and a few were mid-Europeans. As Canadians, Roy and I were looked on as foreigners by all. I was entered in the fourth grade while Roy was promoted to sixth.

It was there at a school athletic day that I first raced against another person to win. Until then, it had been a case of chase or be chased. I won the junior events easily by merely putting my head down and willing my legs to go as fast as needed to stay ahead of everyone else. Roy then suggested to the teacher that I could beat anyone at school, including the senior champion. I won that race too.

Other towns and schools followed: Glendale, Tempe, Chandler, Mesa, Miami, and Globe. We finally settled in Phoenix in a rented house on Monroe Street. For the first time in a year, I felt a strange and unaccustomed sense of security, of knowing when I went to bed that I would spend tomorrow with the same friends. I had no idea what happened to the MGM contract; my father was then working at various construction jobs, mostly out of town.

Phoenix had grown through the cattle and copper-mining booms and was just sitting there desiccating in the desert sun. My playmates were mostly Mexicans, Negroes, and some whites, but my closest companion was my brother Roy. He was taller, older, braver, smarter, and more sensible about everything in general than I.

We lived on the rim of a great desert, in a bowl surrounded by cactus-covered mountains through which small cattle drives took place. Whenever a herd camped on the outskirts Roy and I would be there at dawn, helping with anything we could just to be with the cowboys. They were ordinary men, mostly uneducated and without formal manners; many of them were Negroes, and few had as much schooling as we had then.

Close to downtown on Van Buren Street was the city-owned swimming pool, which anyone could use if they paid. For five cents you could stay all day. In 1930, when I was nine, I took the American Red Cross examination for certificates of proficiency in life saving. I had worked so hard at the programme that I completed the entire senior adult course to receive that highest grading.

There weren't many airplanes flying around Phoenix's small airport, which I visited for the first time by sneaking away from school one afternoon. It had been in the paper that Phoenix would be a stopover point for an air race from California to Texas. I was allowed to sit in the cockpits of three racing airplanes, one of which was being taxied to a hangar. I sat alongside the pilot and held the joystick, as the control stick was then called. That stolen afternoon, for which I was soundly whipped, was to influence my life irrevocably and set me upon a path of high adventure.

The security I felt in Phoenix was, however, only temporary. Once again came the day when my father announced we were moving again. The Belmont Mine at Tonopah, Arizona, had run out of copper ore and the directors ordered it shut down and dismantled. My father got the contract to disassemble it and ship everything out in trucks to another mining operation. This was located in the Big Horn Mountains, some fifty miles north of Phoenix, and had lain idle since the price of copper plummeted at the start of the 1929 stock market crash. It comprised a large mill with sheds, a cookshack, several bunkhouses, and six two-room frame houses in which the supervisors had lived. Father hired a number of trucks and labourers of assorted stripe. Off we went, over desert roads, a strange convoy led by a 1928 Star truck.

We took up residence in the largest shack, which boasted a small kitchen area and two thin-walled bedrooms off a main room used for everything else. The buildings were raised four feet off the desert floor on large pilings to save them from the flood waters that turned the area into a riverbed each year. Roy and I scouted the area the first day and saw rattlesnakes by the dozen, as well as a Gila monster, innumerable lizards, scorpions, tarantulas, birds of prey, and carrion.

I'd heard my mother crying at night many times since we'd left Montreal, but her deep sobs and the irritable remonstrations from my father that first night hurt me so that I cried too because I couldn't help her. She'd left her genteel world some twelve years before and, from that day, had not had a home she could call her own, or mingled with ladies of her quality, or acquired a decent wardrobe, or seen any member of her family. But when daylight came she stilled my tears for her, and with a hug told me she loved us all and was looking ahead to better times and a nice home, where we could all live happily until Roy and I grew up.

My mother's anxiety was increased by our living conditions. So numerous were the scorpions that each shoe was turned over and tapped on the floor before it was used in the morning, and clothes hung on wall pegs at night were shaken out before being put on.

I cannot count the times my mother screamed as scorpions dropped to the floor. But the day she reached to the top kitchen shelf and placed her fingers inside a cup to lift it down, then felt the scorpion curled up in the bottom, will live in my memory forever. She dropped the cup, which smashed onto the floor, and the scorpion skittered away. Then she held her face in both hands and screamed and screamed until I thought her voice would come loose from her body. She wouldn't stop even when Father came running from the mill. It took hours to calm her and days before she was well enough to work around the house. After that incident, she was never the same. There was something missing from her deep violet eyes. It was as though her mind had reached a distant plateau.

We left Arizona within a few weeks, in an old Mormon sedan. We travelled via Chicago, Boston, and New York. We lived in Philadelphia for a time, and then were once again packed into the car and returned to Saint John and my grandparents' house on Paradise Row.

When my father told me I'd be enrolled at Winter Street School the next Monday I was terrified. Throughout my childhood I'd heard him tell horror stories about his years there. Roy was unperturbed; he felt the place must have mellowed in the years since my father was a student. When I begged not to be sent there my father replied, "You've got to be tough in this world to get by, and you always have to stand up to bullies. If you don't, they'll take over the world. What would have happened to all of you if soldiers like me hadn't gone to fight the Kaiser and won?" I was going to tell him we'd likely all be speaking German, but knew I'd get a clip across the ear. Instead I told him that if anyone bothered me I'd stop him—somehow. That apparently pleased him because he clapped me on the shoulder in camaraderie and said, "A chip off the old block, that's what you are."

As a new sixth-grade student and one who had lived in the United States, I was asked, as a gesture of friendship by the teacher, to practise for the role of Santa Claus in the school play. I tried to turn down the offer. The teacher, however, insisted that I take the part.

All went well in class, at rehearsals and on the street, and a hint of a pleasurable school experience loomed as a possibility in my mind until Friday after school. My route home took me past an old lumber yard surrounded by a twelve-foot-high fence into which had been set a double gate large enough to accommodate horse-drawn freighting wagons. As I rounded the corner I came face to face with five older students, the largest of whom was the size of a small horse. Before I could use my fleetness of foot to escape I was surrounded and the shoving began from one to another to another until I'd been spun, whacked, punched, kicked, and left crying in the slush.

"You play Santa and you go under the river ice, you Yankee bastard," the big one yelled as I stumbled to my feet and reeled home.

My mother was all tears when I explained the beating. Roy couldn't understand how it could happen because he hadn't been bothered, and my father was visibly upset that I hadn't stood toe to toe with them and slugged it out.

"You're going to get a boxing lesson, and the next time anyone tries that you'll be able to take care of yourself," he advised sternly. For the next hour I was instructed in the art of bobbing, weaving, ducking, lefts, rights, uppercuts, overhands, straight jabs and combinations, until I could hardly hold my arms in front of me. Just then he slipped a hand between them and slapped me across the face.

"Bastard." The word came off my lips and struck his ears like a round-house blow.

"What did you say?" he thundered at me.

"Bast—" Before I could finish he slapped me right off my feet. I ran from the room and sought my mother, who stood between us and told him not to lay another hand on me.

"He said, 'Bastard,'" my father shouted at her.

I finally made my mother understand that it was the first time I'd used the word and had no idea what it meant. Then I took my swollen body and frightened mind to bed, hoping the troubles would disappear with sleep.

The Christmas concert was set for three o'clock that Wednesday afternoon in the auditorium. Parents had been invited to attend as well as the student body. At two o'clock, as I walked to the boys' lunchroom to get into costume, I was grabbed by the same five seniors and hustled with a hand over my mouth into the wash-room. They dragged me to a toilet, lifted the lid, and held my face just above the water.

"You get on that goddamn stage and we'll flush your brains to Chicago," the big one said, spacing out his words, as he shoved my head underwater and held it there.

Then they all went away, and I sat on the floor, crying from the fear of drowning, from the pain of the kicks they'd left me with, from the fear of what they would do to me if I didn't quit, and from the shame of it all. Finally I cleaned up, stopped sniffling, and walked straight into the lunchroom and up to the teacher. I told her flat out that I was not going to play Santa and that nobody else could make me.

"Why you little..." She grabbed my arm, marched me through the fairies and reindeer and more of the little green elves, up the stairs, into my class-room, through another door into a large, wire-mesh enclosure jutting into the hall. She locked the door behind her and left me in a floor-to-ceiling cage some 8 × 12 feet. On the walls hung wet clothes, and on the floor stood galoshes and smelly lunch buckets. I was in jail, but I reasoned at least I'd live the day through.

When I saw through the mesh my mother, father and Roy coming down the hall, I managed to hide behind some clothes until they passed. Then, minutes later, I heard my parents and the teacher coming back, entering the class-room and then unlocking the cloak-room door. I couldn't hold back the tears and blurted out the whole story. The teacher promised to have the five boys in her office the next day and said they would never bother me again. She insisted, however, that I take the stage as Santa. And take it I did, giving a performance that brought tears to my mother's eyes and even a forced smile from my father.

That night I lay in bed remembering all the times I'd been hit, chased, hurt, and threatened. I figured out that the real reason I'd been afraid was because I hadn't known what was going to happen to me.

Suddenly a plan began to form and I remembered the first time I'd visited my grandfather's house. He'd taken me into the front hallway and pointed to an enormous oil painting of an old-time soldier wearing a kilt and holding a great sword. An assortment of cannons and bodies lay in the background.

"That is Sir Robert Munro," he stated firmly, turning me by the shoulders to face the portrait. "He was a famous soldier who commanded the gallant Black Watch regiment at the Battle of Fontenoy in 1745. Using his own method of alternately firing and taking cover for the first time in a Continental battle, he introduced a system of infantry tactics that has never been equalled. Be proud of your ancestors and learn from their deeds," he ordered.

I had it! I sat up in bed so violently that I half-wakened my brother into an irritable rebuke. Sitting there, I drew in my mind the map of my homeward route from school and planned my battle for the morrow.

It was all over in ten minutes in the principal's office. I told my story to him in front of my parents and the five defiant-looking students, who collectively denied they had laid a hand on me. A file was produced on each of the boys, listing the numerous complaints made against them during their school career by other students, teachers, and parents. The verdict was harsh. The big fifteen-year-old gangleader was expelled from school then and there. The other four were advised that if one valid complaint was ever laid against them during the balance of their school-days at Winter Street, they'd meet the same fate.

In the hallway outside the principal's office I told everyone who'd been inside that the big kid was a coward who kissed girls and was afraid to fight me alone after school without his gang. Then I walked back to my class-room, shouting back at the big kid, "Coward, coward, coward, coward."

At noon I finished whittling a handle on the piece of wood I'd got at dawn from my grandfather's wood-shed. It was about two inches square and a yard long and was made of hardwood. I ran all the way to the locked gates of the old lumber yard. Just around the corner from my enemy's approach path I propped the club behind a telephone pole. I timed, with thousand-and-one counts, how long it took me to run from there to the lane's next corner, where a low, broken fence leaned against a garage behind a scraggly bush. Then I returned to school for the afternoon.

I left right after dismissal at 3:30 and ran the wrong away around the block to the lumber yard lane. I scouted the area for any sign of boys and saw none. Then I waited between two houses until I saw my quarry coming along the street. His head was down and he was moving like an express train. I ran out right in front of him shouting, "Coward, coward, bastard dirty coward," then ran like hell for the laneway. He came tearing after me, shouting and waving his arms. I slipped around the corner, grabbed the board from behind the pole, and waited for him to hurtle around the gate. My timing was perfect. Just as he rounded the pole, my swing reached its ultimate velocity, and the square timber clapped him hard across the stomach and one arm with such force that he flipped over it and landed on his chest in the dirt. Then I raced past him, clutching the weapon and shouting, "Coward, coward, coward, bastard coward." And after me he came.

The fear hit me even as I was sprinting and counting the steps I had to run to reach the next assault point. Right on the number I rounded the corner of the garage, leaped behind the fence, and ducked down. Just then I heard him slamming past the other side of the shed. As he caromed into sight, I stood up and swung the board once more, right at his face. His head stopped but his body kept going. For one moment he was horizontal to the ground, then he fell flat on his back with a great thud and started to scream, holding his head in his hands.

Sensing a trick, I ran as fast as I could towards the street. But when I heard no racing feet after me, I slowed, stopped, and then sidled back warily to the rolling, crying form on the ground. I could see the blood from a few yards away. Holding the board over my head to smash him again if he attacked me, I got close enough to see that he was hurt so badly that he wouldn't bother me any more that day.

A woman ran out of her house and called me all sorts of names, then she helped him stagger inside, where, I learned later, she telephoned the police.

Eventually, the police made their way to my home, and in front of my father, grandfather, and the officer I explained every detail from the day I'd started school through the beating and the threats, the ancestor who had invented the hit-and-run type of warfare, and how I'd planned it all. I was forced to promise never to use such defensive tactics again and I kept my word. I finished the school year, and no one in Saint John ever hit me or called me a name again.

During the first week of January my mother took me aside and quietly told me to say goodbye to my friends, as we were leaving the next day for Toronto. I was tired of moving from one place to another, of being torn apart from children and places I'd come to like. The seed of dislike for my father that had been planted in Arizona grew some more.

We spent the first night in Toronto in a downtown hotel, and moved the next day with our few suitcases into a small apartment on Bloor Street West opposite Christie Pits. There I would be educated for two months in nearby Christie Street School. Two houses away lived a man named Hunter, who advertised on a sign in front of his house that he gave ju-jitsu lessons. I didn't know what that meant, so I asked him and got a tour of his small gymnasium and a free sampling of the ancient Japanese art of self-defence. Gradually I earned enough points taking out his garbage and cleaning snow from his walks to get a half-hour lesson. I learned some slick things, like how to hold a person with only one hand so they couldn't hurt you, and how to break a hammerlock, which was said by other kids to be impossible.

The Depression had reduced tens of thousands of Torontonians to jobless status, and lines formed daily at every church mission for food and used clothing. Coffee and a hamburger were ten cents at lunch counters, sugar was five cents a pound, and you could get a café meal for twenty-five cents.

My father was a skilled cabinet-maker and worked for awhile at the Christie Biscuit Company, making display cases. Soon he went on his own as an entrepreneur. I can remember him disguising his tools and overalls in a parcel and putting on his best clothes to tackle a job. He didn't want anyone he knew to think he worked with his hands, and yet I was proud of his skills. His hang-out during those years was the Sapper's Club on Sherbourne Street. There, World War I veterans used to gather to play poker, drink, and reminisce. He was rarely home until after dark. I expect he lived by his wits in those days.

Mother was just plain worn out. Sometimes I'd see her standing by the kitchen sink holding her head and rocking back and forth as if to make the pain go away. There was pain, real pain. I learned of it when my father met me at the front door after school and told me she had been taken to the hospital for a serious operation. Two weeks later she came home, the top of her head bandaged and sealed with tape. She was very weak and had to stay in bed. Roy and I helped my father look after her. She told us that she'd had an operation on her brain to have a tumour removed. When she was well again, and her beautiful hair had grown back, she showed us the large scar, like a two-inch cross, on her right temple. But she never spoke of her pain.

Every year at the Canadian National Exhibition there were swimming events held inside the breakwater, and both Roy and I trained for them every chance we got at the College Street YMCA. I never once beat Roy in a swimming race—he could go the full length of the pool and back underwater—but in my age group I could beat almost anyone.

The morning before the CNE races started, Mother went to the Women's College Hospital and didn't come home. Father told us at noon that she had to have surgery the next day to remove both her breasts. Neither of us slept that night. We discussed pulling out of the races, but finally decided we could cheer her up by winning. Because my age-class races were held first, Roy was watching as I dived in, stroked hard to the midway point, and then simply disappeared under the water. Lifeguards in boats were stationed throughout the course, and within seconds I had been retrieved unconscious from the bottom. I regained consciousness in the Hospital for Sick Children to learn that my appendix had ruptured in the water. Because I was thirteen, no operation could be performed without the written consent of a parent or legal guardian. Roy had ridden in the ambulance with me, voiding his entry in the races. He told a nurse where my father was working, that my mother was in hospital.

Within minutes the nurse learned that my mother was still in the operating room and that my father, only hours before, had fallen from a scaffold and severely injured his spine. He had been rushed to a third hospital and was also unconscious. My brother was only fifteen and could do nothing to help. I was put on a stretcher and wheeled into an operating room where a surgeon waited for permission to proceed.

My father awakened first and signed the required form. Permission was telephoned to the doctors standing by, who quickly anaesthetized me and operated.

I awoke in a room with fifteen other children and, after a very sick night, felt well enough the next afternoon to talk to the boy next to me, who had osteomyelitis. He explained simply that his bones were rotting away and that he was going to die. And he did, that night. The next day it was announced that the governor general, the Earl of Bessborough, was coming to visit us. I thought he'd be dressed up in his gold-braided uniform and that I could shake hands with him. But he didn't come into the charity ward.

After I'd been there a week I got sick again, and they moved me into a private room on the second floor next to a window with a heavy wire screen on it. The other bed was empty. My brother was let in to see me once in the big ward, and on the day after I got my own room. As he left he gave me a dime because I didn't have any money, although I couldn't spend it. I must have been very ill as it was several days before I was given any solid food. Having lived on liquids since the operation, the one thing I wanted more than anything else in the world was a chocolate bar. Since I knew the nurses wouldn't let me have one, I determined to outwit them.

I acquired a part roll of twine, a pencil, and a scrap of paper on which I printed a simple note: "Here is my only money. Please buy me any kind of chocolate bar. Keep the nickel for doing it and tie the chocolate to this string. Pull it three times when I can haul it up."

Having rolled the dime into the note and tied it up with string, I pushed the little bundle through the screen, lowered it until I felt it hit the sidewalk, then pulled in three feet of string. I tied the other end to the bedstead, and kept jerking the string so that someone would see the bobbing bundle and open it.

It must have been more than an hour before I felt a few tugs. I wanted to pull up the string to see if someone had removed the packet, but I waited and waited for the three pulls. Long after the streetlights came on I started taking it up, knowing somehow there was nothing tied to it and never would be.

I could never wholly accept the confinement of a class-room. It was only through superior grades in geography, history, and English that I managed to graduate from Rose Avenue Public School. The closest secondary institution to my home was Jarvis Collegiate, which Roy was attending for his second term, having completed his first year with the highest class standing. But I had chosen Danforth Tech, where I could pursue a matriculation course to help me with my flying career and at the same time learn the mechanical skills that would permit me to repair the machines I would fly.

I probably would have gone ahead with my plans had I not played touch football at Riverdale Park on a July afternoon. I had grabbed the ball near my own goal, threaded my way through a horde of attackers, dipsy-doodling around, hurdling over and pivoting past them all to score. I had large hands, powerful shoulders, and fast feet, at least that's what the short, barrel-chested man said. He sported the first two cauliflower ears I had ever seen. He asked my name and age and introduced himself as George Stewart, athletic coach at Central Technical School. We talked for awhile. Then he asked me to sprint fifty yards while he timed me with his stopwatch. I gave it my best effort, and he asked if I hurdled. I explained that I'd cleaned up at the big school track meet but had given up those events because I worked all the time I wasn't in school.

In mid-August my father showed me a letter from the board of education, advising that I was to attend Central Technical School in the first year of a matriculation course. This news came as a shock and a disappointment to me, because I'd made friends with a couple of kids my age who were going to be my class-mates at Danforth Tech. I raised a fuss and met George Stewart again. He explained that I had some athletic talents that could be developed into a winning form if I worked hard at my studies and devoted the rest of my waking hours to training with several other boys under his supervision. If I applied myself, he went on, I would be taken on trips to different cities and would win some great prizes and maybe make enough money from it later on to pay for all my flying lessons.

Well, he'd said the magic words. Off I went to CTS. I started training at six in the morning, then after school until dark, five days a week. I was entered in all sorts of school and intramural track events and joined the football team as flying wing when they needed a special speedster. That year I won a CCM bicycle and a chrome-plated Planet racer, clothes, fishing gear, and other great stuff.

Before the next school term commenced, I was ordered by the board of education to enrol at Danforth Tech in the second form. They advised me that due to an error I had mistakenly been sent to Central. Then I learned that George Stewart had died at night on a country road near Paisley, Ontario, when a great white horse jumped over a fence and smashed through the window of the car he was driving.

I gave up track after that and only half-heartedly took part on the school's fencing team. Half-way through the next term I defended myself against a brutal shop teacher, whose response to any student creating a less-than-perfect mortise-and-tenon joint was to jam one of their hands up to the wrist in a glue-pot. He made the mistake of grabbing my left hand, so I hit him between the eyes with my right, knocked him down, emptied the sticky mess on his head, then walked across his chest into the cold, crisp air of freedom.

After supper I left a simple letter for my parents and Roy, explaining that life was too precious not to be lived to its fullest. Then I walked through the cold night to the acrid pungency of the Bathurst Street rail yards, where the freight trains slowed just enough that a fast lad could make it aboard. Two weeks later I was on the outskirts of Phoenix, hours away from my first parachute jump.

EARLY FLIGHTS

THAT NEXT YEAR after my trip to Phoenix, I made the first entry in my new pilot's log-book: "2 August, 1937 -DH60A -CF-APB- .30 -dual- Gillies—local—Heaven!"

The airplane was a 1929 De Havilland Gypsy Moth with an inverted Cirrus engine. Its wings could be folded backwards for towing behind a car, or for storing in a small hangar space. It was a biplane, with two open cockpits and a long exhaust pipe that ran back from the engine within elbow reach of the occupants. No one I knew who flew it failed to sport at least one burn scar on their left arm from inadvertently touching the pipe when it was hot.

I had earned that flight by doing all sorts of general work around Dufferin Flying Service at Barker Field. Timed from the curb in front of my parents' rented home on Sherbourne Street, it was a good three hours to the airport on north Dufferin. I hitch-hiked, trotted, or walked with great, excited strides. About half-way there I'd get hungry and force down some thick tomato sandwiches, pummelled by then into moist balls of reddened dough, and wash away my ever-present thirst with great gulps of rubbery-tasting water from gasoline station hoses. I could have ridden part of the distance by streetcar for a nickel, but every cent that came into my possession went into the bank towards my first paid-for flying lesson.

My second lesson cost me five dollars and left sixteen cents in my bank account. It lasted thirty minutes and took place in a tiny Aeronca C, whose shape earned it the nicknames "airknocker" and "flying bathtub." Two people could wedge themselves with difficulty into the single cockpit, and if the wind and temperature cooperated, the irritable, underpowered beast might be persuaded to leave the ground and maintain flight. Since one set of controls had to be shared between the pilot and instructor, each take-off was an adventure into fear.

It was the worst airplane I was ever to fly. I felt so ill at ease and so uncomfortable that I eventually told Fred Gillies, the owner of Dufferin Flying Service, that I would take no further instruction in it. Instead, I would put my time in on either the Taylor Cub or the Gypsy Moth.

To pay for the lessons I held down five jobs, one after the other. During what little time I had left over between jobs and flying lessons, I'd go to the book department in Eaton's College Street store and start reading the latest best seller, which the public library would not yet have. The first book I read there was John Steinbeck's *Of Mice and Men*. It took me more than a month to finish it, because after a few pages I'd be asked to leave the store. Then I'd walk down Yonge Street to Eaton's main store at Queen Street, and pick up where I'd left off until requested to depart. Then I'd amble across the street to Simpson's where I continued adventuring with big Lonnie. Over a two-year period I acquainted myself with the contents of every best seller as they were published.

By late September, I had logged a further four hours of dual instruction in the Moth and Cub, had completed all my air exercises to Gillies's satisfaction, and had made five consecutive landings that were slick and smooth. After the last of these, Gillies climbed from the plane while we were still on the runway and tapped me on the shoulder.

"Once around, son, once around," he said. I was about to make my first solo flight, a proud moment and a giant step towards becoming a licensed pilot.

I was gripped by a fear such as I had never before known. It wasn't being hurt that I feared, but being less than perfect in Gillies's eyes. But, when the plane's wheels lifted from the ground, my confidence returned. A feeling of pure freedom enveloped me. In my mind's eye I could see the plane with me alone in it, curving around the circuit, turning arrow-true to the runway as its power was reduced. Then it sank into a whisper-light touchdown and stopped in front of the waiting Gillies. Alone I had conquered the alien air.

I was now confident I'd have no trouble getting my licence. I'd spent hours studying the Air Regulations and the Aeronautics Act, upon which the piloting examinations were based, as well as airmanship, theory of flight, navigation, and the rest of the lore of heavier-than-air flight. I had assimilated the knowledge to such a degree that I knew I could handle any question asked of me. It was a satisfying feeling.

Perhaps it was this overconfidence that led me to do something against not only my better judgement, but also against the rule prohibiting student pilots from taking up a passenger. Despite both of these, I decided most generously to give my brother Roy his first-ever flight. We planned the event carefully. Roy was to cross several fields and hide alongside a split-rail fence on the far side of the aerodrome. I would pick him up there before I took off.

The day we chose was clear and warm. When I arrived at the airfield, all looked well. Roy was on his way to his hiding place. It was then I realized that the only airplane available was the Aeronca. It was parked in front of the Dufferin Flying Service office, where several bystanders were gathered with Gillies.

As nonchalantly as I could, I climbed into the pilot's seat, revved up the ridiculous little engine, and taxied off across the patchy grassed field in a cloud of dust and dead grasshoppers. When I reached Roy's hiding place, I pulled up, hoping to screen his movements from the sightseers and owner.

He scrambled onto the seat beside me and buckled up his safety harness while the wheels were still turning. Having completed the cockpit and engine checks while moving towards him, I merely pointed the nose down the beaten track and opened the throttle, certain that no one was watching and that if anyone was, he or she would not be able to see two bodies in the cockpit.

My confidence began to evaporate as we picked up speed. Enveloped by heat-thinned air, the single small wing found so little lift that I found myself within a giant's step of the end of the runway with the wheels still glued to earth. The airplane simply refused to leave the ground.

I could hear Roy's sharply indrawn breaths as clearly as I felt my own. Suddenly I realized that I could neither stop the Aeronca before crashing into the looming fence, nor gain enough speed to clear the low telephone wires that stretched immediately in front of us.

In desperation I pulled back on the stick. The nose jerked up and we vaulted over the fence and underneath the telephone wires. Instantly I shoved the stick full ahead, in blind defiance of the laws of gravity. The two little tires smacked the centre line of

Dufferin Street, compressing the landing gear, which then expanded abruptly to hurtle the aircraft over the wire fence on the other side of the highway. Directly ahead of our staggering mount, which didn't know whether to crash or fly, was a small group of abandoned wooden mushroom sheds, which, magnified by the fear of our imminent collision with them, loomed like apartment blocks.

Roy suddenly grabbed the stick and pushed it forwards. I yelled at him to let go. Just then the propeller passed inches above the roof of the first shed. The wheels touched the roof and rolled along the dried and curled-up asphalt shingles with horrendous grinding and chopping sounds. Just as they ran off the far end, we sustained lift and gradually gained height over the vacant field that lay ahead.

"My gawd, I thought we were going to crash." Roy forced the words past his white, tight lips. "Is this the way you take off all the time?"

"Shut up, goddamn it." I elbowed him in the chest with my cramped right elbow. "And don't ever touch that stick again." But even as I shouted at him above the engine's sound, I was choking down the fear that pushed up into my throat. I knew that if he hadn't kept me from raising the nose too high we wouldn't have made it. Had I succeeded in raising the nose, the little wing would surely have stalled and plunged our fragile craft rather messily through the roof, tail first. And I realized, too, for the thousandth time, that God in His infinite wisdom had given Roy an intelligence superior to my own. I didn't tell him then that he'd saved us both that day. I waited until four years later in a London pub, when I was a blooded fighter pilot and he had just arrived from Canada to commence his operational training as a fighter/bomber pilot.

Gradually, lift overcame gravity. I avoided several stands of trees and some farm buildings, and finally coaxed the recalcitrant machine to 500 feet altitude over open country. Knowing that the people on the airfield would certainly have observed my dangerous and unorthodox take-off, and that they would be waiting for me to return and disembark my passenger, we agreed that Roy had to leave the airplane at another location. Knowing that in any emergency a bad plan is better than no plan at all, I decided to bring the poor excuse for a flying machine to earth in a large meadow alongside the Rouge River, where Roy and I had often camped as Boy Scouts.

The flight there took ten minutes. The meadow, however, was already occupied by a number of beef cattle. I flew upwind atop my selected landing path within a few feet of the ground, while both of us hung into the slip-stream. Roy shouted at the animals to move off and I checked the ground for pot-holes and stumps.

The landing proved uneventful. Leaving Roy on foot some thirteen miles from home, I took off for the return flight to Barker Field. My mind raced to design a plausible explanation for my awesomely dangerous take-off. The idea, of course, was to refute any suggestion that I had carried a passenger into the air. I reasoned that even if anyone in Gillies's group had seen two forms in the cockpit at such a distance, they would not be able to swear the other form was an animate object. My entire future in aviation was at stake. If the truth were discovered not only could I be dismissed as a student, but federal charges could be laid against me by the Department of Transport under the Aeronatics Act. So great was my need to survive the coming questioning that all fear was shoved from my mind.

During the short flight back to the field I removed my large leather windbreaker and old felt fedora, rolled them loosely into an elongated bundle, and tightened the safety-belt of the passenger's seat across them. Getting out of the jacket in flight required my taking both feet from the rudder pedals, sitting sideways on the seat with my feet sticking out into the right-hand slip-stream, and letting go of the control stick. This act resulted in several near heart seizures, following short but violent aerial manoeuvres for which there are no names.

At the conclusion of that challenging experience and with a dwindling fuel supply, I had only a few minutes left before touchdown at the field in which to design an acceptable reason for the plane's erratic take-off. It came to me as I gentled the Aeronca to a feather-light landing, taxied slowly towards the people emerging from the office, and swung into a parking place with the passenger side facing them. There was no way they could avoid seeing that the right seat was occupied.

Unhurriedly I shut down the engine, climbed out, and walked around the tail section to the passenger side. I removed the upright bundle from its restraint and donned the coat and hat in full view of Gillies, who was striding towards me in a most purposeful manner.

"What in hell were you doing out there, you damned fool?" he shouted.

"Damned fool?" I asked in surprise.

"And what in hell were you doing carrying a passenger?" he thundered, his face contorted with anger.

"Passenger?" I stared at him blankly. "Passenger? I was solo. I've never carried a passen.... Ohhhhhh, I get it now." I interjected a chuckle of understanding and nodded towards the others who had joined him. "You were watching my take-off and thought I'd taken a passenger aboard, is that it?"

"You flew right under the telephone wires on take-off and god-damn near through a few buildings." He struggled without success to contain his rage. "You—"

"Okay, that's it!" I pointed a finger at his face. "I get out of a situation that could have wrecked the Aeronca and killed me. When I return it to you unharmed I'm accused of carrying a passenger." I raised my voice to a near shout. "What passenger? You want to know what happened? I'll tell you what happened!" I turned up the volume, waving my arms to emulate his body language.

"I took off my jacket and hat as I taxied out and rolled them up under the right seat belt. Then just as I was about to lift off, the stupid buckle came undone. The whole thing fell on top of the stick and the throttle, so I had to change hands, holding the stick with my left hand under a mound of leather, then fight through the whole mess with my right hand to find the throttle to close it. By the time I got hold of it I was too close to the fence to stop. If I'd tried to stop, I'd have gone right through the fence and into the ditch and that poor excuse for a flying machine would have been turned into scrap. To save the plane, I deliberately lifted it over the fence, bounced it off the highway into the air, and all at risk to my very own life." I paused long enough to refill my lungs. "And then I avoided those goddamn shacks, which have always been a menace to take-offs on the west-east runway. Once I was airborne, I decided I might as well complete the air exercises I rented that useless heap for in the first place." I stopped abruptly, staring at him with an actor's anger, then pushed through the group and into the office to complete my log-book entries.

"Jesus." One of the younger men grabbed me as I passed. "We thought you were going to crash because you had too much weight on board to get airborne. It looked as if there were two people in the plane."

"Thanks!" I bit the word out sarcastically. It was the last line of my charade and left me with a growing feeling of disgust for myself.

I had endangered Roy's life, placed my own in jeopardy, broken a number of valid rules and some federal laws, challenged the immutable law of gravity with wild abandon, and irresponsibly designed and cowardly presented a tissue of lies that would forever stain my honour.

It was late when I arrived home. I felt so low that I woke up a rather irritable Roy to learn that he'd walked only a half-mile before getting a lift. I told him what I'd done after leaving him and how lousy I felt about it.

"You have two options," he yawned, giving me a slice of his wisdom. "Tell Gillies the whole truth from conception to execution, and gamble that he'll forgive you the lie and not stop you from flying, or keep your mouth shut and live with the lousy feeling you'll always have about it." Roy had a way, as always, of getting to the heart of a problem.

For a time, I toyed with the idea of telling Gillies's daughter, Marion, and asking for her intercession. In the end though, I faced my responsibility and decided to speak to Gillies alone.

Before the city was awake I took the streetcar to the end of the line and hitched a ride to the airfield. There was always a special magic present for me around dew-covered airplanes in pastoral surroundings. As the sun warmed the good earth and the striations of ground fog dissipated, I walked to the old Gypsy Moth and reached above my head to wipe a finger through the grease of its rocker arms, which had chattered their way into my heart. I ran my hands affectionately along the cold steel exhaust pipe that had barked its muscular sounds into my ears, then walked to the Aeronca and silently forgave it for being created a less-than-acceptable vehicle of flight.

When Gillies arrived, I gave him a few minutes to settle at his desk before stepping into his office.

"I'd like to talk to you," I said.

He swung his old swivel chair sideways and motioned me to sit.

Without deviation from the truth, I told him in detail what I had done.

He didn't say a word. He just sat there, sideways to me. Slowly he turned to face me.

"Start up the Moth from the front seat." He waved me away with a flick of his hand. "I'll be out when it's warmed up."

Uncomprehendingly I left the office as in a dream, my mind flooded with questions, and did as he instructed.

He was there in minutes. He climbed into the rear cockpit, took the controls, and lifted us off into the rays of the warming sun. We climbed easily to 2,500 feet over open country. Gently Gillies pressed the nose down and then pulled it up into an easy loop, down again with increased speed and up into a perfect roll-off-the-top, followed by a blood-draining figure eight, and culminating in a long and lazy barrel roll, which ended in line with the runway onto which he eased the wheels. Then he taxied back to the tie-down and walked directly to his office.

I followed him in and stood, holding back the bile as he riffled through a desk drawer, found what he was seeking, and, standing stiffly in front of me, pinned the simple cloth wings of the Dufferin Flying Service onto the heart-pocket of my windbreaker.

"Without courage there would be no art of manned flight, and without truth it would lose its purity," he said simply, before walking past me to the hangar doors and awakening the mechanic who slept in a back room.

I made my way deep into the shrubbery behind his office before nausea swept over me, followed by the tears I could not stem, tears of shame, of relief, and of pride. For years I'd been told that real men never cried, and I hated the wetness on my face.

I carried those wings for thirty-five years, until they sank into the winter waters of Long Island Sound after an ocean-storm landing I would never forget. The thought that was given with them I still carry.

I continued to work to obtain money for flying lessons. I held various delivery jobs. On one of them I had a terrible accident. I eventually recovered, and took a variety of odd jobs while I fully mended.

Through a friend, I was hired by a service station owner across from the Goodyear Tire and Rubber Company. By working both shifts, I managed to purchase a 1930 Model A Ford roadster for $50. I put the car into great shape and sold it for $125. With that tidy sum, I bought a 1931 Model A Ford coach, which I also brought to superlative condition.

Wally Everist, who lived near the station and who was related to the owner, introduced me to his sixteen-year-old neighbour, Grace Anderson, who was a student at Mimico High School. I was immediately struck by Grace's auburn-haired beauty and by her outgoing honesty, which brought sunshine into every life she touched. She had a rare combination of caring, humour, and understanding.

Grace and I were soon enjoying each other's company at the soda fountain, at skating rinks, at United Church socials, and at the occasional movie. Since her stern Scottish parents were vehemently opposed to her forming a liaison with any young man, all our meetings were surreptitious.

Sometimes when we were alone, just holding her hand and feeling her squeeze my fingers in simple affection filled me with a desire to be something greater than I was. My determination to preserve my virginity and honour had been tried on more than one occasion, but her presence caused me to treasure my unwritten vow of continence until the day when I would give myself purely to the person I chose to wed.

ENLISTMENT

IN TENNESSEE WILLIAMS'S play *Camino Real*, one of the characters declares: "Make voyages! Attempt them. There's nothing more." Those words, loaded with challenge, approximated my own feelings at the end of 1938, when I bid goodbye to my family and to Grace, loaded up the Model A with my few necessities, and drove north into mining country. I was going against the tide; most people were leaving the north to take up residence in Toronto. They had felt the brutal wrath of a stagnant and putrifying economy and been vanquished by it. I, on the other hand, felt challenged by the new frontier. I knew deep inside that my chances of making money were minimal, but I could not resist the compelling desire to face those conditions and survive the contest.

Kirkland Lake was brought into international prominence by a near-penniless mining engineer named Harry Oakes. Born in Maine in 1874 to a prosperous land surveyor, he graduated from college twenty years later, then wandered the earth in search of a paying mine. In 1911 he came to Kirkland Lake. Detailed geological studies of that area in the Ontario Department of Mines had convinced him that a great gold deposit lay within walking distance of the main street. Five years later he found it, chartered Lake Shore Mines Limited, and brought into production one of Canada's greatest gold discoveries. The man who is credited by others with giving Harry Oakes his start in Kirkland Lake was a rough-and-tumble former circus prize-fighter named Jack Hammell, who would also enter my life, first in Kirkland Lake and then seven years later in Toronto.

I parked the car on the main street and, hoping to get some information on job prospects, went into the town's largest hotel. I found the beer parlour and sat in a corner of the half-filled, filthy room. It reeked of stale beer and unwashed bodies, and several men at a far table were raising their voices. Then a chair was overturned and I heard the unmistakable sound of a fist smashing into yielding flesh. Within moments a great commotion had erupted, with bodies entangling and fists flailing as the combatants shouted insults and hammered each other with anything they could lift. I got up to leave and saw two men spread-eagling a short, heavy-set man against a wall. Another man prepared to smash him in the stomach. Without stopping to think, I pushed through the tables to help the pinioned man. Just as two aproned waiters grabbed me by the hair and arms to prevent me from entering the fray, the victim kicked his assailant in the crotch. Pulling his right arm free, he felled the opposite enemy with a savage blow, then grabbed the remaining man. He kept smashing that man's face into a table until others pulled him away.

The stocky victor had seen me coming at him through the crowd and, thinking I was another enemy, tried to pull himself away from the hands that restrained him. The waiters finally calmed him down and made him understand that I had been en route to his aid.

"You're all right, kid." He poked me lightly on the jaw as he pushed through the crowd and swaggered into the street.

"Who was that?" I asked.

"Hammell," came the answer. "That son of a bitch is Jack Hammell."

I made the rounds seeking work but everyone I spoke with had the same story about Kirkland Lake and the mining towns beyond. They were dead, except for the standard shifts of skilled men who operated the more profitable producers. Whole streets in small communities displayed uninhabited and boarded-up store-fronts. The relief rolls had swelled beyond their capacity to dispense further aid. Some family men had turned to pimping for their own wives to put food into the mouths of their hungry children.

I offered my services at a dollar a day to garages and gas stations and every restaurant I passed, but there were no takers. Finally I moved on to Hearst, where I got a one-day job working in a garage. The owner offered to get me a job at seventy-five cents a day plus bed and board in a bush camp farther north. He also agreed to keep my car while I was gone.

I was hired to cut pulpwood without even a handshake, and joined several older men in an unheated truck for a two-hour drive over ice-rutted roads and then deep into the forest over tractor trails. It was timber reserved for use by the Abitibi Pulp and Paper Company, whose NO HELP WANTED sign I had passed earlier at the company headquarters in Iroquois Falls.

Bush workers were paid two dollars for each cord of wood cut and stacked. The camp consisted of two bunkhouses for twenty men each, built of plywood sides with a canvas top, a cookshack of the same construction, and a log cabin for the super. The quarters were heated with two forty-five gallon fuel drums mounted piggyback and stoked before lights out at ten o'clock.

I didn't remain in the bush camp long after I was injured. I moved on from one job to another, settling for a short time as a kitchen helper at Crawley-McCracken at Round Lake where, after three weeks of ten-hour days, I earned $19. Following a brush with death while attempting to fathom the depths of the abandoned Trout Creek Mine, I decided to go home and return to flying. I was to have further northern adventures, but not before the adventure of war.

My prime goal was to obtain a private pilot's licence, and at every opportunity I took what few dollars I had saved and rented one of Gillies's planes. Little by little, I increased my air time and knowledge of the lore of flight. I also went aloft with anyone who would take me as a passenger, just in case I could learn something new.

The summer grass had been touched by fall's first frost on the day I passed both my in-air and written Department of Transport examinations. A week later, when the postman delivered to me the Canada Certificate Of Competency For Flying Machines No. 3284, I felt both old and rejuvenated at the same time. My excitement was tempered by an involuntary shudder. The dogs of war were being unleashed in Europe, and my youth and experience would be needed by Britain in the conflagration to come.

As the clock hands ticked past the time of no return, and a far continent poised for a genocidal war, Depression-mauled Torontonians responded to the government's avowal to stand by Britain in any conflict with Germany by quickening their step and emanating an alien sense of optimism.

Immediately following Canada's declaration of war against Germany on September 10, 1939, I pocketed my new licence and applied for enlistment as a pilot trainee in the Royal Canadian Air Force. I was refused acceptance on the grounds that I had not completed two years of university. I reasoned that if I went back to school, the war would be over before I even entered college. I therefore applied by letter to the Royal Air Force headquarters in London, England, for pilot training. That same day I visited the British Consulate in Toronto. There, a stuffy clerk advised me that "His Majesty's Royal Air Force is not accepting applications for enlistment from Canadians," and terminated the interview. Undeterred, I offered my services by letter to the air ministries of Finland, Australia, and New Zealand, none of whom responded.

One month after its declaration of war the government of Canada announced the creation of the British Commonwealth Air Training Plan. Canada was to become the training ground for its own aircrew volunteers and those from Britain, Australia, and New Zealand. Volunteers would graduate as pilots, navigators, air gunners, and wireless operators. From the outset, the operation proved a remarkable success, but the time required to build a string of major airfields across the country, and acquire the enormous number of assorted aircraft types needed, delayed the acceptance of aircrew volunteers.

During the next eight months I completed RCAF applications in the names of R. Allen Munro, Raymond A. Munro, A. Raymond Munro, and Allen R. Munro. All received no response. I even drove the 100 miles to Trenton Air Base in my Ford, parked it neatly in the deserted lot, and sought an interview with the commanding officer in hopes of gaining his support for enlistment. He was absent from the base, and I was summarily ejected from it by two service police because I'd parked my car under the flag-pole on the main parade square. Not to be stymied, I hitch-hiked from Toronto to Ottawa and applied at RCAF headquarters in my brother's name, Roy McCrae Munro, without his knowledge. I attached to the form a copy of his birth certificate and a statement of his educational achievement—a senior matriculation with a 91 per cent average. Again there was no response.

Spring passed and the summer of 1940 was upon the land. The evacuation of Dunkirk was completed; the aircraft carrier *Glorious* sank; Italy declared war against the Allies; German troops entered Paris; the Maginot Line was breached; the last of the RAF Hurricane fighters had left France for England; and 477 RAF fighter aircraft were announced lost during May and June.

I waited nine months for a call. Then it came.

When I stood before the flight lieutenant I confessed to having filled out more than one application and told my tale honestly.

"Well now, that's some story," he replied, and pondered for a long minute. "But anyone with spunk enough to try as hard to get into action as you have deserves a helping hand. Now, Raymond Allen Munro, take this first application form you filled out last October, together with those papers you brought with you, and see Sergeant Harvey. I'll have a word with him on the intercom. Good luck to you with your medical. And, Munro, better tell your brother about Ottawa."

I could hardly get the words out to thank him. He waved me away with a smile.

The medical took half an hour. Afterwards I was told to return at two o'clock. At that time I was sworn in as an Aircraftsman Second Class and ordered to report for indoctrination and kit issuance, seven days hence, to the RCAF Manning Depot at Toronto's Exhibition Grounds. My war against the Axis powers had begun.

I completed my senior flying training as a fighter pilot in Saskatchewan. That winter, on graduation as a sergeant pilot, I was given a week's embarkation leave. It was taken up by several meetings with Grace, who was then in her fourth year in high school, a visit to Barker Field and farewells to those decent people who had helped fulfil my dream, a goodbye hug from Mother and simple handshake from Father. I then left for the RCAF embarkation pool at Debert, Nova Scotia, a newly built military base pool, set in a quagmire on the outskirts of an Acadian lumbering and farming community.

The most memorable event of that mud-smothered, two-week wait was meeting Sergeant Pilot Joseph Guillaume Laurent Robillard, a slight, elegant, twenty-year-old French Canadian from Ottawa, whose flying experience equalled my own, as did his lust for adventure. Larry Robillard and I were to have many memorable experiences together, commencing with a dangerous voyage to Iceland, where our ship was torpedoed.

We eventually arrived at the RAF's dispersal depot at Uxbridge, on London's western flank. There we were checked in, photographed, issued with extra battle gear, and assigned to various Operational Training Units. Larry and I were among the fortunate few assigned to fly Spitfires in Scotland, and our joy was so great that we threw our caps in the air and hugged each other. Our excitement would have been tempered had we known that only four of our course would survive. But at the time we thought only that the long wait was over. We were finally a part of the war.

THE
WAR BEGINS

SECONDS BEFORE I CRASHED into a rock-strewn rampart of the Grampian Mountains in Scotland, on a misty day in April 1941, I was busy applying what flying skills I had to saving a fine airplane. There was no time to pray for the safety of my person, let alone the salvation of my soul.

The pre-flight check of the Mk-1 Spitfire, newly delivered to the squadron from a factory rebuild after it had seen heroic service during the Battle of Britain, showed no fault. The fighter's agile sprint to 12,000 feet was exhilaratingly swift. The lumbering Fairey Battle light-attack bomber two miles below flew primly straight along the sea's edge, while I, slanting long across the sun-split sky, which was breasted on the north by a fast-rolling wall of yeasty clouds, attacked the white trailing canvas target towed at safety's length behind it.

The wing's eight guns chattered away their ration of shot into and around the make-pretend enemy. I saved some 400 rounds in the unlikely event I made contact with a real enemy aircraft intruding from the North Sea. Gunnery knowledge and false anger spent, I flew past great storm-clouds and darted into and all about their ever-changing secret places. The fullness of life was strong within me as I rolled and frolicked upside-down beneath the clouds' grey-streaked underbellies, which poured rain onto the jagged, reaching rocks below.

Suddenly there was silence. My fingers swiftly went through the sequence of well-rehearsed movements, but none of the valves and handles responded. My eyes checked the flickering needles, without ever ignoring the plane's position relative to the earth.

A narrow valley, boulder-strewn and fearsome, was to be my landing place. Seconds away from contact with earth, all was in readiness: my harness was pulled pain-tight; the hood was open, flaps were down, fuel and electrics were off. Teetering on the edge of the slowest possible landing speed, the plane and I might just have made it safely down.

But that was not to be. In a compacted sequence of sounds and motions, hidden rocks hammered the propeller and the machine's belly into useless waste. The plane turned end for end and slid uphill in a tangle of shrieking metal until it came to rest inverted, the cockpit's mouth pressed greedily against the ground, suspending me inverted in a web of straps and unreachable releases. Daylight fled with agonizing slowness, accompanied by the sickening torment of my ruptured flesh and the almost rhythmic fainting spells that swept my upturned body. All the while the smell of dripping fuel filled my mind with visions of a funeral pyre.

"I'll get ye oot, lad. I'll get ye oot." A highlander's shouted brogue filtered through my agony.

A new pain came then, sudden and sharp, as the tip of the axe wielded by my rescuer bit into my arm. I waited in horror for the steel blade to touch a rock and dance a spark into a sudden whoosh of flame. Yet I couldn't make my voice protest as the kilted woodsman chopped the broken plane in two. The man's urgent shouted orders to his straining, harnessed horse made me finally realize I was almost free.

At last my tomb was wrenched apart to expose me to the spring rain that washed burbles of blood onto my rescuer's great chest as he carried me child-like to the wagon. The wet gloaming closed around us as we moved slowly out of the valley.

Later he explained to me that he ventured into that wilderness only once a year, to seek wood for carving figures. Fortunately, he had seen my Spitfire falter. When it did not emerge, he began searching.

Late that night, after being transferred from wagon to cart to wagon to car and finally to an ambulance, I was hospitalized in Perth.

At dawn, my friend Robillard flew so close to my hospital window that his Spitfire blotted out the daylight. His airplane crossed my field of view once more in the middle of a long victory roll, and then he was gone.

The damage to my body turned out to be less serious than it appeared to be. Outside of head cuts, a sliced arm, swollen lips, and a cut and stiffened knee, I was in great shape—well enough to be interviewed by a crash investigation officer. Three days later, I was back on station, where I was temporarily restricted to non-flying duties until I was cleared of responsibility for the crash and received medical approval to return to airpilot status.

My Spitfire's wreckage was gathered up by a retrieval crew for examination. My detailed report, together with the findings of the engineers, confirmed that sabotage had been the cause of the engine failure. The engineers found that there had been deliberate interference with the fuel gauges connected to each of the Spitfire's tanks. They both registered full, when in fact one was empty. Instead of having eighty minutes of fuel for the speeds and altitude at which I intended to fly, I had instead taken off with less than forty minutes. My fighter had just plain run out of gas.

Vic Arnold, a fellow Canadian pilot, was killed the day I was returned to flying status. His Miles Master trainer suffered in-flight damage and crashed savagely on the aerodrome. We buried him in a pilot's grave on a spring afternoon as rifles volleyed in the warm rain.

By dinner time, Robillard and I were in trouble. Over lunch we had come up with a scheme that would test our skill and our friendship. We had decided that we would fly our Spitfires in complete unison with me following Robillard's every move for an hour. It was one of those superbly irresponsible undertakings that were the hallmark of unblooded Canadian fighter pilots. It was agreed that there would be no radio conversation between us or with the ground. We would obtain permission from the control tower ostensibly for a low-level exercise in the Grampian Mountains. Then from the moment his aircraft began moving on the runway, I would follow him. We planned to use the battle-tested head signals with which a leader could tell his wing man about changes of direction. There were also fist signals for other requirements.

I tucked my Spitfire up close to his on the runway. With the brakes full on we advanced our throttles until the brakes could no longer resist the enormous energy of the massive propellers. Together we unleashed the Spitfires, lifting the tails into the air and then hurtling arrow-straight down the runway. At the slightest backwards nod of Robillard's head I lifted the wheels of my fighter from the concrete, still flying almost within touching distance of his craft. We were scarcely a man's height from earth when I followed his second nod and raised the wheels.

Every aircraft made has specific speeds at which each manoeuvre must be carried out. One of the written examinations at the OTU was on the correct speeds for every different attitude of our particular airplanes. We had both committed to memory all these vital numbers, but because I could not safely take my eyes from Robillard's head as long as I remained almost glued to him, I had to place my faith in his retentive powers, which I did without hesitation. He levelled out about six feet above the runway and reached quickly behind his head to close and lock his cockpit's canopy. I did the same. But even after my air-speed indicator touched the approved climbing speed of 140 miles an hour, he held his Spitfire at the same height above the ground. We passed the runway's end, then sped across the perimeter fence and between two large trees, level with their bottom branches. Our propellers were still in fine pitch, the throttles giving maximum climbing power to our engines.

I knew by the blur of the passing landscape that we had passed 200 miles an hour. Still Robillard held his airplane flat to the ground; with each second the desire to pull up and away from him grew. Finally the whine of the engine and the whistling blur of the outside view convinced me that I was indeed as mad as Robillard. At that moment his head flicked ever so slightly back, and we arced upwards into the first half of a tight loop. At the top, he rolled off, coming out right side up directly over the end of the runway we had just left. The book speed for that manoeuvre was 320 miles an hour, which all reason told me we had not reached.

Without even a sideways glance to check that I was still with him, Robillard next lowered the nose of his Spitfire and dived between the two main hangars of the air station. Each of us had no more than a dozen feet clearance on either side. Then he began a full barrel roll. We were by this time going over 300 miles an hour, and I had fallen behind. Clinging wildly to his tail, I followed him north into the bowels of the Grampian Mountains.

For the next hour I stayed with him in line abreast, in line astern, in vic formation, and even upside-down through twisting valleys, across marshes, and almost into the tops of trees. Suddenly beneath us was the town of Gallowridge. We brushed the houses with our turbulence at some 350 miles an hour, then lanced between the smokestacks of Culross and straight down the centre of the River Forth with only a yard between our propellers and the water. Suddenly I knew what his last manoeuvre would be: he intended to loop the Forth railway bridge. In that blinding instant I knew that I too was committed to the magnificent folly.

There were three great steel arches spanning the broad river. We went straight for the centre one, passed beneath it, then pulled up as one into a tight, blood-draining loop. Hurtling downwards in the final arc, we bottomed out almost into the water and shot under the span once more. Then spray-high atop the vessel-dotted river past Inchcolm Island, we tucked into a steep right turn to bring us over downtown Edinburgh. Finally we blasted back across the roof-tops to a gentle slow-down before a formation landing on the same runway we had left when we were so much younger.

They were waiting for us as we taxied our Spitfires back: the station commander, the unit commander, the adjutant, and two service policemen. Not a word was spoken. The adjutant merely curled a beckoning finger at us. We followed them reluctantly into the station commander's office, the S.P.s following behind.

We expected that a court martial with dismissal from the service would be our fate after a brief but severe questioning. We stood rigidly at attention before the seated group, to whom we told exactly what had happened.

"You are confined to base until further orders and restricted from any contact with aircraft," was the initial judgement.

The following day Bill Greenfield crashed onto the airfield just a short sprint from Robillard and me. We pulled his body from the cockpit just as the first tongues of flame flickered from beneath the wreckage. Bill was a tough and craggy Englishman whose two purposes in life were to engage the enemy and to live each day to the utmost limit of his capabilities. He was rushed to the base hospital where it was ascertained that several bones were broken. He also had some rather serious lacerations and body bruises.

He was out of the operating room and his old ebullient self when Robillard and I arrived in the early evening with a bottle of banana rum secreted in a gas-mask bag. After the usual amenities and commiserations we got down to some serious drinking, at the end of which we dressed Greenfield in parts of his uniform, smuggled him out a side window, and carried him aboard an Edinburgh-bound bus to a local pub.

The drinks were on anyone who wanted the privilege of auto-graphing Greenfield's casts. The party went on until midnight, when several rather drunken wenches of questionable repute car-ried the unprotesting patient off in a taxi. Robillard and I stayed on with the intention of separating some of the civilians from their money. He had an enormous capacity for fluid despite his slim build, and I bet all comers that he could drink two half-pints of beer, one of mild and one of bitter, one immediately after the other, while standing on his head.

When I had taken all the bets I propped him upside-down on his head in a corner with his feet touching the angled walls above, giving him the stabilization he required. I then passed him two glasses in quick succession. He downed them as though the fluid was being sucked up in a vacuum.

He flipped himself back on his feet, shook hands all around, and then very casually approached the bar, where he ordered another pint. While it was being drawn, he eased himself unobtrusively out of the room and into the toilet where he coughed up the previous intake. When he returned to the bar, he quaffed the third one down in one gulp.

We staggered aboard the last bus back to the base after failing to locate Greenfield. The next day we learned that he'd been found asleep in a hotel wash-room with his pants missing. He was very drunk and offered no resistance to the S.P.s who drove him back to the station hospital.

Greenfield, sterling fellow that he was, refused to name his abductors and even went so far as to cite Robillard and me as being the sole cause of his survival. He went on in his written report to the adjutant to create the illusion that, with an utter disregard for our own personal safety, Robillard and I had entered the already burn-ing cockpit, fought to release the harness that was restraining his unconscious person, and despite fearful heat and the ever-present possibility of an exploding gas tank, removed his battered body and carried it a safe distance from the wreck.

"Nonsense," thundered the station commander at the two of us as we stood at attention before him. "What Sergeant Greenfield has reported is a bag of cocks-wallow and you both bloody well know it. I know what you did. Oh, you pulled him out all right, as any little old lady on crutches could have done, and then, by God, you got him drunk and stole his body, hauled it off to Edinburgh, and sold tickets to see the poor benighted sod all wrapped in bleeding bandages and wet casts. Then to your everlasting disgrace you gave him like a side-show freak to a pack of lascivious whores, who likely starred him in a sex circus, then discarded him in a bloody latrine. Oh, I know all about you two!

"However" — his face lost some of its magenta colouring and his hands stopped trembling — "we shall first deal with yesterday and that fucking idiotic flying circus you two put on. You are now ordered to sleep during mealtimes and take what nourishment you can find after your usual daily classes are attended, at the close of which you will attach yourselves body and soul to Pilot Officer Day. You will serve in the control tower as he sees fit during the hours of darkness. If he determines for any reason that you will pilot a Spitfire he will so order you.

"About the Greenfield affair — as most regretfully I shall always remember it — you will not communicate with him in any manner until he has been released from hospital. You are confined to base until further orders, unless your services are required by Pilot Officer Day. Now get out of here!"

Pilot Officer Day was a lanky and personable young English gentleman who had completed a tour of duty as a Spitfire pilot, and was sent to Grangemouth to pass along his hard-earned skills to would-be fighter pilots like Robillard and me. He was an easy-going fellow with a taste for good wine. When Robillard and I, in a most contrite manner, entered the control tower that evening with a bottle of decent claret we'd purchased with our winnings from the headstand caper, he was captivated by our charm, but refused to remove the cork and sample the vintage while on duty.

The three-storeyed, square, white-painted, wooden tower overlooked the airfield in all directions. It controlled the runway lighting and all radio contact with airborne and ground vehicles, and was connected by telephone to all operations quarters of the station and to the sector's operations room at Edinburgh.

"If the weather remains in this soggy state," Pilot Officer Day waved a carefully manicured hand at the windows, through which we could see that the whole airfield was already wrapped in a damp blanket of mist, "we shall have ourselves a flight this very night. And I shall tuck you two fledgling birdmen under my wings, so to speak, trusting in your ability to maintain an exquisitely tight formation, with the hope that your ability to control an aircraft about the three axes of flight is truly superior to that puerile display of airmanship which I and your other instructors were witness to earlier." This lengthy dissertation, given without inhalation, left me marvelling at the capacity of his lungs.

Just before dark, Day ordered Robillard to taxi Day's own Spitfire and two others, fully fuelled and armed, from the flight line to the readiness area adjacent to the control tower, and to advise the ground crews they were on red alert.

"As of this moment," explained Day, "you may consider yourselves operational fighter pilots, comprising Red Section, and ready to leap at any moment into your aircraft and follow me into the jaws of hell, if necessary. You, Robillard, will be my number two, unless you have forgotten where that position is relative to a vic formation. And you, Munro, shall be my number three. When we leave it will be in a terrible hurry, and because of this unspeakable weather, we shall take off as one, remain together aloft as one, and land as one. Now, is that portion of the exercise abundantly clear to you?"

"Sir." Robillard held up his hand as a schoolboy to a teacher. "If one or both of us loses contact with you, what are your orders?"

"Sergeant Robillard," Day said, leaning back in his chair and pointing his index finger at Larry, "if either of you amateurs posing as professionals has the misfortune to leave my side for any cause, you shall not graduate with your class. Is that quite clear?"

We nodded, elated that courts-martial had apparently been avoided.

"We shall communicate between ourselves on B channel," he went on. "You will not arm your guns until I so order, which is highly unlikely, and you will refrain from uttering any word on the radio transmitter, unless it is to advise me immediately, in a normal voice and with a paucity of words, of the sighting of another aircraft, be it friend or foe. Is that too quite clear?"

Again we nodded.

"From now until that moment arrives, when we shall assume that we have been scrambled to intercept an intruding enemy, you will close your minds to all else except recalling those areas of your training that concern operational night flights," he said, concluding the briefing.

We sat silent through the next hour, absorbed in our own thoughts, interrupted twice by telephone calls from operational control in Edinburgh with information that London was taking a bad mauling from enemy bombs. The true extent of the damage inflicted on that night of May 10, 1941, was not published until after the war. Only then did I learn that 1,212 people had been killed, 1,769 seriously injured; some 2,000 fires had started, and the House of Commons had been severely damaged by bombs. It was the last great raid on London for almost three years. Meanwhile, Hamburg was being attacked by 110 RAF bombers.

An instant after the telephone jangled and Day spoke briefly into it, he was on his feet and headed for the stairs. While the corporal alerted the ground crews to start the engines, I tumbled after Robillard, who was on Day's heels. I zipped up my Irving jacket against the chill night and took the steps three at a time in my downward plunge. The props were being pulled through as we grabbed our parachutes from the port wings where they had just been placed, buckled them on, and clambered onto the wet wing-step and into the damp cockpits, pulling on our helmets which rested on the control column and fastening our restraining harness.

After Day waved away his ground crew, and Robillard and I had followed suit, we began the familiar taxiing-out routine, slipping off the parking brake, opening the radiator shutters fully, and checking the vital air pressure supply which activated the brakes, flaps, and guns. I caught up with Day and Robillard as they turned from the perimeter track onto the runway. When they stopped, I took my position to the side of Day's Spitfire opposite Robillard. We locked our brakes on and cleared the engines, losing ourselves in the tumbling roar of the three mighty machines. Suddenly Day released his brakes, triggering the same action in Robillard and me. With full power fed to the propeller blades, we left the earth behind us, smothered in ear-pounding echoes. We were tucked together as one, enveloped in a black wetness, lancing upwards on a heading that would place us over Edinburgh in three minutes.

"Red Leader here." Day's calm voice broke the tension. "There's a bandit about, a one-one-oh, at low level, inbound. Arm your guns, stay alert, and sing out if you sight the fuckah."

It took all my physical co-ordination to stay beside Day's Spitfire, which frequently appeared as only a shadowy wraith in the enveloping vapours, and to keep a tight rein on my jangled thoughts and on my fear of the shame and discipline that would surely follow if I lost him.

"Steady, chaps." His crackling voice snapped me back to reality.

"We're turning port and descending rather abruptly to angels one on a recip heading." With that terse message he rolled the nose of his Spitfire down into a tight half-turn which left my plane above and behind him and approaching Robillard, who sheared away earthwards to avoid a collision and to catch our leader. I did the same and fortunately recovered my position without accident.

"The fuckah's gone for the deck and hopefully into a hill. We, kiddies, are returning to base." Day's summary of the aborted intercept flushed the adrenalin from my system.

We landed individually, after breaking off from the formation beneath the cloud layer at 400 feet, then taxied back to the revetments we had left only seventeen minutes before.

Monday morning we listened with excitement to a BBC radio report. Rudolf Hess, Hitler's deputy, had flown from Germany in a twin-engined fighter on Saturday evening. He had passed over Edinburgh and abandoned his crashing plane near Glasgow. Hess parachuted onto the Duke of Hamilton's estate, where he was captured, without resistance, by a ploughman. It was clearly Hess's aircraft that Day, Robillard, and I had searched for on our intercept mission.

Of more importance to Robillard and me was news of our posting to No. 145 Spitfire Squadron at Merston, Sussex. We were the only two pilots from our course to be sent to what was then referred to as Hell's Half-Acre.

BADER'S
BUS COMPANY

RAF FIGHTER COMMAND comprised five groups: No. 14 defended Scotland, 13 northern England, 12 the Midlands, 10 southwest England, and 11 the southeast, with the city of London as its centre. The hottest sector of the southeast was immediately east of Portsmouth at Tangmere, where a three-squadron wing of Spitfires, led by Wing Commander Douglas Bader, the legless ace of the Battle of Britain, was headquartered. The wing comprised squadrons 145, 610, and 616, and was affectionately known to the British and distastefully to the Germans as Bader's Bus Company.

Commanding 145 Squadron at the satellite field of March Farm, a few miles to the west, was Squadron Leader Percival Stanley Turner. The squadron's full flying complement was eighteen Mk-2b Spitfires and twenty-two pilots. The planes were originally Mk-1s increased in engine power, with four of the usual eight .303 wing-mounted machine-guns supplanted by two 20mm Hispano cannons, one mounted in each wing. The cannons alone carried 120 rounds of mixed fire-power in the form of tracer, ball, high-explosive, and armour-piercing ammunition, a formidable weapons array in the hands of a skilled pilot.

It was into this illustrious company that Robillard and I were thrown, replacing two pilots who had fallen to enemy guns only days before. Here, too, were the elite of Fighter Command and here also lay the first line of aerial defence for the greatest city on earth and those who dwelled in it. It was, indeed, a holy place at an unholy time.

As part of the squadron, we had many roles. We escorted bombers on daylight raids into northern France in great mixed-wing air armadas, code-named Circus; we made lone convoy patrols over Allied shipping in the English Channel to guard that vital sea lane from air attacks by the Luftwaffe and from sea attacks by German submarines and motor torpedo boats; we flew intrusive sweeps over the continent in either wing or squadron configuration to entice the Luftwaffe into combat; we took part in two-plane search-and-destroy missions into France called Rhubarbs. This last method of attacking the enemy on the ground, and in the air as well if such circumstances arose, was considered by some pilots to be an act of sheer madness or a dirty date with fate and by others as the ultimate in flying excitement. But more often then not it took the life of at least one of the adventurous duo. Cumulatively, Rhubarbs did considerable damage to the enemy and piqued them at times into stupid reprisals that cost them dearly. Such sorties also became a safety valve for those pilots demanding contact with the enemy as a release from the crushing ennui.

Earlier teams that carried out these dangerous sorties comprised Willy McKnight and Ben Brown, and John Latta and Laurie Cryderman. All were killed within weeks.

By June 1941, Fighter Command, having gained air superiority over England, was going on the offensive. History would record that the Battle of Britain ended in late 1940, but for Robillard and me, it was still going on.

Squadron Leader Turner was a superbly trained man of twenty-four with a low tolerance for sloth. His job, as he saw it, was to destroy the enemy from his airplane, killing as many and as often as possible, and wreaking havoc upon the German war machine. His unflinching and resolute leadership caused those under his command to excel themselves as he himself did and to accept his orders without comment. As a result, the squadron was responsible for horrendous losses to the enemy, relative to the numbers of men and machines it lost.

Without knowing it, Turner would keep me alive through my first and most perilous confrontations with the enemy. He taught me by his own indomitable courage that fear was a friend, not an enemy.

We were given our new Spitfires, assigned to us as personal mounts. Mine was code-named SO-B, "SO" being the designation for 145 Squadron and "B" the identity of that particular aircraft. It was, of course, impolitely referred to by all as "B for Bastard." Robillard's machine, SO-P, was its twin. We cared for them as though they meant our lives, which in fact they did.

It was during this mating time of man and machine that Robillard gained a nickname. A Polish pilot, unable to pronounce Larry's surname, found it easier to say "Rhubarb." Later on, Larry would unintentionally invent a new aerial manoeuvre that would bear his name. It was known throughout the war as the Rhubarb Roll.

Days grew into weeks, and life became more uncertain. We flew tactical training missions, convoy patrols, squadron intrusions into France, and jousted with the various enemy fighter squadrons that speckled the coastline from Calais to Cherbourg. Wing Commander Douglas Bader had given our squadron new cannon-armed Spitfires and positioned us as top cover for the wing's sweeps, which meant that we flew in the rarefied air at 30,000 feet, where we used up fuel at a rapid rate, shortening the planes' range and operational usefulness.

It was from this position that we followed Turner into attack formation to defend the bombers against enemy fighters that tried to dive on them from above. Consequently our squadron saw less action on a one-to-one basis than the lower-flying Spitfires and Hurricanes, but on occasion violent dogfights ensued. The first enemy fighter I fired at was an Me-109. It had cut in front of me, and I had made such an abrupt turn to starboard to follow it that I stalled my aircraft. It flipped over into a spin that took 10,000 feet to recover from.

The radio transmitter was alive with chatter from the squadron's pilots, some engaged in individual duels with the enemy and others calling out positions of German fighters.

"Look out, Blue Leader. Bandit at three o'clock."

"Two 109s front and centre," Turner's voice crackled, as I struggled at full throttle to reach the skirmish almost two miles above me while watching for enemy fighters.

And then it was over. The squadron reformed and headed homeward with several fewer Spitfires and the men who flew them than had taken off only one long hour before.

We paired up for several routine convoy patrols over the next two days, not being required to defend the shipping against an enemy attack, and carried out two more sweeps without firing our guns. Then the squadron joined 610 and 616 for a wing venture into France. We had a major scuffle with several squadrons of 109s. I managed to elude one in such a violent turn that, in trying to follow me, the enemy pilot slammed into another 109. They spiralled downwards in an ever-tightening circle as I sought out the bulk of the squadron to rejoin them.

Newcomers to a front-line squadron were usually blooded in the position known as Tail-End Charlie. This plane brought up the squadron's rear and weaved back and forth in search of enemy aircraft. Its pilot was responsible for alerting the squadron to the enemy's presence astern, if indeed the pilot survived, as he often didn't when an enemy attacked from out of the sun. Robillard and I were seldom spared that job in early June. The physically debilitating and dangerous assignment brought us closer together, as did the sometimes snobbish attitude of the British, who kept the Poles, Czechs, and us two Canadians at arm's length.

When weeks-old letters arrived from home, I learned that my parents had moved from Toronto to a house on the bank of the Severn River in the Muskoka area. Pictures showed Mother relaxing on a lawn swing near Father, who was holding a finny monster he had just caught from the river passing by the back door. Roy had enlisted and was stationed at Carberry, Manitoba, undergoing his service flying training, and was pleased with his progress. He hoped to be selected as a fighter pilot but doubted he could get a transfer from the twin-engine course he had been assigned to. The letters from Grace were buoyant and detailed the events that filled her high-school days, plans for the summer holidays, and her thoughts about either continuing her studies at university after graduation, or fitting herself into some business role. She sounded bright and cheerful and untouched by the global conflict in which I was so enmeshed.

I had never spoken of love to her, although I had on occasion intimated that I cared for her in my own imperfect way. Her letters filled me with a desire to hold onto that which had been so comfortable between us. I decided one afternoon to write before the sun set and tell her in simple words that my life would be the better if she would wait for me to return, when I could speak to her of my inner feelings and my hopes for the future.

I committed a cardinal sin on my return from my last sweep with the squadron in June. During that mission I had again been Tail-End Charlie. Turner had us all tucked in together in a near-perfect vic formation, and I was holding position as the last airplane on the starboard side. The beautifully formed arrowhead shape arced gracefully around the airfield and lined up into the wind for the touchdown. Each pilot watched the one ahead for the almost imperceptible signals that started and ended the turns, the lowering of the landing gear and the flaps, then the final forward head nod for the kiss to earth.

A sudden splash of yellow against the brown-green grass, dead in line with the Bastard's scything propeller, triggered my reflexes into instant action. I rammed on full throttle and hauled the stick hard over and back as my Spitfire's starboard tire roiled the air above the head of an unsuspecting tractor driver, trapped in his own deafening world of rumbling exhausts and chattering mower blades.

Moments later, I too landed. Even before I'd disengaged myself from the cockpit, Turner was there, tousled red hair matching his mood. He jabbed his pipe-stem at me.

"Well?" he thundered.

"Well, what?" I parried.

"You fucking well know bloody well what!" he exploded.

"But—" I tried to explain.

"You fucking well broke formation, that's bloody well what!" He was apoplectic.

"But if I hadn't bloody well pulled up, I'd have bloody well creamed that stupid son of a bitch and killed myself," I shouted at him.

"That's *my* responsibility, not yours." Turner bit off the words and spun away. I knew then I'd lost my chance for a Rhubarb flight with Robillard—a flight we had both requested. What I did not know was that on the morrow I would face my greatest ordeal.

I drew a mid-morning patrol of a convoy of merchant vessels moving through the English Channel between the Isle of Wight and Cherbourg, under low cloud cover and occasional showers. Since most of the cargo ships had some form of armament, whether it was a single deck gun or small arms, and since the two Royal Navy ships packed a medium wallop of fire-power and were always trigger-happy when any aircraft was thought to be near, it was prudent to identify oneself as a friendly presence *outside* shooting range. But since enemy radio installations along the French coast monitored the sea traffic's radio chatter, it was imperative not to break radio silence. My arrival time on patrol was pre-arranged with the convoy commander, but even after I had ventured close enough to let them identify my aircraft as friendly, I stayed far enough away to ensure I wouldn't get hit if they started firing.

I'd been circling the convoy, paying special attention to the south where the French coast lay bathed in rain, when suddenly the radio transmitter channel connecting my aircraft to the convoy commander's vessel and the navy ships came alive. There was a crackling interchange of terse messages concerning the positive sighting of a submerging German submarine immediately to the northeast of the convoy.

I shoved on full engine power even as I started a low diving turn to place me in line with the U-boat. I saw it at once, dead ahead and submerging, with only the rail of the conning tower still above water. Spray was breaking over it from the speed of the dive. My thumb was already positioned for firing the two cannons. I triggered them into a short burst, but stopped when I saw that the first shells had churned up the water beside it because of my awkward firing angle.

With throttle full on I pulled the Spitfire up into a loop. As I came out of the overcast towards the almost submerged submarine a second time, I eased my thumb to the centre position of the firing switch to bring all four machine-guns into play with the cannons. Only an outline of the enemy remained above the sea as I centred the target in the glowing gun sight and brought the cannons to life.

There was one hell of an explosion, and the Bastard lurched up and backwards as though it had been slapped by the hand of Thor.

Assuming I had been hit by a German fighter, I pulled the Spitfire into a tight steep turn to port. But the plane was not handling properly, and as I tightened the turn, satisfied that no tailing enemy could get his sights on me, I glanced quickly to my right and saw a hole large enough for a pony to jump through torn completely through the wing only a few feet from the cockpit. Pieces of the wing's aluminium skin were being peeled backwards by the roaring air and ripped off as I reduced the power and pulled the turn even tighter.

With the Spitfire standing vertically on its side, shuddering on the near edge of a high-speed stall that would send me out of control into the sea only a few hundred feet below, I craned my neck to try to spot the fighter that had nailed me. My mind was alive with the options. I could not hold the tight turn with the damaged wing, yet if I broke out of it I was a sitting duck. I could not parachute into the sea, because the chute would not deploy in time. Even if it did, the German pilot would likely have shot me full of holes while I was hanging under it. And even if luck was with me and I made it into the water safely I would have drowned, because my life-jacket was full of the holes it had suffered while standing in as the sergeant's mess dartboard. I momentarily considered edging lower to the sea in the steep turn, then straightening out to get close to the convoy, so I could set the plane down on the water. That would have been a death sentence as well, because a Spitfire sank in less than a minute, and no vessel would dare stop for a rescue. Also I would have been taking the fighter within range of ships that could not fire at my attacker without hitting me. My only option was to try to get him to overshoot me, and then either get lucky with a salvo as he passed or ram him in the side.

In anticipation of taking the latter course, I pulled the quick release on the Perspex canopy and lost it to the slip-stream, chopped the power off, and slipped the landing gear lever into the down position. It was like hitting a car's brakes at high speed on dry pavement. I tensed for the shellfire I felt sure was coming. Through the dizziness I was suffering from the sustained high G-loading in the steep turn, I shouted, "Why in hell is this happening to me?" I should have known, but had not lived long enough to have learned, that the time I spent on asking why was time I should have applied to some superior airmanship. My error flipped the Spitfire upside-down.

With both hands on the stick I pulled with all my strength as I kicked full left rudder, horsing the Spitfire back onto an even keel. I was still flying at a sickeningly slow speed just above the surface of the sea.

It was then I heard myself asking the unforgivable: for God to help me in a contest with death that I felt I could not win. It wasn't fear of the pain that I would feel, or that others would feel at my passing, that caused me to pray. Life was, to me, the second greatest adventure; death was the first. Yet I had scarcely begun my earthly quest. It was for a chance to fulfil my prime purpose in being alive that I asked for help. And the act left me suddenly ashamed.

I shouted my rejection of it into the tearing wind and damned myself for the cowardice of asking. Then I gentled the shuddering craft and set the retracting lever to raise the wheels into their wing recesses. But they would not rise. The mechanism had been damaged by the explosion.

Still I waited for the bullets to enter my back. When no pain came with the rattle of gun-fire or the whine of bullets ricocheting from the armour-plate, I yawed the airplane slightly to each side to bring the sky behind me into view in the mirror above my windscreen. There was nothing. No enemy, no convoy, nothing moving. I was alone, out of sight of land, hidden by mist, somewhere east of the Isle of Wight and captive aboard an aircraft that took all my strength to hold in level flight.

In one flash of pure brilliance it came to me! I had not been attacked by an enemy fighter at all. Instead, a high-explosive shell had somehow detonated inside the mechanism of the starboard cannon.

A split second later the Spitfire shuddered violently as another large strip of wing cover was whipped away. The Smith clock on the dancing instrument panel showed that I had been airborne for fifty-three minutes; sixteen of them en route to the convoy, thirty-one in circling, and six year-long minutes in attacking the submarine twice, turning repeatedly to shake my supposed attacker and to clean up my act for the ordeal that lay ahead. I gentled the nose to port and started home.

My squadron's airstrip was worn into the sparse grass of a farmer's field near Chichester in southern England. It was a sight I wanted to see more than anything I could remember. But as each long minute passed, my nausea increased. The Spitfire kept rolling onto its back, and my strength ebbed from fighting to right it. After another vicious half-roll, during which I viewed the earth from upside-down, I saw the distant landmarks I so desperately sought.

With what I knew was the last of my strength, I muscled the Spitfire right side up. I was close enough to the ground to read the squadron letters SO-A on Turner's Spitfire, and to recognize his coverall-clad figure running in the direction of my possible crash site. Instinctively I gave full attention to the frightening undulations of the damaged aerofoil, which was determined to part from the fuselage.

My wounded craft then sought the earth and folded its broken wing a breath away from a safe landing. It impaled itself on hard, unyielding, man-made things, breaking its back in a final, wrenching crash. I was mercifully unable to sense my hurts, as Turner reached the truncated fuselage and crawled beneath it to free me from my harness. Then he carried me to the oncoming ambulance.

I awoke without pain in a cheerful Chichester hospital room to learn that my injuries had been repaired and that I would eventually be none the worse for my ungentle meeting with the ground. The list of hurts was not unanticipated, and consisted of concussion, a smashed kneecap, dislocated elbow, swollen feet, severe cuts on both thumbs, shrapnel shards in my right leg from the exploding shell, and a back bent awkwardly out of its normal alignment. It was late afternoon when Larry arrived, a look of concern etched on his face.

"Well, buddy," he asked solicitously, "how are you feeling?"

"Terrible, rotten, lousy, and I hurt all over." I was exaggerating a bit but the drugs in fact had begun to wear off.

"Turner's coming over soon to find out what happened. The Bastard's a write-off. The starboard wing broke off when you landed."

"The goddamn cannon exploded and I almost bought the farm," I explained between pulsations of pain. "I couldn't jump as I was too goddamn low, and I couldn't ditch because the wheels wouldn't come up. When I ran out of options, I decided to try for home base."

We talked for a few minutes, then he was asked to leave by a nurse who came to take the pain away with another blessed needle.

Turner arrived that evening, brusque and forthright, enquiring briefly into the state of my health and insisting that I would be physically able to get back to flying duties in short order. He asked for a detailed account of the convoy patrol and the explosion. He was particularly interested in how the damaged wing affected the performance of the Spitfire in flight. I told him as much as I could about the chain of events and about my concern that the wing would fall off at any moment.

"You're just bloody lucky, Munro. A high-explosive shell exploded in the breech of the cannon, blew that all to hell, then riddled the main spar with shrapnel, all but cutting it in half. Some of the flying metal damaged the small rear spar. Shrapnel sprayed all over and through the side wall of the cockpit, and the starboard wheel was blown off with its axle. Had you put any further strain on that wing before you landed, you'd be on a slab in the morgue. The only thing holding the wing together was the aluminium skin." He lit his pipe.

"Why did it happen?" I asked him.

"Since the war started a number of aircraft have been lost because of exploding cannons. Most of the pilots died. The few who survived baled out. So until yours arrived back here intact, we couldn't determine the fault. When I know more about it, I'll tell you. And the brass from Group are talking it up about your sticking with the machine and getting it back so we could have a look at it. They think you put up a bloody good show. You'll be hearing more about yesterday." He blew a cloud of cheap smoke into the air as he sauntered out.

Almost to the day seven years later in Vancouver, he told me about the English machinist who worked in the munitions factory that made the type of high-explosive shells that had taken the Bastard's life and nearly claimed mine. Every so often this Nazi sympathizer would craft the nose of one high-explosive shell slightly larger than the specifications called for, just large enough that it would detonate itself as it was rammed into the gun barrel. Because inspections were carried out by supervisors infrequently and at random, none of the defective shells was ever spotted and all made their way into British weapons. The Bastard's broken cannon and the salvaged shell casing were the clues that led to the culprit, and to his arrest and eventual conviction, the penalty for which I was never to learn. Twice, then, I had been the victim of sabotage.

Turner also told me that he had been instructed on that July day to commend me in an official manner for my actions. "I had a choice between putting you up for a commission or for a medal," he said. "I chose the commission because I had learned that your brother had just graduated as a pilot officer. And with luck you'd have many more opportunities to earn a gong."

"Well," I remonstrated over drinks, "I'm grateful to you for many things, but I do think you should have given me the choice."

"Why?" he queried with a laugh. "It was none of your fucking business."

The next day was a bad one for the squadron and a very bad one for Larry Robillard. The events of the day would soon become the basis of a Canadian adventure magazine article, would bring him the Distinguished Flying Medal, would set the stage for an audacious endeavour, and would give him the title of Ottawa's Ace.

I learned about the day's events that evening from a pilot who came to visit me. Apparently the wing's three squadrons had been assigned to act as forward cover for a bombing raid on a target near Lille, 200 miles from base on the border of Belgium. Robillard flew as Turner's wing man. Almost immediately after crossing the French coast, they were engaged by enemy aircraft.

With a trio of Me-109s slanting at them, Larry broke into a sharp turn amid the crackle of gun-fire and found himself near a parachute. Thinking the man dangling underneath it was Turner, and seeing an enemy fighter boring in, Robillard tackled the enemy from astern in a vertical dive, striking it several times with cannon fire. The fighter exploded and the German pilot was seen baling out. As Robillard started to pull out of his dive, he was overshot by another 109, which turned away from him. He followed it, firing, until it too rolled over on its back with smoke streaming from it and plunged earthwards.

Suddenly shells began striking his airplane from behind and ricocheting off the armour-plate guarding his back. He twisted the Spitfire away and into the face of three more German fighters. He held the gun button down and headed straight for the leader. Just as they were about to collide and with the enemy's fire coming directly at him, he was through them, or so he thought, and into the clear. He went into a steep dive to escape when more bullets reached into his airplane. Suddenly the left wing was blown completely off. With Larry trapped in the cockpit, the Spitfire SO-P twisted into its death spiral only seconds above the earth.

"It wasn't the C.O. under the chute," explained the pilot who had brought me the news, "but a pilot from 610 Squadron. The C.O.'s plane had been hit and was on fire, but as he started to bale out, a 109 made the mistake of flying in front of him. Turner slipped back into the cockpit and blew the enemy fighter all to hell, then dived his plane straight down until the fire went out. He then flew it back to base."

"Any hope for Larry?" I could easily imagine Robillard's feelings during those last moments, being so fresh myself from holding the hem of death's mantle.

"No parachute was seen," the pilot explained And he left to keep a well-earned date with some aged ale.

During my recovery Bader was shot down, and some of the starch went out of the Tangmere Wing; Iceland was occupied by U.S. forces; RAF Ferry Command was formed; Stalin was named commissar of Russia's defences; the RAF bombed Cologne; the Germans bombed Leningrad; and Roy graduated near the top of his wing's class as a fighter/bomber pilot. He was posted to Charlottetown, Prince Edward Island, for a course in general reconnaissance, then shipped to England for operational training with the RAF. The letters from him and my parents and Grace bolstered my spirits during the boring hospital routine, which was punctuated only by daily physiotherapy treatments on my knee and back.

WAR-TORN
SKIES

IT WAS LATE in September 1941 and I was a week away from a medical board that might see me discharged as fit for flying duty. Late one night I was seated in the hospital lounge playing bridge.

"Hi, Ray, how's everything going?" a voice behind me asked.

"Great," I answered without turning my head. "And how's it with you?"

"Couldn't be better old sp—"

Then it hit me with an almost physical force. It was Robillard's voice! I spun around so fast I fell out of the chair. As I rose from the floor I saw him, slim and straight and looking great. Our arms reached around each other unashamedly and we hugged. I kept shouting at him to tell me he wasn't a ghost, that it was the real him.

We sat on my bed while he picked up the thread of his adventure after confirming that what I had been told concerning his fate was correct. When he went into the spin, he had tried desperately, without success, to jettison the Spitfire's hood. The airplane had been descending too fast and the G forces caused him to black out. Then an explosion dismembered the fighter and flung him through the whistling debris into free air. He came to immediately, pulled the rip-cord on his parachute, and moments later landed barefooted near a railway line on the edge of a farmer's field. He ditched his parachute and started along the tracks, coming face to face almost immediately with a young boy. Speaking fluent French, Robillard identified himself and followed the lad, Jean Couderc, to his home. The boy's parents were members of the Resistance and helped Larry escape into southern France. From there he climbed the Pyrenees, travelled across Spain to Gibraltar, and was flown back to Britain by the RAF.

Robillard had received almost £200 in back pay. With that, we escaped from the hospital and headed for London and the Strand Palace Hotel, where we spent five days looking up old friends and generally carousing.

Robillard returned with me to Matlock. He had two days left before he was required to report back to 145 Squadron, and offered to accompany me to the hospital to face my punishment. The officer in charge had been a senior surgeon with hospital administration experience before the war. He was a thorough gentleman and most casual considering his position.

"You have admitted absenting yourself from this unit without permission, sergeant, and you have honestly explained your reasons for doing so. There is no doubt in my mind that your recent escapade was the stimulation you required to get you back on the track. You appear to be physically none the worse for your adventure." He spoke in measured tones. "What you both need is a good night's sleep. By mid-morning the required paperwork for your dismissal from Matlock Hospital will have been prepared, and a travel warrant readied for your return by train to Catterick. You, sergeant"—he nodded to Robillard—"will have to make your own way there as I have no jurisdiction over your comings and goings. That is all except goodbye and good fortune to you both."

Outside we collapsed in a paroxysm of joy. After a filling meal and hot baths we slept and dreamed the dreams of innocents.

Before dark the next day we were clapping the backs of those few pilots who had lived through a time that most men only read about.

Turner professed little interest in my return, preferring to have a rather spirited conversation with Robillard about the last flight they'd had together, when SO-P went to that great aerodrome in the sky. He then straightened himself up, causing us to come to some semblance of attention, and gruffly advised Robillard that he'd been awarded the Distinguished Flying Medal.

"Now, you two, it's a new ball game here. We're converting to Spit 5s and we'll be the operational squadron in this sector. There are a lot of new hands here and I don't want any of your bad habits brushing off on them. Now get out of here and get to work."

The conversion to the new model was simple. My own new machine, coded SO-V, was brilliant in its handling qualities and forgiveness of human error. The main advantages of the Mk-Vb (a Model 5 Spitfire with four machine-guns and two cannon) were a more powerful engine and a defroster built into the windscreen.

Our first assignment was clearly intended as punishment for our misdeeds. Commencing at dawn each and every day, we formed a two-plane squadron that served as fighter protection for the coastal convoys. Enemy gunboats seldom dared attack our shore-hugging coastal shipping, but Heinkel 111s sporadically bombed and strafed Allied shipping during daylight hours when enough cloud settled over the water to provide an instant escape from our Spitfires.

We continued in this assignment throughout the late fall. Each day as we struggled to warm our bodies with mugs of steaming tea, we hoped that no enemy would dare enter our sector in weather so foul. But daily the orders came to patrol the ever-increasing number of convoys shipping the varied menus of war, and daily we thrust our protesting bodies into damp clothing and wet metal cockpits, patrolling ever farther from land. But while those periods of snow-lashed rains and gale force winds sapped our skills and energetic spirits, they also grounded the seldom venturesome Luftwaffe pilots.

So boring did the routine become that we pleaded with Turner for a remission of our sentence, to no avail. That each flight eastward over the North Sea could spell death was an unspoken thought, as was the truth that our far-ranging Spitfires, linked to the convoys' armed escorts by a fragile radio thread, were the deterrent that kept the seamen afloat.

Enemy pilots from Luftflotte 5 had learned through bloody experience and heavy losses to sneak in low and fast under a protective overcast for one slashing attack on only the most vulnerable ships, then dart swiftly away into cloud on a hurried course for home, knowing they were safe from our Spitfires, which had no on-board radar.

Distant, changing forms dissolving from sight behind walls of greyness were all we usually saw. Our guns were fired most frequently in frustration and anger with the convoy commanders, who more than once had erringly loosed their shot at us.

In December, a telephone call came from Roy. He had just arrived at Uxbridge, the RAF base from which all pilots were dispatched to Operational Training Units. The adjutant approved a twenty-four-hour pass for me to meet him. I was there on the parade ground the next morning as he received his orders to proceed to No. 3 Photo Reconnaissance Unit at Bournemouth on the south coast of England.

We had a high time in London, dining at a fine restaurant, drinking great ales in assorted pubs frequented by RAF personnel, and catching up on the myriad things that had happened since we last met. We parted near dawn at the railway station, never to meet again.

When night bombing attacks against industrial targets in the Midlands increased, Larry and I were given a new assignment. It was our job to patrol the Darlington sector at varied altitudes during certain hours of darkness and to sprint aloft individually on intercept missions as ground radar stations plotted the enemy nearing the coast.

This new assignment was a welcome change from the pre-dawn risings, and we took great pleasure in lying in bed until noon, then disporting ourselves at various endeavours until evening, when we would prepare our eyesight for the coming operation by wearing dark goggles while relaxing to the gentle music of the BBC, or harangues from Lord Haw Haw.

We had few calls to attack enemy planes. More often than not, the German pilots would jettison their load of bombs into the sea and head for home at the first smell of a British night fighter. It was a dedicated airman of the Third Reich who dared penetrate inland Yorkshire.

Late one snowy night, after an already-extended patrol at 25,000 feet, I was directed by ground radar to approach the city of Darlington. Suddenly I was caught in scattered anti-aircraft fire aimed at an enemy bomber also approaching the city. Robillard meanwhile was on the ground, starting up his aircraft to join me in the attempted intercept.

The thundering exhaust of the great Merlin engine masked the scimitar sound of the shilling-sized piece of shrapnel that pierced my Spitfire's tender skin and severed the metal line between the plane's air compressor and its two storage tanks. A slight flicker of all three needles on the instrument panel's air pressure gauge told the story. High above the earth I lost the use of my four Browning machine-guns, two Hispano cannons, wheel brakes, the wing flaps, and two landing lights. I tried to trace the complicated pneumatic system in my mind, but gave it up as an exercise in futility and advised the ground controller that I was out of action.

He accepted my report rather coldly, and I was left to orbit a moon-splashed cloud while Robillard streaked upwards from the black airfield below through the deep overcast that hugged the frozen earth to attempt to intercept the raider, who by now was fleeing homeward in dense cloud.

The night landing of a Spitfire onto an unlighted, snow-blown runway through near-zero visibility was a challenge to any airman's skill. But take away the wing flaps to slow the plane's forward speed, and the brakes to rein the rolling juggernaut to a standstill before the runway ended, and all the cards are stacked against the pilot.

As I had so many times before—falling backwards from the Waco's wing onto the Arizona desert, watching as my Spitfire met the Scottish mountain's face, and landing the Bastard on March Farm's hardened earth—I tasted fear. I wished myself away from white hospital sheets, from the sound of guns, from the mangled bodies and flaming planes, from sinking ships, and from grey-clad forms falling in puffs of dust on alien roads.

Suddenly the night sky was too black, the radiumed instrument dials too bright. The twin tongues of flame from the exhaust ports of the twelve-cylinder engine were too easy a target for enemy guns; my body was too warm under the fleece-lined flying suit, and the flat voice of the controller giving me compass headings was irritating to the point of hatred.

The wheels locked themselves grudgingly into landing position, and I ripped back the canopy to suck in great draughts of brittle air.

"And God plants fear in every human breast as surely as he plants hope and courage," the line crowded away the tension building within me, as I slanted the Spitfire's nose into the sick vapours.

At 200 feet above the whitened earth with an air speed of 120, the pressing darkness spit me out to the welcome sight of the dimly outlined airfield. I was almost rifle-true to the runway. With power off and the nose slightly high to kill off the excess speed, I rapped the Spitfire's wheels smartly onto the frozen surface. The plane bounced once and then settled into a great scything turn, removing itself obliquely from the runway and tearing across the airport's empty centre like a loco steer until it ran out of speed and shuddered to a halt.

Robillard landed later, his guns unfired. The world had turned full circle on another day.

Quite unexpectedly, orders came the following day for Robillard to present himself to No. 72 Squadron, a formidable Spitfire unit operating from Biggin Hill in 11 Group. We belted back a few beers that night while reminiscing over our times together.

The next day my knee suddenly swelled to such an extent that I couldn't bend it. Somehow it had been damaged when it had been struck by the control stick during the violent landing my Spitfire had made two days earlier. I was grounded while X-rays were taken and assessed. Next, an infection in both legs put me back in hospital for another three weeks.

During this time the squadron's pilots began aircraft-carrier take-off instruction from a short section of an unused runway. Word leaked out that we were going to North Africa with our aircraft aboard a Royal Navy carrier and would fly them off the ship's flight deck in the Mediterranean Sea to our new land base. I also learned that applications were being accepted by Group for transfer to a special unit. A limited number of battle-tested pilots would fly Hurricanes in Russia against the swelling German tide. Having had enough as a youth of desert sands, I volunteered for the Russian expedition. To my surprise and delight I was accepted, albeit on a verbal basis only, with confirmation to come in several weeks' time.

Upon my discharge from hospital I was assigned as a check pilot to monitor the instrument-flying practices of the squadron's new pilots. To do this, they flew blind under a special hood in a low-winged training plane. On my first flight the pilot was a Pole whose English was restricted to four-letter words. He had already been grounded on two occasions by Turner for improper aerial conduct.

Our flight began uneventfully. Soon he was flying the airplane over open country at 1,000 feet on the various compass headings that I fed him over the intercom. My knee still troubled me, and to ease the pain I undid my safety harness and adjusted myself half-sideways on the parachute pack.

For one weird moment I was a-tumble in the cockpit, then I was hurled from my seat into the cold slip-stream. Instinctively I twisted my body to regain equilibrium. The leaves of the notebook I was still holding fluttered in the wicked wind, and with some fear I realized I had left the airplane and was in free fall.

I felt for the rip-cord, pulled it immediately, and was slammed down into the harness as the parachute opened. I drifted with the wind onto a large flat field, where I landed painfully with both legs doubling under me. I got to my feet immediately, only to fall again because my damaged knee would not support my weight. Then I felt a new pain, drawn in a straight line across the bottom of my stomach.

Reason told me, and the Polish pilot later confirmed, that he'd peeked out from under the hood and seen me ahead of him in a relaxed position. Thinking I was not paying proper attention, he had pulled the plane's nose up sharply to alert me, then rolled it onto its back and shoved the stick full forward, not knowing I had freed myself from the restrictive Sutton harness. I went out of the cockpit like a cork from a champagne bottle, my stomach knifing along the top of the front windscreen.

The airplane meanwhile came past me in a screaming dive. The pilot threw the hood off to see where I was. When I waved him an "okay" sign he promptly cut the engine, curved down in a long spiral, and landed near me. I field-packed the parachute and walked painfully towards him.

I suppressed my desire to punch his nose from his face only because I hurt too much to swing. Instead we fought our way past the language barrier and agreed that if Turner learned of the event we'd both get the chop. We decided to keep quiet about it, and he flew me back to base, where I planned to return the parachute to the packing station with the lie that I had caught the rip-cord on a cockpit projection.

As I stepped from the wing, however, I felt a large area of wetness inside my trousers. Thinking the unthinkable, that I had evacuated my bladder during the excitement of the moment, I unbuttoned my fly and recoiled at the sight of a blood-soaked shirt and underwear. I couldn't see the source of the gore so I hurriedly sought to reassure myself that I had not been sexually dismembered. Knowing that there was no acceptable way I could explain my injury to the station medical officer, I ordered the Polish pilot to run for his motorcycle, get it back pronto, and take me with great haste to any doctor in Catterick. While I clung desperately to the pillion seat with one unbendable leg stuck out straight ahead and blood running into the other shoe, we roared past the startled gate guard onto the main highway.

Within minutes I was on the examination table in a doctor's office, naked from the waist down. The doctor was suturing a three-inch gash that had come within a hair's breadth of emasculating me. He had frozen the area before working on it and, having a sister resident in Toronto, was decent enough not to ask any questions concerning the matter, assuming, I suppose, that I'd received it in some unmilitary situation and did not wish it on my record. I made the Polish pilot pay the doctor £4 and was back on base within the hour, placating the gate sergeant with the promise of a free airplane ride.

The next morning I couldn't straighten up or walk. I stayed in bed until a hospital orderly came. I showed him my swollen knee and he bandaged it up and gave me some pills, but it was a week before I was back on my feet.

Almost immediately I was sent off in the same Miles Magister from which I had so carelessly been ejected, to pick up a newly posted pilot from Northolt air station on London's western skirt and return him to Catterick. The weather grew so bad en route that it was dangerous to proceed, so I set the airplane down in a large field as a precautionary measure. The landing was smooth enough until the roll-out, when the starboard wheel caught in a large rodent hole, slewing the plane to an abrupt stop. After I examined the undercarriage for any sign of misalignment or hydraulic fluid leaks and found it to be perfectly sound, I taxied the plane to the far corner of the field and waited out the filthy weather.

Some two hours later the overcast had lifted to what I guessed to be about 500 feet. I warmed up the engine and pointed the nose down my pre-selected take-off track, which was into a slight wind and over ground I had walked several times. The plane gathered speed quickly, but just as I started to raise the nose, the starboard undercarriage leg collapsed with a violent snapping sound, canting the flailing propeller and the lowered wing-tip into the hard earth, flipping the fuselage end for end and sideways, rupturing the fuel tank to drench me in gasoline, and jamming my feet past the rudder bars.

When I heard the ominous crunch of the oleo strut being torn from its junction, I reached to kill the plane's electric power, but failed in my attempt, as I had already been trapped out of reach of the master switch. My legs stayed locked behind the twisted metal despite my muscle-tearing efforts to free them. My senses exploded as the rasping fumes attacked my lungs. I heard screams, and even knowing they were mine I couldn't stop, as my mind's eye saw the first flame escape the engine's shell.

A pair of hands extending from khaki sleeves came at me from above to undo the Sutton harness while a hard voice commanded me to be still. Fingers fumbled inexpertly with the parachute harness quick-release knob, then two arms pulled me from the smashed cockpit and dragged me along the ground. As the world swam into full focus I saw a second soldier emptying a fire extinguisher at the crumpled fuel tank.

I fought my way through an enveloping sickness as they carried me to the floor of a tarpaulin-covered truck, one soldier holding me from rolling around and the other driving away from the wreckage, which I could see growing smaller through the open rear flap. I was twenty-five miles northeast of my destination of Hornchurch fighter station, but only five miles from the small RAF station of Hatfield where a base hospital was located. The soldiers' fortunate passing had undoubtedly saved my life.

After I'd been stripped and examined by two doctors I was advised that both my knees had been hammered out of shape; my feet swollen from breaking the rudder pedals; hot oil from the cracked engine had burned my legs; my head could not be turned without severe pain, and I bore some facial damage. They assured me that there were no injuries to my person that could be classed as terminal and that on the whole I had been a most fortunate young man to have escaped so lightly.

My squadron's adjutant, who was advised by telephone of the incident, dispatched an accident investigator to interview me. He arrived the following day and let me know that Turner already had been posted to Northern Ireland as senior training officer for 82 Group. In a short while he would leave there to command 411 Squadron. I was not required to attend before a board of enquiry and was relieved of all responsibility for the crash. But the group of doctors that convened to review my medical history with the RAF determined that I was unfit to continue flying. Despite the fact that I argued heatedly with the senior hospital authority, his decision was firm. I became so upset at what I considered to be an unfair and unwarranted act that I finally stormed into his office and invited him outside for a real old-fashioned punch-up to show him just how fit I was. That ungallant gentleman immediately placed me on charge for threatening an officer, for insubordination, and for several minor offences, all of which I freely admitted when questioned by the station's commander, who confined me to my ward for the duration of my recovery as punishment.

Three weeks later I was back on station at Catterick in charge of the airfield's control tower and staff. Those pilots who had been accepted for fighter operations on the Russian front had left the base; 145 Squadron was en route by sea to North Africa; the Polish pilot who had flung me into space was in jail awaiting trial for a sexual attack on a Darlington girl; and Roy was completing his operational training at Chivenor on torpedo-carrying fighters. Robillard's commission came through, and I asked the records sergeant to locate and process my own commissioning papers, which he had side-tracked at my request some months previous. I then bought a new uniform.

During the ensuing weeks my body slowly rebuilt itself, but my mind still rejected the decision that prevented me from flying. I wrote to assorted persons within the RAF and even to my member of Parliament in Toronto, all without result.

Bad news filtered back from the operational front. Of the twenty-five pilots with whom I had chased the shouting Scottish winds aloft only a breath of time before, fourteen were dead. (Another seven were yet to die.) My shift in the tower left me a good deal of free time, much of which I spent in the parachute section, where I learned the art of packing them, knowledge that I would put to good use in later years.

In early March 1942, I received notice that I was to be returned to Canada and the jurisdiction of the RCAF. While the thought of being home again gave me great pleasure, I could not accept that my flying war was over. With two weeks of non-duty status ahead of me, I toured several air stations to visit old friends. From Oaking-ton, near Cambridge, I flew on a night trip in one of the largest of the RAF's bombers, the Short Stirling. Navigator of J for Juliet was Nick Durban of Portage la Prairie, Manitoba, whom I had come to know at Manning Depot. We had a fine time in a pub the following night. As I left the station two nights later, he took off for a target deep in Europe. His airplane, with its crew of seven, was never heard from again.

At month's end, I boarded an American transport vessel at Greenoch, Scotland, for an uneventful trip to New York. From there I travelled by train to Montreal, where I was met by Ian Sclanders, a senior reporter for the Toronto *Daily Star*, sent to interview me about my war experiences. That night, when we parted, he told me that if I was ever interested in a job at the newspaper to let him know. At that time, however, I expected to remain in the RCAF until the war's end. I still hoped to be reclassified as medically fit to fly. But I would not know for thirty-six hours what non-flying assignment would be handed me, nor where I would be stationed.

HOME AGAIN

MY POSTING was to the repatriation depot at Ottawa's Rockcliffe Airport as the adjutant. My first order of business was to take the week's leave to which I was entitled and head for Toronto. From there I was driven by a friend to Orillia where my parents were.

Their Severn Bridge home had burned to the ground only a week earlier, and they were awaiting an insurance settlement that would allow them to start a new life on the outskirts of Orillia. Since there was little I could do to help, I took a bus to Toronto, telephoned Grace at her home the next day and arranged to meet her downtown that afternoon.

I asked her the age-old question and she accepted. That same afternoon she found an engagement ring she liked and which I could afford; then I rented a car and drove her home to New Toronto, where I met her parents. We gently told them of our long relationship and of our intention to marry within two weeks.

We had decided to find an apartment in Ottawa, where I planned either to continue in the military in a non-flying capacity, or to become a civilian in the general work-force. While I stayed in Toronto with friends, Grace made plans for a wedding in the United church where she had been baptized.

Suddenly I was summoned to report for duty within twenty-four hours. We went to the minister's house, explained the situation, and were married in his living room. Within the hour we were on our way to Ottawa.

While "For Sale" and "To Let" signs speckled the lawns of most smaller communities, Canada's major cities suffered zero-vacancy rates in 1942. The influx of workers employed to feed the maws of the furnaces fired to white heat to meet the demand for war supplies caused the shortage. Some foods and articles of clothing were rationed, as were gasoline and alcohol. Double-breasted suits were placed on the restricted list along with cuffed trousers. The punkish ne'er-do-wells of the period adopted a uniform of baggy, tight-cuffed pants and knee-length, oversize, single-breasted jackets called zoot suits. The Great Depression had ended.

We finally found a one-room tourist cabin on Ottawa's outskirts. I put in my daily stint at Rockcliffe and searched for more suitable accommodation at night.

While I was pushing other servicemen's papers around in Ottawa that spring, my brother Roy was acquitting himself admirably as a torpedo bomber pilot out of Malta against the Axis powers in the Mediterranean. By the new year, Roy would be promoted to flying officer, complete a tour of operations, and return to England for special training to instruct others in advanced torpedoing techniques. Roy walked away from two serious crashes, while at least half his squadron was lost to enemy action. During February, March, and April 1943, he survived three more crashes as an instructor.

In March 1942, Larry Robillard received his decoration from King George VI. He then returned to 72 Squadron as a flight commander. He was involved in escorting Commander Esmonde's ill-fated Swordfish torpedo bombers back from France after their valiant attempt to stop the major German warships, *Scharnhorst, Gneisenau,* and *Prinz Eugen* from slipping into the Atlantic from the Channel. In April, Larry destroyed a fourth enemy fighter and probably another. He returned to Canada on a Victory Bond tour, and we were reunited in Ottawa where we spent our leave together.

Turner, meanwhile, was in Malta, commanding 249 Squadron with Canada's top fighter pilot, George Beurling, on his team. After chalking up two more victories, he would go on to North Africa to teach fighter pilots how to destroy German tanks with cannon-armed Hurricane fighters. He survived two serious crashes: one in Malta when he was shot down, and the other in the desert when he collided with an enemy tank while attacking it at ground level.

After a few months in Ottawa, my non-flying status was reconfirmed by a final medical board. I was offered the opportunity of retiring to the reserve, or remaining in the service at a desk job. After Grace and I talked over the pros and cons, I decided that I should first call Ian Sclanders at the Toronto *Star* and take him up on his job offer.

He was delighted when I phoned and arranged for an interview with Gerry Brown, the city editor. My commanding officer, Squadron Leader Christie, was all heart and gave me two days leave to look into the matter. I appeared in the news-room in uniform, spent an hour with Brown and Ken Edey, the managing editor, and emerged with the promise of a junior reporter's job as soon as I severed myself from the service. Within three weeks, I had terminated my commission. I presented myself to my new employer and began another career. It would last seventeen years.

When I started work there as a cub reporter in the summer of 1942, the Toronto *Daily Star* was as holy a place for a novice newspaperman as Bader's Bus Company was to a fledgling fighter pilot. I inherited the desk used by Ernest Hemingway and an Underwood typewriter once used by Pierre Van Paassen, both of whom left their indelible marks on the map of world literature.

I have heard it said that newspapermen are lucky because they meet such interesting people. The reverse of that is more likely true: newspapermen are lucky because *they* are such interesting people. I never met a dull newspaperman. Tired, disillusioned, broke, and drunk—but never dull.

The editor of the *Star* was Harry C. Hindmarsh, who was also the publisher's son-in-law. In charge of all news and features was Ken Edey, the managing editor. Subordinate to him was Gerry Brown, the city editor, who was responsible for the gathering and writing of all local news and was boss of the reporting and photographic staff. His assistant was Ian Sclanders, and lower down on the pecking order were the editors in charge of telegraphed news, sports, regional happenings, social events, and artwork.

My immediate superior was Brown. His counterpart during the night shift, Stu Brownlee, had no hiring or firing authority and only a skeleton staff that drifted in and out of the news-room.

My salary was $17 a week, for which I was expected to work at least sixty hours. Grace and I rented a simple bachelor apartment on Earl Street for $10 a week. We watched the remaining seven dollars very carefully because we had a baby on the way.

After a short-lived first assignment, I was sent to Toronto's City Hall news bureau as a student to learn from the senior reporter the art of court reporting. Every hour of every day was filled with civil or criminal cases which I listened to, assessed, made notes on. Then at night I retired to the press room to write my stories, which I left for the bureau chief to review and criticize. I graduated to the general reporting staff and regular assignments after I covered three major court stories in one day, writing them all because the two staff reporters didn't show for work. The paper used them without any serious rewriting. With the promotion came a raise in salary to $25 a week. Grace bought herself a new dress and I began to take the streetcar every day.

A girl, whom we christened Joanne, was born to Grace in early February 1943. That marvellous addition to our family made me even more determined to expand my horizons and to seek ways of upgrading my status as a news reporter and increasing my income. I made it abundantly clear to Jim Kingsbury, the new city editor, that there was no task he could set for me that I wouldn't complete to his satisfaction. I covered innumerable situations for the *Star*, never failing to bring back the story to which I had been assigned. The result of my efforts was another raise, bringing my salary to $32.50 a week, the stipend for intermediate reporters. This added income permitted me to make a down payment on a 1935 Ford four-door convertible, which I used on *Star* assignments to offset the monthly costs. Because I was using the car for news gathering, I qualified for a "B" gas ration, which gave me ample mileage.

Some of my assignments for the *Star* stand out in my memory either because they brought me into contact with interesting and special people, or because they started me down the path to a type of reporting that would become my specialty.

One such assignment involved the Bank of Commerce.

"Munro!" Kingsbury's call from across the city room brought me to his desk in short order. "What's the tallest building in the British Empire?"

"Bank of Commerce," I responded.

"Right. How tall is it?"

"Four hundred and seventy-five feet," I answered.

"Well, get over there with Joe Perlove and find out what those men are doing hanging from ropes near the top. And take a photographer along in case one of you falls off."

Joe Perlove was a middle-aged byline writer with a mind like a pepperbox pistol and the soul of a poet. The photographer was Gordon Powley, whose hands trembled so badly that he'd been nicknamed "Shaky."

We'd ambled only half the distance from the Star building when we saw several forms swinging from tiny bo'sun's chairs near the top of the structure. We avoided checking in with the superintendent's office, entered an elevator, and bade the operator take us to the building's thirty-fourth floor, telling him we merely wanted some pictures of the city's skyline. On disembarking we noticed an open window at the end of the south corridor with ropes dangling in front of it. Joe and I looked down from the opening but our attention was immediately drawn by a yell from above. By craning our necks we could see an overalled man in a wooden-seated sling chipping loose mortar from between the huge stones that made up the structure.

Perlove tried to interview the man but his shouted questions were blown away by the wind. In desperation he waved the man to lower himself to our window-ledge. After he had answered Perlove's questions, the man suggested they trade places.

"To hell with that!" Perlove demurred. "But Munro here was a fighter pilot. He's used to height. Get out there, ace." He pushed me towards the open window. "Show us how to fly one of those things. Get some pictures of him out there, Powley." He moved away to give us room to operate.

Realizing immediately that every word I spoke and the manner in which I uttered them would be repeated verbatim to the rest of the *Star* reporters, I responded by merely saying, "Excuse me." Then, biting back the small fear that started niggling at my insides, I climbed through the opening and onto the simple inch-thick wooden seat, holding myself in place by the ropes that crossed in front of me.

"Pictures, Powley," Perlove shouted at the photographer, who was having trouble forcing himself to lean through the opening above the street on which ant-like figures could be seen moving.

I had a grasp of the new medium in moments, and to add some spice to the recitation I could see forming in Perlove's mind, I swung myself out and sideways towards another window. I missed my target slightly, however, and wound up bouncing my feet off the lower pane of glass, then flattening myself against it as a baby would against a father's chest.

Before I could bounce away and arc back to where Perlove and Powley were waiting to grab me, a short, florid-faced, balding man yanked up the lower sash.

"What in hell do you think you're doing?" he yelled.

"Departing," I answered as I kicked myself away from the stone-work in a swinging curve and into Perlove's waiting grasp.

By the time I had climbed back inside the building, I had placed the face, the name, and the circumstances under which I had seen the man in the window before. It was Jack Hammell, the man I'd tried to help in the beer parlour fight in Kirkland Lake.

Leaving the visibly shaken newspapermen I located the office in which I had seen Hammell and was confronted by a hatchet-faced woman who demanded to know whom I wished to see and why. I was explaining that I had not seen Mr. Hammell for some years and just wished to introduce myself in passing when he stepped from an inner office. Before he could speak I offered an apology for my sudden arrival and departure at his window.

"It was a newspaper assignment for the *Star* on which I got carried away," I tossed the pun at him, "but I came to see you because I remembered the time you whipped three miners some years ago in a Kirkland Lake hotel. It was in the early winter of '38 and—"

"I know, I was there," he interrupted my narrative, "but I don't remember you."

"I thought you were in trouble and I tried to get through the crowd to help you. When you'd punched them out you came at me until the waiter explained that I was a good guy."

"Yeah, I remember now. But you were just a skinny kid then, no more than sixteen. Well, nice to see you again. The *Star* you say, a reporter?"

"Yep. I've been there since I left the air force."

"Maybe we'll meet again." He shook my hand. "Leave your name with my secretary, will you?"

On my way out I noticed that the glass door was filled from top to bottom with the names of mining companies, the first one being Pickle Crow. He was, I learned within the hour, the toughest, most successful, and wealthiest mining magnate in Canada.

In order to improve my financial standing even more, I decided to learn the art of news photography. Not only could I make more money as a two-way newspaperman, able to act as both reporter and photographer on most assignments, but I could do commercial jobs on my off-duty hours. The only acceptable camera for the job, how-ever, was a 4 × 5 Speed Graphic, which cost five months' wages.

My lucky day arrived when Charlie Stead, the *Star*'s art editor, permitted a small crap game to develop in his office during an army enlistment party for a staff cameraman. When the dice came to me I threw two dollars on the floor and wound up winning the photographer's Speed Graphic outfit.

I had seen enough press pictures being taken to know the fundamentals of the art, but I persuaded Kingsbury to assign me for a month to Tom Wilson, the *Star*'s aging chief photographer. I had no sooner commenced the apprenticeship when Kingsbury directed me and two senior reporters, Alf Tate and Dick Sheridan, to Toronto Western Hospital where Wilson had just been taken, seriously ill and in need of blood for an immediate operation. We were typed and I was the match they were seeking. Within minutes I was stripped, gowned, laid on a stretcher, and wheeled into the operating room alongside Wilson and connected by tubes for a direct transfusion. Just as the anaesthetic mask was placed on his face, he half-smiled at me, but after a while we were disconnected because he had died on the table. Alf Tate later was to board a USAF weather plane for a *Star* feature, enter the eye of a hurricane off Florida, and disappear forever, and gentle Dick Sheridan would pass on from disease the following year.

I was in the news-room one night when a call came from Midland, telling me of a passenger vessel overturned in Georgian Bay with a heavy loss of life. Only Gordon Sinclair and I were available, so Stu Brownlee, the night editor, sent us there in the *Star*'s chauffered car to cover the tragedy. On our arrival Sinclair ordered the driver and me to wait for him outside the mayor's house. I stayed for a few minutes then walked to the next dwelling, hoping to find a telephone on which I could call the police, harbour-master, and fire department. A light shining between the closed doors of the garage caught my eye, so I entered and was faced with the body of a man, hanging by his neck from a rope near an overturned barrel. He was cold to the touch. I went back to the mayor's house and called Sinclair outside.

"There's a chap next door you should see right away." I urged him to follow me, and pulled open the door so he could view the body.

"You son of a bitch," he snarled. "Help me cut him down."

I held the body while Sinclair stood on the barrel and sawed through the rope with his penknife. Then he called the police. The deceased was a senior officer from the death vessel.

We had the story wrapped up with a full complement of pictures and were back in the office before dawn. So pleased was Ken Edey, the managing editor, that my salary was raised to $50 a week, only $10 less than that of a senior reporter. Of equal value to me was the transfer to a normal work schedule of days, subject only to emergency call-outs.

By December Kingsbury felt I was competent enough with both typewriter and camera to send me by plane to Ottawa to interview and photograph some returning war heroes.

At dawn on Monday, December 22, 1942, I seated myself aboard the Trans-Canada Air Lines Lockheed. Two other passengers turned out to be Captain Morris Griffiths of TCA and Captain Jack Sharpe of Atlantic Ferry Command, old pre-war flying friends. Morris's younger brother Harry, a civilian employee with Ferry Command, had fallen from a Boston bomber on the outskirts of Montreal a few hours earlier, and was in critical condition in Ste. Anne de Bellevue Military Hospital. Morris had been told that his brother had fallen without a parachute but up to an hour ago was still alive.

I asked their permission to stick with them for the story, got approval from Kingsbury at Ottawa, and before noon was rushing to Harry's ward.

Morris asked the doctor how his brother was.

"Judge for yourself," he was told as we were shown into a darkened room.

"Hello, Harry. It's your brother Morris," Griffiths whispered to the still form on the hospital bed.

"Well, it's about time you arrived," replied a very healthy-looking eighteen-year-old, who sat up and gave us all a wide grin. "When's the party?"

A picture of Harry sitting up in bed grinning made page one of the *Star* the next day. TORONTO FLIER FALLS FROM BOMBER, LIVES, read the headline. The copyrighted story, carrying my "as told to" byline, was sold by the *Star* across the world at a handsome profit. Everyone wanted to know how he had survived.

The story, as Harry told it to me and I told it to the world, was that he had been kneeling on the front entrance hatch of the bomber, speeding along on the test flight 7,000 feet above the ice-coated Lake of Two Mountains, just west of Montreal, in the pre-dawn darkness. The ground temperature was below freezing. Harry had been wearing flight coveralls and was connected to the pilot by an intercom system. Suddenly, the hatch fell away and he fell out. He managed to grab the edge of the frame with one hand, but his radiophone connection was torn apart. While he clung by his finger-tips, his shouts for help blown away by the slip-stream and covered by the roaring engines, the pilot, John Gerow, noticed two strange things simultaneously: the draft of cold air from the forward section, into which he could not see, and a nose-heaviness of the airplane.

From his position Gerow was unable to identify the problem, but he guessed what had happened and immediately slowed the air-craft's forward speed, lowered the wheels and flaps, and let the plane sink as fast as possible towards the frozen lake below. He had eased the speed back to 150 miles an hour and had the heavy attack airplane within ten feet of the ice when suddenly he felt the nose lift, just as a small treed island loomed ahead. Instantly he pulled the plane up to clear the obstacle, raised the flaps and wheels, and radioed Montreal airport for immediate assistance for Griffiths, whom he knew had fallen onto the ice.

Within half an hour, searchers found Harry, unconscious, at the end of a half-mile path sliced through the thin snow by his speeding body. He was wrapped in blankets, and his frozen extremities were bathed in cold water. Within an hour he was in the hospital.

Three days later I was back in Ottawa to complete another assignment. While killing time in the railway depot, awaiting the arrival of the train I would take back to Toronto, I met and inter-viewed Raymond Massey, the actor, then a major in the Canadian Army. After he left, I was leaning against a closed ticket wicket when I heard a telephone ring, then a man shouting in disbelief, "My God, when? A troop train? Oh, Jesus! Dozens dead? Right away!"

When I banged on the glass so hard I almost broke it, the green blind was raised and a pale face appeared.

"Where is it?" I demanded.

"Almonte," he choked out the word. In spite of a raging blizzard, I went directly there by taxi.

It was a scene from Dante's hell. A fast-moving, fully loaded troop train had smashed into a local passenger train as it stood in the station, boarding more travellers returning to Ottawa.

Hundreds of tons of charging steel and scalding steam had ploughed into the last three coaches of the passenger train, hurling people through the roofs and walls like rag dolls into the snow.

Uncomprehending children and adults alike were trapped, many under enormous weights. A whole night and part of a day would pass before equipment would free them all and their dead companions.

Troops and passengers from the killer train joined with unhurt passengers and the residents of Almonte to rescue the living. The dead were stacked like cordwood first along the track side, and later in the town hall, the community's morgue. The small hospital was jammed to overflowing with injured. Some died waiting to be treated.

I knew then, for the first time, what awesome damage the high-explosive shells from our Spitfires' wing cannons had done to German troop trains. And for one moment I was torn between putting the camera aside and lending my strength to help lift a caved-in coach roof from atop hundreds of people, many screaming and many dead. In that small way, I thought, I could help to expiate my wartime sins. But my job was to be the historian of that terrible event, to record on film the happenings, the suffering, the moments of pain and terrible anguish, and the uncountable number of heroic events, large and small, that held the death toll down to an eventual thirty-six.

I moved as if in a dream from one viewpoint to another, operating the camera as a mechanical device and myself as an omniscient being, framing each event in the viewfinder and not tripping the shutter until that precise moment when anyone seeing the published picture would know its story without reading beneath it.

I climbed through a jagged hole in the roof of the second coach and lowered myself into the near-darkness, illuminated only by the lights of rescue vehicles caroming off the twisted, whitened ceiling. I could get no farther than two seats down the aisle because of the jagged steel and splintered wood, but in front of me sat the body of a man with no head. Lying on the next seat was a woman, quite dead, her legs drawn upwards and spread open revealing the tiny feet of a dead child, breached in birth and cold to touch. I photographed it all, clenching my throat against the sickness I could not allow to happen.

When I had taken thirty-six pictures, I wrapped the film holders and a numbered sheet that identified each as accurately as possible in two blood-streaked pillowcases I found frozen in the snow. I folded and refolded them around the film holders into a tight package, bound it with surgical tape, and addressed it to Kingsbury.

"Take this to the Toronto *Star*," I told my taxi driver, "and give it personally to the city editor whose name is on the front. Do not let it out of your sight or open it. He will pay immediately for your return trip, and I will be waiting for you here when you return."

He agreed, and at 6:35 the next morning he dragged himself in front of Kingsbury, handed over the film, and collapsed. He was an elderly, one-legged man, and had broken his artificial limb while digging the taxi from yet another snow-filled ditch en route. But he'd given his word and kept it.

The night's ordeal did not end with false dawn, or the arrival of a team of *Star* reporters and Norman James, unquestionably the best all-round press photographer in Canada, who listened carefully to the description of my photos then drew his own plan of film coverage.

Then we saw it together, the tiny child of perhaps two, clad in a once-blue snow suit, unbendable in frozen death, clutched to the chest of a grim-faced soldier whose tears had drawn whitened lines across his cheeks. He wouldn't release his grip until his arms were pried away from the body. I learned later that I had unknowingly photographed the boy's father earlier, upright in death, near the dead woman, his wife.

It was over for me when James arrived, because I had to reach the *Star* with the rest of my pictures and give them the information I had for the overall story. When the first train paused on its westerly run I boarded it, after leaving the taxi driver's name with James, who cared for him in a grand manner when he returned, as he promised he would.

The train made two lengthy stops en route to Toronto. At each one I called the *Star* and read my notes to the rewrite men. The story reached the newspaper's first edition, lumped in with numerous other reports that took *Star* readers right to the scene. A full page of my less gory pictures were used, some of which sold around the world.

When the Canadian Pacific Railway released its official casualty list, they numbered thirty-six dead and almost 200 badly injured. No cause was immediately given for the disaster, but on January 6, 1943, nine days after the crash, John Howard, the conductor of the CPR's special troop train No. 2802, took his life by jumping into the Rideau River from a bridge only a few miles from the crash site. I was there also to capture that second tragedy on film. He left a note for his son, stating it was not his fault but that history would not record that fact to clear his name.

Another bonus was added to my next pay-cheque, together with a "well-done" note from Kingsbury, and I was given further photographic assignments, either alone or in company with a reporter. Much of the trauma associated with providing responsibly for my family on inadequate finances had dissipated with the raises and bonuses. My photographic techniques were now good enough that I was able to get some small commercial jobs, from which I made enough profit to maintain my valued equipment. My parents had bought and refurbished a country home at Atherley, and Roy was continuing his adventures as a Beaufighter pilot operating out of England. Except for occasional overnight trips on out-of-town assignments, or early morning calls to major news breaks within the city, I led an eight-to-five existence. This rare freedom gave my life an almost holiday feeling, allowing me evenings and weekends with Grace and our child. For the first time since our wedding, I could enjoy a feeling of companionship and fatherhood.

ON
ASSIGNMENT

EARLY THAT SPRING of 1944, the *Star* toyed with the idea of acquiring the latest in walkie-talkie equipment to use for fast-breaking news stories in the downtown area. The equipment had been tested with some success between Bloor Street and the *Star*'s news-room. Reporter Clifford Trevor was assigned the task of testing it from Centre Island, two miles away in Lake Ontario, and I was assigned to take a few pictures of Trevor.

Bundled up against the cold winds that chopped the icy lake water into tiny white-caps, we boarded a launch operated by an elderly skipper. Near the harbour's centre the skipper called to us that he'd seen a canoe in the distance a moment before and that it had vanished. We sped to the scene but only the bow of the boat was still above water. There was no occupant in sight. While Trevor gave a running commentary to the news-room, I slipped out of my coat and shoes and plunged over the side, hitting the frigid water fast and knifing deep beneath the surface. It was a long shot and it paid off. Underwater I ran into a still form that I managed to bring to the surface, only to see the launch pulling away in a huge turn. I held the man's body in my arms and kept treading water to keep him afloat. The launch overshot us on its first pass, but on the second moved in close enough for the skipper to toss me a rope. Once aboard, I worked continuously to revive the unconscious man while Trevor took pictures and called the *Star* on the new walkie-talkie. The *Star* alerted the harbour police, who came alongside in their launch and took over the resuscitation, then took off to meet a waiting ambulance.

Within the hour I had returned to the office in dry clothes to learn that the man I had pulled from the depths was conscious and expected to live. He was a badly injured war veteran who had limped away from his hospital room with one leg in a steel brace, made his way to Centre Island, borrowed a canoe, and struck out for the mainland. I never saw him again, but I learned that he survived and returned to hospital for further treatment. The story was plastered across the front page of the second section with pictures of me holding him in the water, then straddling him in the boat.

As though I were the precursor of disaster, one untoward occurrence seemed to follow another. The Norwegian Air Force in Canada had been training at a base near Gravenhurst called Little Norway. When the RAF asked for the services of its trained pilots, an official going-away ceremony was designed and presided over by the future king of Norway, Prince Olav, who attended with his wife, Princess Martha, and their two small children. Commander of the force was Colonel Ole Reistad, who prepared a cordoned-off area on the lip of the airfield, then gave the signal for his airmen to commence a display of low-level flying. What he did not know was that prior to the flight, many of the pilots had been into the aquavit.

I was there representing the *Star* as photographer with Marge Earl as reporter. Alongside us were Yousuf Karsh and his brother Malak, who was a commercial photographer, and Roy Taché, senior cameraman for Associated Screen News, which was seen in movie-houses.

The aircraft had been airborne less than a minute when they began performing ground-level aerobatics, flying upside-down at man-height and acting in a most dangerous manner. Taché's newsreel camera was whirring and I was taking pictures along with the others when suddenly, no more than fifty yards away, two inverted aircraft smashed into each other.

As in a dream, I felt myself running towards them, watching one airplane shed a wing and the other crash nose down. Even before they struck the ground I was half-way there, and as the first slither of flame licked upwards into the pilot's cockpit I was undoing his harness, hauling him out, and dragging him away from an explosion I felt must surely occur.

It was over in seconds. The fire crews had the flames out immediately, and the pilots were rushed off in ambulances.

After the mess was cleaned up, both the prince and the colonel thanked me over a drink. I felt embarrassed because the effort had not been as fraught with peril as it might have appeared, nor had I been harmed in any manner. Nevertheless, Prince Olav promised to send a token of his appreciation through Colonel Reistad. It was thus that I later received a pair of silver-brocade wings of the Royal Norwegian Air Force, with authority to wear them.

More than once during my years on the Toronto *Star* luck placed me at the scene of a fast-breaking story. One such instance found me in Detroit on my way back from another assignment. A small riot had erupted the previous afternoon on Belle Isle, in the Detroit River. A black man had been accused of assaulting a white girl and a fight ensued between military personnel and black civilians. When I read about the story I grabbed a cab and directed the driver to the bus terminal. En route he stopped at a major free-for-all in the middle of Woodward Avenue and refused to continue. He said that a bunch of white girls had been raped by a gang of blacks the day before at Belle Isle, and that trouble was starting up in the city. I sent him back to the hotel with my suitcase, uncased my camera, and headed for the action. Within minutes I was surrounded by hundreds of battling men, black against white, stabbing, clubbing, and shooting at each other.

The streets were alive with hatred. All about were dead and beaten bodies, overturned cars, and burning and looted stores. Many cars had been set afire, some with the occupants still inside. I photographed every horrible sight that came into my viewfinder, ever mindful of the film supply I had available. In front of me a surging crowd of hundreds of whites stopped a streetcar by brute force. Shouting, "Niggers, niggers, there's no one aboard but niggers," they then turned it over and threw gasoline bombs into it. It was like watching a newsreel unfold in a theatre and being unable to halt the carnage. And I knew that any interruption on my part, to save either black or white, could mean my death.

"Take a picture of me killing this black fucker," an overalled white man shouted at me as he smashed a hammer deep into the skull of a kneeling black man, while his companion jumped in front of me to stop his friend being identified on film. I ran then, and lost them both in an alley, where I was cut off by two burning cars jamming the exit. I went up a fire escape, through a building and out onto a side-street, then boarded a streetcar that was still moving. Within the block it had been slammed into by two cars and halted, while a mob smashed through the front windows and hauled the black motorman through the shattered glass. His blood drizzled over them before they stomped him into a bundle of mush.

In one block I'd counted twenty-nine overturned cars, most on fire, three streetcars on their sides, a large bus with a black man squashed beneath the wheels, and finally a squad of policemen, some armed with shotguns and one with a sub-machine-gun. They blasted one black man through a store window, then caved in the skulls of two men who suddenly ran out of a burning store.

A V-shaped wedge of men in working clothes, led by a burly man wielding a huge wrench, charged another bus. On board there were only two people: a black man and woman. Neither made it off alive: the man was clubbed to death in the doorway, and the woman was raped to death by a line-up of cheering whites.

I rounded a corner and came face to face with a black youth, who ducked behind me, screaming, as a knife-wielding white man came head-on at me to get at him. I shoved my camera at his face and threw up my right arm to deflect the downwards slash of the knife. I heard two screams, the first as the flat bed of the Graphic smashed the attacker's teeth, and the second as the point of his knife entered the boy's arm at the shoulder and slid down the bones to the wrist. I grabbed the knife from the attacker's hand as he fell to the pavement.

The boy hugged me with his good arm for support. I stuck the knife in my belt for protection, then dragged him into a doorway. As two policemen trotted past, I grabbed them, and one tied his belt around the boy's shoulder while the other ran with him in his arms to a squad car. Their car was just then being set afire with a gasoline bomb, so they stopped another car in the street, commandeered it, and drove off at high speed. I never knew if the boy lived or died.

I ran out of film just as the army arrived. From a street phone booth I called Kingsbury collect and spoke for half an hour to the rewrite desk. Each paragraph was set in type as it was written. They played it big, with an eight-column headline and my first major byline, which included my name above the four most important words of my short career: "Toronto Star Staff Reporter."

When I got back to Toronto that night I processed the film immediately. The pictures sent shock waves through the newsroom; many were so violent they were classed as unusable. One photo of a burning car with a black man inside was used across the full width of page one. Also on page one was another headline: STAR REPORTER SEES DETROIT RACE RIOTS. A second story carried my byline with the same four memorable words below it; and was accompanied by a picture of me, holding the knife I had taken from the boy's attacker.

The final toll was twenty-nine dead and more than 700 badly injured. My pictures were sold throughout the world, including to *Life* magazine. That week I was offered a job as a full-time photographer on the *Star* with a contract that would earn me more money annually than the city editor. I accepted it without hesitation.

I had planned a surprise Christmas Eve party for Grace and had invited some of her friends from high school who had seen little of her since our marriage. Just as the first guests arrived, I answered the telephone to hear my father's voice, half-strangled with emotion.

"Ray," he said, "your brother is missing in action. We have just received a telegram from the War Office."

"When ... how ... ?" I heard myself asking.

"Two nights ago." I could hear the strain in his voice. "Over Norway."

"It'll be all right," I told him. "You'll see. The old Munro luck will take care of him. He's probably in a warm bed in a P.O.W. camp right this minute. In no time at all you'll hear that from the Red Cross."

He didn't believe the hope I gave him, nor did I. I knew in my heart that Roy was gone.

I rang off and ordered myself to put on a pleasant face for the evening and to tell Grace only after everyone had left.

The next morning we drove to Atherley and tried to comfort my parents. I knew my father wished it could have been me instead, while in my own heart I shared that desire. A letter reached them some weeks later from Roy's commanding officer telling them that he had volunteered, with his English navigator Bruce Conn, to fly at low level across the North Sea at night in their Beaufighter, carrying a special torpedo with which they were to sink a particular enemy vessel hiding in a fiord. They did not return.

It was not until after the war that I learned that Roy's aircraft received a direct hit from anti-aircraft fire while on its torpedo run, exploding it in the air. Both men were killed instantly. Later, the wound caused by Roy's death would be reopened when the government gave Mother a Silver Cross medal and those honours Roy had so properly earned.

Had Roy been a story-book hero from my formative years whose face I had never seen pictured, I could have identified him without hesitation from a phalanx of marching men, as I did at Uxbridge when I travelled from Catterick to meet him the morning he arrived from Canada. I saw him as Roland at the pass, taller, more resolute yet jauntier than the officers surrounding him, his brick-coloured hair escaping from his forage cap, and the crooked smile I knew so well unmasking his joy at finally arriving on our war's doorstep.

After Roy's death, I buried myself deeper in work, riding each day into the ground at full gallop and straining the close relations I had with my fellow workers. I seemed to have been invaded by a compulsion to complete every task assigned to me in a faultless manner, striving to be superlative in every assignment I took. Before Roy's death I had seen my life as flowing through a series of pleasant years towards a grandfatherly ending. Without Roy, my once-placid nature turned aggressive and assertive. I placed myself in more perilous situations than before, and did so without reasoning out the potential for personal harm.

To keep my hand in at flying, I began taking paying passengers for night flights over Toronto, usually making little more than the rental cost of the airplane. I had met actor Pat O'Brien and his wife Eloise a year before when I had happened across their reason for quietly visiting Toronto every year. They were caring for the financial support of two hopelessly crippled children of desperately poor parents. I promised to keep their secret. Pat had been smitten by the flying bug when he made a movie with James Cagney about U.S. Navy pilots. He flew with me on two occasions, the last at night, and performed credibly with the dual controls.

Among the other film stars I met and flew, generally on daytime flights over downtown Toronto and around the Harbour Islands, were Randolph Scott, Frederic March, Beatrice Lillie, Ned Sparks, Jerry Colonna, and Frances Langford. I flew the last two during a visit with Bob Hope, and Patty, Maxine, and Laverne, known as the Andrews Sisters.

Rob Roy was born to Grace in June 1945. For weeks after she was listless and short of breath. I insisted upon a complete medical examination but she refused, having had two in the previous few months. Then a series of sudden headaches hit me with sledge-hammer blows, and violent spasms gripped my stomach. The military doctors at Christie Street Hospital blamed wartime traumas and present working stress for the headaches and the stomach pains, which turned out to be an ulcer that had settled itself into my duodenum.

I withheld these problems from Grace, and as she gradually improved, we selected a building lot and contracted for a home to be built. It was on Old Orchard Grove, overlooking pleasant rolling fields, and would cost $12,000. But as the frame of the house took shape, Grace's health deteriorated until I knew she needed a holiday away from Toronto and the children. Kingsbury agreed to let me undertake a month-long roving assignment by car to Mexico. I would be in daily contact by telephone with him and with our parents, who were sharing the responsibility of caring for the children.

In Mexico, Grace worsened so we returned immediately to Toronto. I sped her directly to St. Michael's Hospital, where she was diagnosed as having advanced tuberculosis. It was shattering news. I refused to return to the *Star*. Instead I spent the days caring for the children while the house was completed. In the evenings I sat with her, until she was taken by ambulance to the sanitarium at Hamilton, where the proper facilities were on hand to treat her. Because of the serious drain on my finances I finally returned to work, but drove to see her most nights. She was always bright and cheerful with me, but she was torn apart by her desire to see and hold her children, who were not permitted to enter the hospital. On weekends I would drive Joanne and Rob to stand beneath a balcony outside her room. They waved to each other, but always ended up crying. On the way home the headaches would come again with loathsome ferocity.

I resigned from the *Star* in a friendly, gentle manner, despite the remonstrations from Kingsbury and Edey and an unpaid mortgage I could not handle. That week, when I went to the bank to explain my position and to seek a solution, I was advised that the mortgage had been paid in full by cheque from the *Star*. That solemn, gaunt, great, and good Harry C. Hindmarsh had ordered it as the *Star*'s parting gift to me.

Grace died in the spring of 1946, and I buried her in a pleasant spot where the trees touched each other softly and sunlight awakened the flowers. I stood by the grave numb with anguish, hating God for taking her and thanking him for halting her pain. With her passing went a part of me that no one else would ever see or have.

I had no desire to become a commercial photographer and wanted no interruption of the time I could spend with the children, who were cared for in my absence by a fine Scottish nanny. To satisfy the new financial demands, I took a position with the *Globe and Mail*, as both a pilot and a crime photographer, under a contract that lasted four months. Then I sold the house and moved with Joanne and Rob to my parents' country home at Atherley.

At the end of the summer I left Toronto for a journey through Mexico that I hoped would be a rejuvenation of my mind and spirit after the indelible losses I had suffered.

MEXICAN
ADVENTURE

I CAME AWAKE HEAVILY, sick from the smell of stale vomit hanging in the air, and with the feeling that I wasn't alone. I longed to sink back into a comatose state, but my aching bladder won the battle.

Grasping the metal bedstead above my throbbing head, I hauled my torso upright. As I did so, I looked directly into the eyes of a hairy spider as big as a longshoreman's hand.

The skin on my scalp grew tight and cold, and the short hairs on the back of my neck stood stiff with fear. For another frozen moment my heart paused, then with a violent wrench of my body, I broke the hypnotic spell and smashed my way across the room to flatten myself against the opposite wall.

As if stunned by the abruptness of my lunge, the spider twitched its plum-sized head to fix me yet again with its malevolent stare. I slowly tied the end of the wash-bowl's worn towel into a large knot and just as slowly eased it into the clogged sink to weight it with moisture.

The spider must have sensed I was going to kill it because just as I leaped towards it with a mighty overhand swing of the sodden knot, it skittered sideways. But it wasn't fast enough. I smashed it again and again until no form or shape remained, only spattered blood and brown fluids and tufts of fur fouling the wall and the splintered floor. Then a nausea I couldn't control swept over me.

Events of the previous day swam slowly out of my sickness.

The streets of Mexico City had been alive with scuttling taxis. Peasants squatted on street corners offering piles of fruits and village crafts. The neon sign advertising my cheap hotel's watering hole had lost two letters. It proclaimed itself to be the " ETROPOLE AR."

The muted, coloured lights behind the shelved bottles signalled each other dimly in the thousand blue mirrors pasted to the walls and pillars spaced among the near-deserted tables. I nursed a drink at the stand-up bar while settling my mind to act on the problems closing tight around me.

I'd bought the first new civilian Jeep delivered in Toronto, then driven it south across the broad chest of America and deep through Mexico to the border of Guatemala. There, a simple incident occurred that restored my reason and stopped me from running away from myself.

On the coastal road that wriggled uncertainly through the state of Chiapas, in southwest Mexico, lay the village of Tonalá, located on the rim of the Gulf of Tehauntepec. A mile or so to the east rose a steep-sided hill that urged me to challenge its gradient with my four-wheel-drive vehicle. Before committing myself to this contest, I reconnoitred the surface of the approach to the slope. It was smooth, dried clay, not unlike one side of an Egyptian pyramid lopped off half-way up. I planned to take a clear run at its base in high gear and advance up one side as far and as fast as I could, gearing down as gravity overcame thrust. And if I couldn't make it to the top, I'd twist the Jeep quickly around and roar back down like a rocket. I figured it would be one hell of a ride both ways, and worth remembering.

I lashed my suitcase and duffle bag securely to the rear floor, revved up the engine, and roared across the hard-packed sand at fifty-odd miles an hour. I had almost reached sixty about half-way up the slope when power loss forced me to gear down into second. Still holding at thirty, I roared over the curving lip of the crest and before I could hit the brake, I was airborne. The Jeep cleared the top of the hill with the engine spinning the four wheels at least three feet off the ground. Then it headed, nose down, into the largest man-made reservoir I'd ever seen.

I was still in second gear with the gas pedal floored when the Jeep went under. The water closed over my head, and with a solid *thunk* the Jeep stopped on the silted bottom in an upright position. I floated up from the seat, and with one kick I was on the surface, a dozen feet from the mud bank. Then the humour of my ridiculous escapade overcame the self-pity I had been wallowing in, and laughter about my own frailties cleansed my mind and nourished it.

It was dark and I was $40 poorer before the waterlogged Jeep was removed by a team of villagers. They piled aboard it and with a still-wet teenager driving, hurtled down the awesomely steep hill in neutral gear. They tore across the desert's floor, then slammed into a barrel cactus. Their bodies flipped through the air like chaff in the wind. They picked themselves up laughing and pushed the machine for a mile into the village and the security of an adobe shed. The following day, two bright young mechanics dried out the engine and fuel lines, and I drove at dusk into the mountains, on the first leg of my return trip to Canada.

A week later I was deep in reverie and pleasantly relaxed by the potent tequila I'd been sipping since I'd entered the Metropole Bar.

"What are you drinking, old man?" the shadowy figure standing next to me asked.

I ignored him. The second time he spoke, less friendly than the first, I turned away in physical disregard of him.

"Don't turn your back on me, my friend," he spaced out the words with a *tap, tap, tap* of a forefinger between my shoulder blades. I hadn't quite swung full to him when a name matched his tanned, moustached face. It was Errol Flynn.

"Do that once more," I waved a finger under his nose and smiled, "and I'll order a double on you."

"Double it is, barkeep. And another for me." He beckoned the bartender.

"Passing through?" I asked incautiously, not admitting his name.

"Some business hereabouts," he replied.

We chatted easily for awhile about trivial matters. I told him I was a pilot, rather than scaring him off with any hint of my journalism background. Then I bought a round, telling him honestly it was the last treat my dwindling budget could stand. He leaned closer.

"Let's sit down," he said most confidentially, "and let that bag of fat who just came in do the buying." He nodded to a squat man in a well-cut suit.

We made our way past the newcomer, Flynn affording him both a full-face and profile view as he passed. The man stared after him in disbelief.

"Now, here's what we do, old cock." The actor tutored me point by point. When he finished outlining the plot, I walked slowly towards the wash-room past the fat man's table.

"Pardon me," I interrupted his gaze, which was still fixed on Flynn. "Are you waiting to see Mr. Flynn?"

"Then it *is* him. It *is* Errol Flynn!"

"Yep. Thought you were the chap he was meeting here from L.A. Mr. Flynn doesn't know his face, only his name. Sorry," I apologized.

He grabbed my sleeve. "Jesus, but I'd like to meet him."

"I don't know," I deliberated. "We're talking business, and when that chap arrives, we'll be leaving. Besides, Mr. Flynn is likely to get ugly if you butt in on him." I paused and took a half-step away, then stopped and asked, "What's your name? Maybe I can fix up a quick introduction."

"Harrison. Harold Harrison, from Denver," he blurted out.

"Okay, Harold," I restrained him, "Let's say we're old friends from before the war. We haven't seen each other since '39. Munro's the name. Ray Munro. Okay?"

"Great, Ray. Jesus, great," he breathed. "Let me send over a drink."

"Okay, but you'd better sit tight till I come back. I'll tell Flynn I know you and you'd like to meet him. You tell the waiter to keep the drinks coming on your tab," I suggested.

"Jesus Christ," he moaned in ecstasy. "Wait'll I get home. They'll never believe this!"

"What line of work are you in?" I asked the parting question.

"Embalming," he beamed. "Wholesale, to the trade. Here on holiday. Have to leave tomorrow."

Minutes later Harrison was seated beside me and across the table from Flynn. When the waiter arrived the undertaker asked for our pleasures. Flynn ordered two more doubles of Black Label scotch and the same in tequila for me. The undertaker reached over with both hands and took one of Flynn's in a near caress.

"You a fairy or something?" Flynn smiled the question at him as he pulled his hand away and wiped it across his chest in an exaggerated manner.

"Oh, my, I'm sorry," the fat man said. "But I'm so excited at meeting you, sitting with you, talking to you, that I just can't get hold of my emotions."

The booze kept coming fast and free, while Flynn probed mercilessly into the dark corners of the undertaker's business world.

"What the fuck is a wholesale undertaker?" Flynn kicked off his questioning. Harrison explained that he operated under contract to a number of funeral directors. They did nothing but pick up corpses from their places of death and drive them directly to him. The funeral directors charged the bereaved for the most expensive coffin, chapel services, limousine use, and graveside personnel they could sell, paying the undertaker for any facial reconstruction, prettying up, and embalming that was agreed upon.

"Great business," Harrison slurred. "And lotsa money in it."

"You know what you look like to me?" Flynn asked with a half-smile. "A necrophiliac." As abruptly as he made the statement, he turned to me and asked if I'd meet him the next day for lunch in his suite at the Hotel de la Reforma, then the most fashionable residence in Mexico City.

"Bring your log-book, old sport," he cuffed me on the shoulder as he passed. "I might have something interesting for you."

"Son of a bitch," the fat man breathed in disbelief. "Did you hear what he called me?"

"Sure. He figures you mess around with some of the bodies under your care and control. Do you?"

"That's a hell of a thing to ask," the fat man retorted. "That's sick." He stroked his hair and fussed with his breast-pocket handkerchief, which he used to mop his forehead. Then he ordered yet another double for me and a Manhattan for himself. "I'm not even going to think about Mr. Flynn again because he's a vulgar, filthy-minded man."

He was lying. I knew he was already designing stories he'd tell when he got home. Contrived tales about Flynn's sexual mores and those of his associates.

I knew I was drunk as soon as I rose from my chair and had to steady myself on the back of another. When the undertaker insisted we drive to a distinguished restaurant for a thick prime steak "cooked the good old Texas way," I couldn't resist the invitation.

He drove his Cadillac through a maze of unlighted streets to the city's edge and then along a rough road. I soon slipped into an alcoholic doze.

I felt the car stop and then felt his hands squeezing my inner thighs and then his fingers fumbling eagerly at the zipper of my trousers. As I came groggily out of my stupor and tried to struggle free from beneath his heaving bulk and slowly rotating hips, his slobbering mouth touched mine.

I freed one arm and drove my fist hard into his ear. Suddenly I fell backwards through the car door, which my twisting body had somehow unlatched. Together we rolled in the night-shrouded dust until, in an explosion of pain, I twisted away. His hand still refused to let go of my genitals. I smashed his face with my fist and broke his hold. Kneeling in agony, I held his filthy fingers on the sill of the car beside me, raised the inside handle to the locking position, and slammed the heavy door shut on them. Then I lurched off towards the city's distant lights, remembering with full clarity a terror-filled night in the Arizona desert when I was so young and so alone.

Long after my rage had passed, I could hear his screams in the distance. My physical pain continued in waves even after I threw myself fully clothed onto the bed I took in a filthy hotel on the city's rim.

After I woke and met and killed the spider, I headed back to the Metropole Hotel by a series of hitched rides. My room was on the second floor rear and overlooked the owners' chicken yard. I planned to catch a few hours' sleep before meeting Flynn at the Reforma, but I was intercepted in the hall by two uniformed police officers who blocked my passage. They were short, dark, unsmiling, and each carried a pearl-handled Colt .45.

"Señor Morro?" the nearest one asked.

"*Nieves*," I used the slang to deny the question. "Mun-ro, Señor Mun-ro." I stepped between them with a *por favor*, but they grabbed me hard, one on each arm, and fumbled for their handcuffs.

"What the he—!" I shouted before the one with the plate-sized belt buckle slipped an arm around my neck. I threw him off against the wall, then made the mistake of turning my back. I was hit over the head with what I later learned was a wooden stand.

"*Quemarse, quemarse.*" I heard a far-off voice spitting out the words as a sea of pain buried me. They each took one ankle and towed me like a hog to slaughter down the stairs, my head bumping on each step. On the sidewalk I could hear people, but could not see them for the blood that filled my eyes. I never lost consciousness, even when they cuffed my hands behind me and one of them rammed something hard into my stomach. It robbed me of breath and caused me to vomit into my lap. Then, mercifully, there was no more pain. The next I knew, I heard the sound of rapid Spanish, felt the handcuffs being brutally removed, and knew the hard coldness of a stone floor on my face.

The cell into which I was thrown was as large as a mediaeval banquet hall. Twenty or more male prisoners walked or sat slumped against the wall. I could do little more than crawl to it and lever myself into a sitting position. I felt my swollen face, sucked a loosened tooth, and tried to pat back a flap of scalp that had been peeled away by the blow. There was no water to drink or wash in. There was no toilet, just a sewer opening in the floor that was piled around with human faeces and which drew swarms of huge, buzzing flies.

The afternoon dragged through a nightmare of frightening sounds and half-dreams into the long night. My treasured RAF watch had disappeared along with my wallet, which contained $300 U.S., $20 in traveller's cheques, and around $30 in pesos. They had somehow missed the lone five-dollar bill in my other side pocket. Gone, too, was the heavy gold seal ring given to me as a family tradition on my twenty-first birthday.

Dawn's first light was accompanied by the slamming of doors and stomping of booted feet. Then the great metal door at the end of the corridor swung open. A number of ill-uniformed men entered and, without speaking, herded us against the wall. I was manacled with leg irons, as were the others. Our feet were connected by a chain. Leading upwards from this chain were others that split into Ys and joined the cuffs attached to our wrists. Then a stout rope was passed through the chains to link us together. Our clanking line was marched through nearly deserted streets to a large wooden gate set into a whitewashed wall. Later I learned that this was the central gathering place for all those arrested on criminal charges in the city during the previous day. Here we were booked and fingerprinted. Here I had my first verbal contact since I'd been asked my name in the hallway of the Metropole Hotel.

"Hey, *mocoso gringo* [slang for snot-nose], you got some money? I get you cigarette and fix your head." The ill-uniformed guard held out a hand.

I fished out the five-dollar bill and tore it in two, handing him the smaller piece.

"*Médico*," I said and waved the bigger portion.

"*Sí, pronto.*" He was gone like an obsequious ferret, returning minutes later to help me to my feet, steer me out of the still-guarded cage and into a dingy room in which there was a dilapidated barber's chair overseen by a perfumed Mexican dressed in a wild sports shirt and army pants. He told me he was a barber, seated me in the chair, and gently scissored the hair away from the wound. He bathed my torn scalp with water from a steaming kettle then tenderly rubbed some kind of oil around the open wound.

I asked for a mirror, and after locating a hand-sized square of reflecting steel he breathed on it, wiped it, and handed it to me. I couldn't believe I was seeing myself. My face, where it had been smashed into the cell floor, was dark blue and swollen. My left eye was almost closed; there were several holes in my lower lip where my teeth had punctured the flesh; and when I tilted my head to see the throbbing wound on my head, I recoiled in alarm. A triangular flap of skin lay askew on my swollen scalp.

When the barber finished his work, I thanked him, shook his hand, gave him my half of the five-dollar bill, and indicated that the guard had the missing piece. I was then taken to the courtyard and pushed into line near a long table.

When I heard my name I remained still. Only after it was shouted a second time and pronounced more correctly did I walk to the table. My entire right hand was pressed flat onto an ink-pad, then again onto printed paper.

I stood looking in wonderment at the discoloured palm and then, as if I were playing a role on-stage, I leaned across the table and drew my outstretched fingers down the chest of the khaki-clad officer.

In that frozen moment I felt pure, strong, vindicated, and scared all at the same time. Had not a commanding voice from a second floor window issued a stern order, I might well have been brutalized beyond identification. The order was to have me escorted immediately and unharmed into the presence of the director of the police barracks.

There I was introduced to a prestigious American-educated Mexican lawyer named Carlos Santiago. I explained in detail, without deviating from the truth, the events that had led up to my arrest, including the attempted sexual assault on my person.

Señor Santiago, in turn, explained that the American undertaker had been found at dawn with his broken fingers clamped vise-like in the door of his rented car. He had been treated and then driven to the airport to catch his flight to Denver. But before leaving, I learned, he had laid an assortment of charges against me and Flynn. Two policemen were sent to take me into custody, and another was sent to invite Flynn in for questioning.

Unfortunately for that officer, Flynn had been working out a duelling scene in his suite with a rapier. In between thrusts and parries, he was disporting himself with an overripe starlet in the bedroom, then refreshing himself with some liquor. When the policeman arrived, he faced a somewhat inebriated Flynn in the suite's open doorway. When told he was wanted for questioning about the abuse suffered by the undertaker, Flynn pressed the point of the naked blade firmly against the officer's chest. Flynn then forced the officer at sword point backwards into the elevator, through the lobby, and out onto the busy Paseo de la Reforma. Outside, Flynn swatted him on the buttocks with the blade before striding back past an applauding gallery in the lobby.

The management of the prestigious Hotel de la Reforma were not amused. They ordered Flynn to vacate the premises and never return. He did so ungraciously, setting up housekeeping in a classy brothel only a few blocks away. Using the parlour as his command post, he called the head of the great Mexican film studio where many of his movies had been filmed. He expressed his intention to cause any number of future films to be made in Spain if I were not located immediately and given instant freedom with my honour intact. Those powerful figures whose investments in Mexico's film industry had to be protected at all costs immediately retained Señor Santiago.

"You are free to leave with me now," the lawyer explained. "I will have you driven to the Red Cross hospital where your injuries will be cared for. Shall we go?"

"No," I stated flatly. "I am indebted to you for your efforts in straightening this matter out, but until I receive back the items that the two arresting officers stole from me, I am not leaving this office."

Señor Santiago expressed his dismay. "Tell me what is missing."

He made a list of the items I enumerated.

"Will you accept my word that before this day ends, I will have recovered these items for you?" he asked, holding out his hand.

"Of course," I responded, placing my hand in his.

At the hospital I was cleaned up and my scalp was sutured. A putty-like substance was moulded over my lower teeth to hold the loosened tooth in place.

By mid-afternoon I was back in my room at the Metropole Hotel. One eye was closed almost shut by the swelling of my purple-sided face, my bottom lip protruded grotesquely away from my teeth, which were capped with a large gob of reddish-brown cement. A large white patch over my head wound was set into a much larger shaved area. My shirt was stained with blood. I took four of the pain-killing pills the doctor had given me, slopped down a full glass of water, and offered myself to Morpheus.

I slept without remembrance and awoke with a dry throat and a sense of being stared at. Seated by the bed was an enormously large Mexican woman. She leaned over and gently pressed me back to a pillow that had not been there when I lay down. Smiling, she waddled to the bathroom where she took a bottle of beer from the sink, removed the cap, and slipped the opening past my lips. It was cold and delicious. I held the bottle and drained it, then motioned for another.

"*Nada, nada, nada.*" She waved a finger at me.

When she gently lifted me to a sitting position on the bed, I realized I was absolutely naked. My hands flew instinctively to cover myself. She laughed, disappeared into the bathroom, and turned on the taps in the tub. I wrapped the blankets around me and staggered to the window. It was still light, and the chickens were pecking and chatting as I eased into the steaming water.

Señor Santiago startled me with his sudden appearance in the bathroom as I finished soaping and washing my abused body for the second time. I had also removed the stabilizing cement from my mouth.

"I trust you slept well," he offered politely, "because you have used up a whole day of your life."

"You mean?" I queried.

"Twenty-five and a half hours ago you threw several chickens and the bedclothes from the window and collapsed on the bed. The woman who has been caring for you is the bartender's wife. Mr. Flynn has received several reports on your progress. If you are well, I will take you to him." He passed a bath towel and retreated to the bedroom while I dried.

"I have no clean clothes to wear," I called to him.

"Shortly your entire wardrobe will be here, washed, cleaned, and pressed. The blood-stained shirt and trousers have been replaced with cotton tans. One of your shoes was badly damaged, but we were able to replace them with another pair. Since you wear a size 12 narrow and only Mexican giants are of that proportion, we could find but one pair of exquisite handmade alligator shoes, which I hope will be acceptable," he apologized.

"I can't afford such luxuries, as you well know from my financial position," I reminded him.

"It is paid for by others as your hotel bill has been. Your Jeep is in Mr. Flynn's care. And here"—he opened his brief-case and removed a wrapped package—"are the items you were concerned about."

They were all there: my watch, ring, wallet, cash, traveller's cheques, and the wad of pesos. "How, where ... ?" I had a sudden lump in my throat.

"It is done, Señor Munro. Those who hurt you unnecessarily after they had subdued you in the hall and then stole from you are at this moment in custody."

"What will happen to them?" I asked.

"It is not for me to say, and you will have no further involvement with the matter. Your passport has been returned to the hotel's safe and all charges against you have been withdrawn. You are at liberty to remain in Mexico as long as your visa permits. If, while you are in my country, you have any police problem, of no matter what nature or severity, be it day or night, you have but to show my card." He passed it to me. "Advise the officer in charge that I represent you and must be contacted immediately."

After a fine lunch at Ciro's, the most luxurious restaurant in Mexico, Santiago took me by taxi to the address where Flynn was staying, which he claimed was the most exclusive whore-house in Mexico.

"Keep in touch." He waved me to the front doors.

"Ah, Señor Munro, but you are hurt worse than I thought," said the pleasant, well-groomed lady in her middle thirties who opened the door. "Mr. Flynn is in the large suite at the top of the stairs to your left. I will be there shortly."

The door was ajar, but I knocked rather loudly, having in mind Flynn's predilection for sexual divertissement.

"Is that you, Munro, old sport?" he called out cheerfully. "Enter, enter, my dear friend. Come into my office."

I followed his voice through the sitting room and into an enormous bathroom lined with huge, coloured tiles. Flynn was in the tub, a long thin cigar clamped in his teeth. Wearing granny glasses on the end of his nose, he held a sheaf of papers in one hand. Facing him, and underwater only to the nipples of her plentiful breasts, was an auburn-haired nymph.

"Don't just stand there, old cock. Meet my secretary, George. George, this is that Canadian who got me into all that fucking trouble. Sit down here." He motioned me to pull up a little bathroom chair. "And what are you drinking? Scotch?"

I nodded and he shouted out the order. "Marcie, get your ass in here and look after my guest. He wants scotch. On the rocks?" He looked at me for confirmation. "On the rocks doubled. Now"—he settled himself deeper in the water—"tell me in detail exactly what you did to that whore-master bastard faggot of a body-fucker."

Still reeling from the shock of the scene, never before having been in the same room with a man and woman in the same tub, and totally unprepared to hear such vulgarities spoken in the presence of a female, I recited in detail the events that transpired after Flynn left the bar.

"Did he do it, I mean did he really do it to you?" George interrupted.

"Jesus, George, let the man finish the story." Flynn splashed water on her breasts. "Continue, sport," he directed.

"To answer your question, George, no, he did not get to me, if I might put it so delicately." I finished my story.

"Well, it's all behind you now." Flynn drained his glass, then began to massage George's crotch with a bar of soap. "What are your plans?"

"In a few days I'm going back to Canada. It'll take me about ten days in the Jeep, but I'm in no hurry. Then I'll look around for a flying job, or maybe start a small bush operation. The tourist business is set for a boom in the north country with all the Americans looking for trophy fish and heads."

"Got enough money to get you back?"

"I'm okay," I responded. "I'm still indebted to you for putting me back to square one after the undertaker caper."

"Great movie scene that! Slamming the door on the bastard's hand and then locking the car up and tossing the keys away," he roared, adding a dimension to the actual occurrence. "Great scene, I must remember to use it in a movie. Meanwhile there's something I'd like you to hear. A dear friend of my father's named Carlos y Gama has a handsome spread in the mountains about 150 miles south of here. He's got an airplane but no pilot. The American who flew it got into the cactus juice, stole Gama's car, and ran it off a very high cliff. The new pilot won't arrive for a couple of weeks. How'd you like to fly for him until his new man comes?"

"Great idea. But I'm not licensed to act as pilot in command of any aircraft registered outside Canada or the U.S."

"That's no problem." Flynn laughed. "The plane isn't registered. Never has been. At the end of the war it was sold as military surplus in Texas and flown here. It's a Stearman and that's all you need to know. You got any Stearman time?"

"All I need for the job." I gave him a run-down on those I had flown.

"I don't know what the job pays, but it sure as hell'd be an adventure. If you want it, tell me now. You'd be doing me a favour."

"Sure, thanks," I accepted. "When do I start?"

"Tomorrow. If you leave tonight, you'll be there by noon."

"What will Gama say about your hiring me?"

"Sport, you've got the job. Gama will be waiting for you." He leaned forward and tweaked George's nipples.

"I'll need the keys for the Jeep." I delayed his sexual attack. "And directions to get there."

"Go south to Iguala and ask for his rancho. The keys for the Jeep are under the left front tire. It's behind the house." Flynn directed me from his knees.

"Thanks again. And goodbye, George." I eased out of the room to the sound of violent splashing.

High in the Colorado Mountains of the western United States, spring sunshine kisses the virgin snow-fields into streams of crystal water that swell together, giving birth to the Rio Grande. The Rio Grande is wed with the Pecos River twisting out of Texas. Renamed the Rio Bravo, and sick from ingesting a thousand miles of stolen silt, it probes the dry wasteland of Mexico like a giant worm, in a restless quest for the sea. The widening river tests the long-dead sands of Chihuahua State's northern desert, rimmed on three sides by the rugged Sierre Madre Range, and finds its escape through a mountain pass into the Gulf of Mexico.

Twenty-three degrees of latitude south of the big river's source, cradled in the mile-high lava fields of Guerrero Province, the ranch I sought bordered on a tributary of the Rio Balsas. It was near Iguala, 150 miles below Mexico City by twisting mountain roads. As the sun reached its zenith over the ranch gate that loomed ahead, a

Mexican in coveralls stirred himself from the shade of a tree and waved me to a full stop. He slid in beside me and pointed towards a private road.

In the shade of a tile-roofed hacienda, a compact middle-aged man in shorts and sandals offered his hand.

"You must be Señor Munro. I am Carlos y Gama. I am pleased you came so soon. You will lunch with me when you freshen up."

Over coffee he read my adventure-stained pilot's log and then with some deliberation remarked that although his new pilot from the United States would arrive in two weeks' time his flying requirements could not wait.

"I will now show you the Stearman airplane." He steered me to the hangar. "It is maintained by my ranch mechanic from manuals for the airframe and the engine, which I translate for him into Spanish. He brought you from the gate, his name is Alfredo, and he speaks no English. The Stearman was flown here by an American pilot who bought it after the war. It is three years old and parts are flown from Texas when they were needed."

He paused and then went on. "You will look on this machine as a truck of the sky. It is not a toy with which to play. You will fly it from here to there and back again. You will fly only when you are told and only where you are told. You will keep no record of the times you fly it, or the places you land. You will not speak of your work with any other person except me. You will write no letters and you will drink no alcohol. You will pass the keys of your Jeep to me, and it will not be driven while you are in my employ.

"You will be paid $50 U.S., in pesos, for each round trip you complete. You will receive all your money the day you leave. You will live in a room by yourself and you will take your meals alone. You may ride certain of the horses as far as the fence when you choose to exercise, but you will not leave the estate. And lastly, you will keep yourself distant from all others here. Is this agreed?" He sounded like Barton McLean playing the role of a prison warden in a 1930s grade C movie, but I curbed my initial feeling of hostility if only to find out what in hell the job was all about.

"First off, what cargo do I carry to where and when?" I asked.

"What you transport is mineral in bags, and that is all you need to know about the cargo. You will fly from here to a map point over there." He waved a hand in the direction of the Pacific Ocean. "From there you may go on to another map point and back to here.

You will make the trip once and sometimes twice a day if the weather permits."

The airplane was stock USAAF except it was painted with shiny black enamel and was devoid of all identifying marks.

"It's not necessary for me to license this airplane," he halted my question with a lie. For the next hour we discussed technical matters from a well-thumbed operational manual. I was surprised to learn it had a 220-horsepower Continental engine instead of the 225 Lycoming I'd been used to sitting behind.

It was clean inside and out. The front cockpit had been faired over with a hinged cover that unlocked to show that the seat and stick had been removed in favour of a sturdy wooden box bolted to the floor-boards. That container was padlocked through a sliding bolt. The propeller blades were free of nicks, and the engine was clean to the touch. Even the spark plug leads had been wired on. I felt a growing respect for the former pilot and the silent Mexican mechanic.

The rigging wires seemed a trifle slack to my pull and the tires appeared too soft, but the engine oil was up to the mark and clean. The gas tank proved full to my probing finger. When I paced off 1,500 feet or so on the hard clay runway, I noticed with satisfaction that it was clear of trees at both ends. There was a gentle westerly breeze trifling with the wind-sock.

Gama offered me a leather flying helmet that would hold the gauze patch in place over my stitches. He then told me to take off and to return and stop in front of the hangar.

There are a number of ways to lift off an airplane, but from a 2,000-foot elevation off an oven-hot clay strip without a head wind, you need all the help you can get. I ran the engine full up and then to magneto check speed. When the oil was hot and pumping through its veins, I worked out the controls and opened the throttle wide with the brakes full on. Buried in the trembling roar, I eased the joystick ahead and raised the tail wheel from the ground, then slipped the brakes and roared down the strip. In the 450-horse-powered Stearman I'd flown but once, given zero altitude, on a cool morning, I would have been off and climbing out in 300 feet. But not this baby. I'd eaten up half the runway and was all set to abort and hit the brakes when the nose-heavy beast broke loose from earth in a sluggish climb that put the upper wing almost level with the hangar roof as I passed it.

I nursed the plane to 1,500 feet over the rancho, then bottomed out under fat clouds and gentled through some turns, always fighting the nose heaviness. I landed then, abusing the brakes to stop the lunging roll just past the hanger doors.

"You had trouble?" Gama asked.

"Well, it puts on a good act sitting there in the sun, but it flies as if a circus fat lady were sitting up front."

"She is." He motioned Alfredo to open the front cockpit cover and the box lid inside. "That," he said, pointing to full grey sacks, "weighs 250 kilos. It is heavier than any load you will ever carry for me. You also had a full load of fuel."

It didn't take an engineer to tell me that the plane was all heart if it could pull 270 pounds over its designed gross weight to the cloud base, while out of longitudinal balance as well.

"You fly well," Gama told me. "Rest now. We will talk tomorrow."

The softening violet light of the fading afternoon showed the fine-scaled map of Guerrero's 27,000 square miles to be rich in detail. Señor Gama's horny fingernail traced the rancho's location on the southern half of the twenty-mile-long tableland that fell off four sides around from Iguala on the north, sliding off southward into the Rio Balsas in the distance. In the floor of the deep valley to the east of the rancho a small river cut its way due south into the Balsas. A great plateau shaped like a bear's paw lay to the west, and directly across from that highland's middle toe was the Rio Sinuoso, at whose source was the first airstrip I'd tackle. It was thirty feet wide and 1,500 feet long, lying at an altitude of 3,703 feet on a spoon-shaped mesa. Overshoot and you went straight down onto the rocks a quarter-mile below. Also flowing into the Rio Balsas, directly opposite Gama's property, was another small river, Pinta Brava.

All in all, it was a healthy flying situation. Four small rivers flowed north and south into the Balsas. Each leg of the trip, from the ranch to the Balsas, to the site of the first native village and on to the junction of the Sinuoso and the landing strip at Teotopec Camesas, were equal to about twenty-five miles. The round trip would cover something over 200 miles and take about two hours' flying time.

Gama instructed me to make my own map from his. He told me what to do if I encountered cloud cover and could not complete the round trip. "I will know where you are, and when you should arrive here. If you do not arrive, I will find you."

I must have looked sceptical, for he pointed to a short-wave radio aerial I had not seen before.

"Radio," he smiled. "We are all connected by radio." Then I realized how Flynn had spoken to him from Mexico City when I'd seen no telephone lines in that mountainous area.

We took dinner on the patio. It was served by a huge, unsmiling woman who I learned was Alfredo's wife.

"My servants know some vulgarities taught to them by the American, but they do not know their meaning." He walked me to my room. "They are as children. We will now be friends and trust each other's word. One last thing," he paused, "you will fly tomorrow morning."

I slept badly and awoke to coffee and a bowl of hard rolls and boiled eggs.

"The supplies will be unloaded and the box filled with 140 kilos," Gama instructed me. "You will fly directly back here. Perhaps later in the day you will make the trip again."

I had expected a "*vía con Dios*," but he merely walked away towards the hacienda.

The Sierra Madre Occidental Range stretches down the west coast of Mexico from the American border to about the twentieth parallel, where it becomes the Sierra Madre del Sur. South of this dividing line, the tortured land is made more desolate by volcanic outpourings and debris. A thin, irregular strip of lowland separates this tail-bone of the Canadian Rockies from the Pacific Ocean. But only from aloft can you see the canyons that shame those of Colorado, the lowland valleys carpeted with wet greens and vivid flowering plants. Jaguars roam beneath wild palms and banana trees in the shimmering veils of mist created by tall, splashing waterfalls.

Below me the Rio Balsas swam its path to the sea. The trees thinned out along the sidehills and heated air rose from dead ashlands to meet moist Pacific air and form clouds such as only Constable could paint. North along this tortured spine, sick and sleeping white-capped volcanoes rise to more than 18,000 feet.

I spotted the first habitation, a cluster of matted huts encircled by vegetation. With some trepidation, I flew into the canyon of the Rio Sinuoso. It was clear as a bell, and I climbed higher than the runway at Teotopec and looked across its eastern ridge to see the metal buildings shining in the sun.

It was just as Gama had described it. I dragged the airstrip twice slowly to get the lay of the land. It was like the buttes I had known as a child in Arizona.

There were three men waiting. One waved me to a stop near the smallest building, and the others stood near a pile of small grey sacks.

"*Buenos días,*" I called out cheerfully to the darkest one. He didn't answer, just waved me away from the airplane. Fishing out a key-ring, he unlocked the inner box to remove the cargo. It had to be dynamite the way they handled the boxes and there was no doubt about the cargo they loaded. It was silver concentrate. I had guessed that, when Gama told me I'd be carrying minerals and when I'd been forbidden to go here or there and do this and that. This too was the reason why the plane was not permitted to refuel away from the rancho. Gama wanted to reduce the plane's range. This realization gave me some concern for the accuracy of the fuel gauge. I promised myself in the future to check the tank with the old dip-the-finger method before each flight.

Knowing the runway quit cold in 1,500 feet, I was off the ground in a third of that distance and climbing away, in a height-grabbing turn, from the crazy jumble of rocks that ended far below. The flight back was as uneventful as the flight out. During that trip, and the next, which came after lunch, I fought crazy thoughts that filtered through my mind about the cargo. Others had done it, but with gold. Planes had been hijacked and pilots with conspiratorial crews had flown off into setting suns with untold millions to Rio, Buenos Aires, or some other sanctuary that thumbed its nose at extradition.

"Never steal anything—small," the qualifying phrase slipped into my thoughts as I forced my mind to stay on a moral course, allowing it to touch only briefly on a hypothetical plan for diverting such a shipment as a mere exercise for the imagination.

At dinner I was questioned about my flights. Gama asked me if I knew what cargo I was flying. I told him, and he confirmed my guess, then went on to tell me about his father and the family silver business. We chatted briefly before he told me I would fly the next day.

In bed, I rolled the situation over in my tired mind. Silver sold at nearly a dollar a U.S. ounce, so one plane-load of concentrate would total about half the $5,000 for pure silver at legal price. I drew a map of Mexico in my mind and measured off 600 miles north to the closest Texas landing point. Knowing that Mexico and the States were like blood-brothers when it came to extradition, I discarded that as a possibility. Six hundred jungle-covered miles in the other direction was the Guatemalen border. And what would a thief have to look ahead to if he made it there? A *gringo* with a load of silver in a stolen airplane would have his throat cut at high noon in a town square and lose everything. To boot, on either side of the dirty little hamlet of Iguala lay a bloody ocean. The Stearman had a full-tank range of less than 500 miles. I went to sleep with the knowledge that Gama was nobody's fool.

The following day I flew two more flights, and the next day I flew from Teotopec to Patichla and back. The day after that it rained so I didn't fly.

The next morning, while running up the engine for a pre-take-off check, I heard a strange sound and dismissed it as nothing. I heard it again while slanting up the valley to Balsas, yet as suddenly as it came, it went. On my return, somewhere over Huatla, a ticking sound came from somewhere ahead of the fire wall. Again, it was gone before I could analyse it. It came on stronger almost immediately, an uneven beat that sent little tremors through the engine mounts into the airframe, up my toes on the rudder pedals, and through to my fingertips on the stick. All the gauges were in the green, and the load up front was below weight limits and cinched down tight.

Wham! Wham! Wham! The three hammering blows were underscored by a tearing, clanking, metallic shudder as the left glass plate of the windscreen disappeared. The vibration grew until the shock-mounted instrument panel danced crazily out of focus. I chopped the throttle and pin-pointed a narrow strand of beach at river's bend. I knew the Stearman would flip over on its back when it hit the sand, even stalling it in low and slow, so I cinched the shoulder harness tight, even as the shuddering stopped completely.

With 2,600 feet showing on the altimeter and still losing height, I eased on the throttle to feel the vibrations return with the increase in engine revolutions. Because of the plane's weight, it would take a speed of seventy miles an hour to hold that altitude and get me back to the rancho, forty miles distant and only 500 feet lower.

As I approached the strip, I could see Gama and Alfredo running from the hacienda; they must have heard the Stearman thrashing through the air from several miles away.

It could have been a lot worse. It could have killed me. The propeller spinner had gradually worked its way loose after losing one metal screw, then another and another. Centrifugal force had finally ripped the thin aluminium cone away from the last of the retainers and flung it outwards to meet a propeller blade, from which it chopped two inches. The spinner, crushed into a projectile, was hurtled backwards at gunshot speed into the corner of the windscreen and then past the tail-bracing wires. The lopsided propeller set up an imbalance, increasing the vibration as engine power was applied. It reminded me of the occasion in 1941 when I touched the tip of my Spitfire's propeller to the surface of the English Channel.

"You are fortunate to have survived the incident," Gama ventured as he poured me a small glass of mescal, offering a saucer of salt and quartered limes to complement the fiery drink. "And I am fortunate that you decided to fly the Stearman back instead of trying to land it in the mountains. Why did you choose to fly home?"

"Survival," I explained. "The ball of metal smashing through the windscreen didn't hurt me and I could see it had not struck the tail. The only problem affecting the handling of the airplane was the propeller imbalance. The most damage that could do—unless the crankshaft failed and the whole assembly flew off and struck the airframe—would be to put the crankshaft out of true. By reducing the engine revolutions to the minimum required to maintain height, there was little chance of losing all engine power. As a last resort I could have landed on a sandy riverbank or in shallow water." I did not tell him that a slight possibility loomed during the homeward flight of excessive vibration cracking the welds of the engine mount, causing the whole engine to fall off.

He explained that the engine would have to be sent to Texas to be repaired and that it would not be ready before the American pilot was due to arrive. He apologized for the termination of my employment and invited me to stay on as a guest for a few days if I chose. There was no reason for me to remain, so I told him I would start back to Mexico City at dawn. I was paid $200 U.S. in pesos, and the keys to my Jeep were returned.

Mexico City's streets were clogged with honking vehicles as I inched along the Avenida Insurgentes looking for a route to the northeast section of the city near Alameda, the location of the Metropole Hotel. I wanted to see the bartender's wife, Marie, and thank her with a small silver gift I'd picked up in Cuernavaca.

I couldn't have been travelling more than five miles an hour when a motor-cycle cop urged me into the curb with a wave of his arm. Still hurting from the abuse of the last policeman who'd stopped me, I did as directed. The officer parked his large silver Harley Davidson in front of the Jeep.

"That is a Jeep, *señor*, no?" A gold tooth showed front and centre as he flashed a broad smile.

"*Si*." I responded with a smile of equal size. "You speak English well."

"*Da nada*," he beamed. "I learn some good words in Nordamericano mine I work."

"Why did you stop me?" I asked pleasantly.

"Want to drive Jeep." He rotated the steering wheel.

I relaxed. "Sure, go ahead. Try it out." I vacated the driver's seat and helped him in. He was all hands and feet; pressing the horn, depressing the clutch, pushing the brake, working the gear-shift, and switching the lights on and off. I started it for him, led him through the forward gears, and watched with trepidation as he lurched it out into the traffic, barely avoiding a collision with a small truck. He was gone from sight in a moment, so I sat side-saddle on the Harley contemplating the day ahead. First to Marie, then to Señor Santiago, and finally on to Flynn at the whore-house. I noticed that it was 12:30.

By 1:15 I was irritated at being treated in such a cavalier manner, cop or no cop. When 1:30 came and went I got angry enough to crank up his machine and go looking for him. I got lost immediately, despite my best efforts and directions from several puzzled pedestrians, who couldn't understand why a civilian American (likely they had never heard of Canada) was driving a Mexico City Police Department motorcycle.

When I saw the light blue globe outlining the word *Policía* hanging in front of an old building, I pulled the machine to a stop, parked it directly in front of the main doors, and strode inside. It took a moment to sort out the uniforms. Finally I selected an older man with a silver bar on each shoulder.

"*Por favor*," I said. "One of your policemen has taken my Jeep, together with my personal belongings. I'd like to have it back, now."

A strange look crossed the officer's face. He pulled me away from the crowd and led me to a desk. "I speak English good and understand it if you speak slow."

I explained clearly and distinctly the situation exactly as it happened.

"And you took the police motorcycle and drove it around the city?" He seemed incredulous at my audacity.

"Of course I drove the goddamn thing. I was looking for the son of a bitch who took my Jeep." I hit the desk with my fist.

"You can't steal a policeman's motorcycle for any reason." He shook his finger under my nose. "And you will not strike this desk. You are a thief and you are going to be held until this matter is investigated. Now, where is the stolen motorcycle and where did the theft take place?"

"Jesus, Jesus, not again." I held my head and rocked back and forth.

"You will not speak the Lord's name in vulgarity," he shouted at me.

I fumbled my wallet from my hip pocket and fished out the card given to me by Señor Santiago.

"I was told to present this card, at any time of the day or night, if I had trouble with the police." I handed him the card then sat down and put both feet on the desk.

He read the card, looked at me quickly, and then dialled a number on the desk telephone and turned his back on me

"You will wait here," he ordered after a short conversation.

In a few minutes he returned with another officer, a higher-ranking one.

"*Por favor*," the newcomer offered. "Your name please and your passport?"

I gave him the blue book, stared right between his eyes and said: "My name is Munro. Not Moon-row, or Morrow, or anything else but M-U-N-R-O. I want only the return of my personal property, a Canadian-built Jeep bearing an Ontario licence plate. It was removed from my possession, in this city, at 12:15 post meridian time this date, by a uniformed officer of your traffic department. Now is that clear enough or do I have to draw pictures for you?" I added, emboldened by my own assertiveness. In my youth I was nurtured by two beliefs: that God Almighty hated quitters and that no defence existed against the truth. "Now, call that number." I stopped to wait for his reaction.

"You have my apologies, Señor Munro, for any inconvenience that officer has caused you. Your car will be delivered here in minutes. You are free to go, with our apologies, of course." He handed me my passport and Santiago's card.

My Jeep was outside at 2:30, the two bags still secured to the rear floor. There was no sign of the offending officer or his motorcycle. The lieutenant stared coldly after me as I joined the traffic towards the Metropole Hotel.

Marie was not there, nor was her husband, so I left my gift with a simple note. I telephoned Señor Santiago's office to thank him once more for the exercise of his awesome powers, but he had just left the city for Mazatlán. I drove to the Georgian home in which Flynn had held court in the bathroom, and learned that he had left the evening before to join his father in Acapulco.

So I drove out of the city and through unnamed villages and dry wastelands and across mountains to Querétaro, San Luis Potosí, Monterrey, and across the border at Nuevo Laredo and into Texas. There I ate the thick prime steak, "cooked in the good old Texas way" that the fat undertaker had promised, but not provided. I slept round the clock in a motel whose sign read "AIRY ELL" and laughed softly at the humorous possibilities, at the adventures I'd begun at the " ETROPOLE AR," and then, loudly, at myself.

DOWN AND OUT
IN VANCOUVER

AFTER SPENDING two months in Orillia, reminiscing about my past adventures and watching my finances disappear, I decided that it was time to find a job—preferably in a balmier clime.

Knowing that Errol Flynn would have heard high praise for me from Gama, I asked Jack Carr, movie critic of the *Star*, to track him down. Flynn, it turned out, was on location in Tucson, Arizona. He took my call in his trailer and listened to my request.

"Leave it to me, old son," he replied. Then he asked if I was qualified to pilot an RC-3 amphibious airplane. I assured him I was. He next asked if I could get to British Columbia for several months on short notice. When I told him I could, he told me to expect a call within a few days.

The call came three days later from the secretary of a Los Angeles businessman. He had sunk a fortune into turning a surplus U.S. Navy ship into a floating palace, and planned to use it to transport motion-picture personalities and others of comparable wealth from L.A. to Alaska and back. My job would be to pilot the passengers on sightseeing flights during the voyage, transport stores and ship's officers from point to point, and be on hand in case of emergency. A raised deck had been constructed on the fantail for the airplane, so that it could be lowered into and recovered from the sea by an electric winch. The contract was for three months and called for me to board the ship at Coal Harbour in Vancouver by 8:00 A.M. New Year's Day, when the ship would depart.

I confirmed my acceptance by telegram, sold my Jeep, arranged for the financial care of my family, settled my debts, and bought a one-way Trans-Canada ticket to Vancouver. I had four days to reach the gangplank, and $260 in my pocket. My father had even offered to drive me to Toronto International Airport.

We left Orillia before dawn in his 1940 Chevrolet sedan and were going at fifty miles an hour along an asphalt highway when I felt the rear end of the car swing ditchward. I heard my father stomping stupidly on the brake pedal and knew that we had hit a patch of black ice.

The outer wheels hit the soft shoulder, and the car flipped in two complete side rolls, crushing the roof over my head. It then sheared off a telephone pole and finally crashed into an enormous tree, which hit almost dead centre on my door. I heard my collar-bone snap in two and felt the jagged end puncture the yielding flesh. The pain came then, hot and hard, and my head swelled to near-bursting from a dreadful weight upon it. It was my father. He'd been knocked unconscious and thrown on top of me. The smell of raw gas from the ruptured fuel tank strangled me with fear until I passed out.

My father came to and somehow managed to extricate himself from the tangled wreckage. Weakened by the loss of blood from a head wound and myriad cuts from sharded glass, he nevertheless managed to flag down a passing truck, and within the hour firemen had pried my unconscious body from the twisted hulk and delivered me to the emergency ward of the Barrie General Hospital, some fifty miles north of Toronto's airport.

When I came to, I was on a table stripped of my clothes, which were piled on a nearby chair. My torso was enshrouded in a green gown violated by a large red stain across the right shoulder. I was alone. As I tried to raise myself I could feel a thick pad pressed tightly about my injured shoulder. Slowly and carefully, I slipped my legs over the side of the stretcher. When they touched the floor, instead of supporting me, they bent, rubber-like, and I slid to a sitting position on the cold tiles, where I waited, holding my breath against the pain that never came. Whatever shots they'd given me had taken it all away, although I was weak and unsteady.

Then the realization came to me that if I didn't get out of there fast I'd miss my flight and the job I needed so desperately. I tried later with modest success to replay the whole scenario, which included gathering up my clothes and the small suitcase that lay nearby, donning my trench coat over the hospital garb, and walking crabwise out of the hospital and into a taxi. We drove to the Toronto airport via a liquor store, where I bought a mickey of rye.

There was a definite rule about taking any alcohol on an air-liner for in-flight consumption, so I secreted the glass flask in my inside jacket pocket, removed the screw-cap, and rammed a couple of straws I'd picked up at a lunch counter through my folded-over lapel buttonhole and into the brew. Each time a wave of pain struck I'd take a long pull on the rye and loaf off again into nirvana.

It was a strange noise that awakened me. It sounded like the rise and fall of several discordant notes, which echoed, then faded into nothingness. Even after I'd fought my way through a gagging sickness and forced open my eyes, I could see nothing but an expanse of tan punched through with uncountable, tiny holes. With my peripheral vision, I saw motion. As I turned my head to stare into the face of a uniformed man, I suddenly knew I was on a stretcher in an ambulance.

"Stop this goddamn truck," I shouted. "Stop the goddamn thing and take me back to the plane or I'll sue the goddamn socks off you!"

He told me I was hurt and that they were taking me to the hospital. I again threatened them. It took a good ten minutes to convince them that I was indeed in full command of my senses, and that, while I was injured and in some pain, I was not going to the hospital.

Having learned I was in Winnipeg, and that the airplane had left, I had the ambulance drop me at a cheap hotel. I checked in at the desk and paid five dollars in advance for a room. While I slept, a maid checking the room took one look at the large area of dried blood on my shirt and summoned the house detective. After convincing him that my condition was not the result of foul play, I had him phone to confirm my continued flight to Vancouver.

A major snowstorm had closed the airport, he reported, and all flights were cancelled.

"The good news," he told me, "is that the train leaves in forty minutes. You've got a seat if you can get to the station in half an hour."

The revised timetable would now place me in Vancouver one full day ahead of schedule, or so I thought, as I eased my body into the lumpy seat. Physically, mentally, and financially, I was in rough shape. My collar-bone had broken loose from its coagulation of blood and was working its jagged end out of the surrounding flesh. I would never be able to put on a good enough act to fool the ship's commanding officer. He would, I knew, take one look at me and refuse to let me pilot the aircraft.

I slept fitfully until dawn. When I awakened, my right arm and shoulder were totally numb. In a panic I lurched through the coaches like a drunken seaman until I found the elderly conductor. He urged me into his own sleeping compartment, sent a porter to fetch my valise, and within a few minutes returned with a slim, young man whom he introduced as a medical doctor. When I asked the doctor's name, the conductor explained that the young graduate was concerned about the possibility of a malpractice charge being levelled against him as he was not licensed to practise in any western province. And because my life was not in jeopardy, his ministrations could not be classed under any Good Samaritan Act. My only option, had the young man not volunteered his skills, would have been to leave the train at the next community with a hospital and seek surgical attention.

The young doctor examined me and explained that my clavicle was fractured. It should be properly treated, he insisted, but he did what he could. He bound it in such a way as to immobilize the whole arm against my chest, thus causing the two ends of the fracture to remain in a static position, although overlapping each other.

I still might have made it to Vancouver on time, but it seemed that even the weather was conspiring against me. In the foothills of the Rockies, the train was stopped in an isolated valley by a storm that was sweeping western Canada and had intensified into a howling gale. Enormous amounts of snow had been whipped into huge drifts that swallowed up whole railway tunnels and miles of mountain track. The conductor broke the news to me that nothing short of a miracle would bring the train into Vancouver before late afternoon on New Year's Day.

I arrived in Vancouver too late to catch the ship. Remembering the young doctor's advice I went to the emergency ward of the general hospital. There I learned that the medical treatment I required would cost $150 in advance. I had only $90 left so I walked back out into the swirling snow and slush-covered streets.

I was in deep trouble and in severe pain. What's more, I had let a man down who'd stood up for me. I was running out of money and knew not one soul in Vancouver.

I bought a paper and consulted the classified ads. Within an hour I had a room and the use of a hall telephone in a workingman's home. Then I sought out a cut-rate drugstore and bought a week's supply of gauze pads, antiseptic soap, and adhesive tape for my shoulder. After that I forced down the fifty-cent special in a Chinese café.

The city was deep in the throes of a post-war recession, and advertised jobs brought lines of hollow-eyed veterans. From a loquacious librarian I learned that the powerful *Daily Province* newspaper had dominated the local readership for years, but that a recent printers' strike had reduced it to second place. The rival *Vancouver Sun* had stolen many of its subscribers and advertisers by acceding to the union's demands. The waiter in the beer parlour of a flop-house adjacent to the Sun building told me that the undisputed boss of that flamboyant paper's news-room was a hard-drinking, tough-talking former sports writer named Hal Straight. He was said to operate on the premise that the fastest way to the top was over the underpaid bodies of his underlings.

I plotted my course of action most carefully. My extra suit went into a one-hour dry-cleaner's for a quick revitalization. I solved the major problem facing me by unbinding my broken shoulder, dressing properly on top of it, and then placing my right arm in a simple triangular sling. I planned to tell my prospective employer that I had only a simple elbow sprain which would disappear overnight.

Straight's office was a glassed-in room in a corner of the fourth floor editorial department. I recognized him from the waiter's description. My plan was to knock once, walk right in, and introduce myself quickly. Before he asked my reason for being there, I intended to explain that with my experience as a photo-reporter and pilot I could open new worlds of news gathering for the *Sun*.

I made my way across the cluttered, noisy room gritting my teeth against the pain in my shoulder. The knob was on the right side of the glass door to Straight's office. I gripped it inexpertly with my left hand and twisted the handle. Then I stepped briskly forward, intending to push the door ahead of me. The door, however, opened outward, and did not budge. Instead I lurched completely through the glass.

The crashing sound brought a sudden silence to the usual bedlam of the city room. At first, all was quiet except for the ring of a telephone and the chatter of the Teletype machines. To this were then added the scurrying of many feet and many voices asking, "Is he hurt?" This minor panic was followed instantly by a bull-like bellow from Straight.

"Forget that 'is-he-hurt' bit. Find out if the bottle's broken!" he thundered.

While the janitor cleaned up the mess, Straight explained that he had thought I was delivering the bottle of bootleg whisky he'd been waiting for. We lied to each other a little, and within an hour I was hired at $65 a week as staff pilot and aerial photographer. I was to start the following day. He called in Himie Koshevoy, the city editor, who immediately let me know that he had no need of a staff pilot and distrusted airplanes. Straight told him to make full use of my talents anyway. Then I went back to the rooming-house and changed my bandages.

The next day Straight arranged with B.C. Airlines for me to have use of any of their aircraft, and he gave me the newspaper's airborne camera, a Fairchild K-20, which required two hands to operate. It was designed to be held with the left hand, while the right operated the pistol grip that both tripped the shutter and wound another frame of film into place. Clearly, it was not intended to be used by someone who was flying an airplane at the same time. I eventually mastered the technique, however. I would turn my torso at right angles to my hips, open the pilot's window, and hold the long, heavy camera in the freezing slip-stream. To make sure the pictures were sharp, I had to avoid touching the camera or my arms to any part of the plane.

To compensate for the fact that I needed both hands for the camera, I cut a three-inch section of rubber from a motorcycle inner tube, which I slipped over my right leg just below the knee. When I was ready to take pictures, I would slide the band over the top of the joystick. That way I could fly the plane merely by moving my feet on the rudder pedals and rotating one knee to change direction.

Soon I was covering stories regularly, and Himie Koshevoy mellowed enough to increase my salary by $10 a week, a lordly sum in that economy. This additional income allowed me to buy a 1938 Chevrolet coupe and move to more amenable quarters.

The *Sun* was owned by the Cromie family, with Don, Sam, and Peter, the sons of the founder, operating the company. The father, it was said, had been the front man for a political party that bankrolled the newspaper. When the party became successful, the elder Cromie told the politicians to go to hell. When they asked for the money back, he kept it all himself.

Don, the publisher, was said to be irritable and shrewd. Middle brother Sam, the assistant publisher, was depicted as an overgrown, affable playboy with a penchant for chesty blondes. The youngest brother, Peter, was quiet and worked in the accounting department.

I'd seen the publisher at a distance, but had not yet laid eyes on his brothers. One rainy morning during my first month at the paper, a man rushing carelessly from the front door of the Sun building slammed into my damaged shoulder.

"You stupid bastard," I yelled at him. I leaned against the stonework to keep from falling.

"What did you call me?" my assailant shouted.

"I said you were a stupid bastard, but I was incorrect: you're an ignorant, stupid bastard."

"I know you, you're ... you're ..." He paused, then shouted, "Air force! That's it! The air force. You were that adjutant at Rockcliffe."

It all came back to me. When I'd been stationed in Ottawa, a drunken young pilot officer from the public relations branch had entered my office with his tie done in a bow and his hat on backwards. He had also been holding a bottle of rum and singing snatches of "The Harlot of Jerusalem." Since I'd heard more than 100 verses of that vulgar song, did not drink rum, and was singularly unimpressed by his assertion that his father owned a newspaper, I suggested he do a swift 180-degree turn and head for his bed. He gave me some smart talk, so I had him arrested and detained, ordering his release without charge when he sobered up.

"You had me arrested in Ottawa, remember?" he recalled correctly, and in a snotty tone asked what I was doing in Vancouver.

"I work here. I'm the pilot," I answered, nodding upwards to the Sun sign above the portal.

"Well," he said with a now-I've-got-you-by-the-balls sneer as he stepped into the street, "I'm one of the publishers." I knew then my days with that firm were numbered.

The results of my early airborne assignments had been highly successful, but Koshevoy had not relaxed his efforts to fail me on a flying assignment. When the largest battleship in the world, the USS *Iowa*, was a day away from Vancouver harbour on a training exercise, he assigned me to find and photograph it.

"It's somewhere out there." He waved an arm in the general direction of the Pacific Ocean. "Somewhere at sea off Cape Flattery.

I can't spare a photographer so take the aerial camera and get me some decent pictures for the final edition."

The fact that the only aircraft available that day was single-engined and on wheels didn't seem to bother him. It gave me some cause for concern, however. I knew I would be subject to the vagaries of offshore weather and the ever-present possibility of mechanical failure. I also knew that the tenuous link between me and the Patricia Bay airport radio station would be less than secure when I left the safety of the American coast. I accepted the assignment without comment, determined to give it my best effort. I knew I had little chance of success but I hoped that when I returned, if I hadn't been swallowed by the intractable Pacific, at least I would be able to hold my head high in defeat.

I topped off the tanks and made sure the Mae West life-jacket I always tucked under my aircraft seat was in working condition. Then I filed a flight plan with the Vancouver tower to Patricia Bay airport on Vancouver Island some sixty miles south. My idea was to refuel there and head due west along the lower coastline of Vancouver Island for about fifty miles, then cut across the Strait of Juan de Fuca to the most northwesterly tip of America, desolate and uninhabited Cape Flattery and head seaward from there.

The radio in my aircraft was a fixed-crystal Narco Superhomer that transmitted and received signals in a line-of-sight manner over relatively short distances. It would be useless once I was over the ocean, miles from the nearest receiving station. I reckoned my maximum air time at six hours if I loafed along at 65 per cent power. Taking the twenty-knot head wind into account, I calculated that I could fly 150 miles out to sea before reaching my point of no return.

The cloud layer was light at 2,500 feet so I pointed the nose west and began a climb to 10,000 feet, locking the radio on the distress frequency as a ridiculous last resort in the event of engine failure. Two hours after leaving Pat Bay I was about eighty miles from the Washington coast. I began flying a large circle some twenty miles in diameter, knowing that my flight time for this search manoeuvre would be about one hour, after which I would head back to land and admit defeat. Soon the cloud base beneath me began to hamper my view of the ocean. I dropped under it and flew the remainder of the arc at 2,000 feet despite the roughness of the air.

Near the outer limit of my radius of action I saw it. Like a beast from the deep it lay near the horizon, steaming almost towards me on a converging course. I headed straight for it, unlimbering the K-20 camera and securing the joystick to the inside of my right leg with the rubber band so I had free use of both my arms.

We closed in fifteen minutes and I took three shots of her as she ploughed through the heavy seas. Then I levelled out even with her deck. When I was close enough to fill the whole viewfinder, I took a picture of hundreds of white-clad sailors lining the rail, waving their hats at the plane. After shooting the rest of the roll from different angles, I set course for Pat Bay and landed there with thirty minutes of fuel remaining.

One hour and fifteen minutes later I was in the *Sun*'s dark-room processing the photos. Then I made up a series of 16 × 20-inch prints of the best angles, and with time to spare before the final edition's deadline, I walked casually past Koshevoy's desk, slid them across to him, and continued out the door to a fine restaurant where I had a great meal with a decent bottle of wine, which I charged to the *Sun*.

The paper played the event up big. The whole of page one above the fold was given over to a huge picture of the USS *Iowa* while the other pictures I took were used almost as large on the inside pages. There was a story, too, about my flight out over the ocean to find and photograph the ship. Koshevoy never said a word to me about the pictures or the story. He'd lost again, and I knew it was only a matter of time before another trap would be set.

Before I ever saw Vancouver I had heard it said that the city was gutsy, brash, wet, dirty, scabrous, perpetually beautiful, and perpetually drunk. I found it to be all these things and more. I also found that it had an effect on me. For the first month I remained in mind and in practice a prim and rather proper easterner, but soon my character changed to meld more with that of my peers and our environs. I doubt, for example, that earlier I would have gone along with the events surrounding the transmission of the first wirephoto in a western Canadian newspaper.

The Sons of Freedom sect of the Doukhobor communities in the fertile Kootenay Valley district of British Columbia held Krestova as their central point. From there they avenged themselves on anything and everyone whom they chose to see as the enemy, including members of the two other sects, the Orthodox and the Independents. All came from Russia around the turn of the century and

Raymond Munro's Spitfire—code-named SO-B and
nicknamed the Bastard—at 145 Squadron's airfield in
Merston, England.

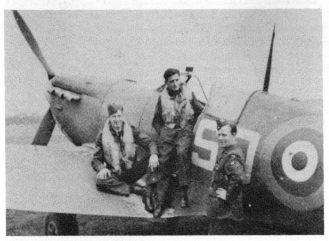

Seated on the wing of his second Spitfire, code-named
SO-V, is Raymond Munro with Larry Robillard (centre)
and their armament expert.

Raymond Munro in a bo'sun's
chair on the Bank of Commerce
building during an assignment for
the Toronto *Star* in 1942.

August 1, 1942: first day as a cub
reporter for the *Star*.

Marilyn Monroe entering the Vancouver Hotel dining
room with Raymond Munro and actor Rory Calhoun.

As editor-in-chief of the *Chatham Daily News*, Munro promoted a move towards world happiness, talking by telephone with world leaders to gain their sanction.

With Sheikh Suleiman al Huzeil in the Negev during a tour of the Arab-Israeli war zone as a military correspondent.

Norman Jones (left) and Raymond Munro, after man's
first parachute descent onto the north polar ice-cap, in
the shadow of the North Pole, March 31, 1969.

Raymond Munro (left) as a bush pilot in northern Quebec with two prospectors, 1968.

As Expo 67 Polar Ambassador, Raymond Munro piloted geophysicist Ivan Christopher on the first leg of the 12,000-mile midwinter flight through the high Arctic, to honour the nation's early bush pilots.

The lift-off of Canada I from Ireland, for the first and
unsuccessful attempt at crossing the Irish Sea to England. The aerostat went down off the coast of Wales. The
co-pilot, Norman Jones, was rescued by RAF helicopter.
Munro stayed with the downed craft until he was rescued with it by a freighter.

In the fall of 1968 Raymond Munro and his teammate
André Coté were involved in a HaLo (high altitude,
low opening) parachuting experiment.

settled in various parts of the United States and western Canada as farmers in private communities.

During 1948, widespread violence flared again among the Sons of Freedom. I was assigned to fly Ted Greenslade, a reporter, and Dave Buchan, the chief photographer of the paper, into the area with the first portable wirephoto machine we'd ever seen. It was a cylindrical device operated by electricity into which was placed a glossy photograph. Then by means of a pulsing light directed at the print, it would transmit a copy over a long-distance telephone line to a receiving machine in the *Sun*'s dark-room. It had worked well on field tests, but this would be the first time a news picture would be transmitted for publication. The assignment was to capture a newsworthy photograph immediately upon arrival in the troubled area and transmit it back to the *Sun* for use on page one of the last edition.

We took off from Vancouver at dawn and flew 300 miles across the Rockies to Nelson, where Greenslade and Buchan contracted for taxi service on a twenty-four-hour basis, then headed for a liquor store and a hotel in that order. I hangared the airplane and hired a guard for it, then joined the news team. They were well into the sauce at what they called a planning meeting. The wirephoto transmitter had been set up in a hotel room and connected to the telephone. All they required to activate it was a glossy photograph and a long-distance connection to the *Sun*. After a couple of drinks, Buchan and I came up with a scheme that would make Greenslade the prime subject of the first-ever news picture sent by telephone to the *Sun*—a momentous occasion.

Our first moves were to rent the modelling services of a buxom lass of ill repute and to purchase a foot-long souvenir-type bow plus an arrow tipped with a suction cup. Then we drove to the outskirts of the city into pastoral surroundings, stripped Greenslade to his waist, and sprawled him backwards over the bole of a huge tree. The suction-cup arrow was fitted tightly to his forehead and a half-empty bottle of liquor was held to his lips. The lady of the afternoon stripped to her waist and was manoeuvred close to the glassy-eyed Greenslade. In her hand she held the bow as though she had just released the arrow. Then she expanded her chest and Buchan took the picture. We loaded ourselves into the taxi and raced back to Nelson. Buchan developed the negative and made a print in a local photographer's studio, while I telephoned Koshevoy in Vancouver and told him to warm up the receiving machine, because Buchan would be transmitting a great news picture within minutes.

In Vancouver, we learned later, Himie gathered together in the thirteenth-floor dark-room the publisher, the managing editor, a number of department heads, and two visiting ladies from the Carnegie Foundation in New York. He ushered them into the tiny room and turned off all lights except one small red bulb, then threw the switch on my telephoned command and waited. When the beeping stopped on their machine, signifying that the picture had been received on the sensitized paper, it was stripped from the drum and slid into a tray of photographic developer by the dark-room technician.

All heads craned to watch the historic event. Slowly, like a wraith appearing from a fog-bank, the forms of the two persons in Buchan's picture swam into view. There, for all to see, was a wildly laughing woman, huge breasts jutting forward, and Greenslade, obviously very drunk and appearing to have been disporting himself, with the tiny arrow stuck into his forehead between his crossed eyes.

Having been up most of the previous night preparing for the venture, we all went to bed and refused to answer the continually ringing telephone. I arose at three in the morning and took the airplane off for an aerial scouting expedition.

Just before dawn, while circling an area near Thrum, I saw a huge agricultural complex explode into flame. I circled it for some twenty minutes, taking pictures of the awesome sight, then flew west across the mountains to Kelowna to avoid the bad weather that was covering my inbound route. Two hours later I experienced some difficulty in controlling the airplane, as the wheels touched the runway and swung me off the centre line to a swivelling stop on the grass verge. A popping sound above my head alerted me to a circular fracture in the Perspex roof, radiating from a half-inch hole.

An examination revealed that one of the tires had a bullet hole in it. The bullet had entered it from the bottom, ricocheted off the metal hub, and then passed through the top of the tire. Another bullet had passed through my open window and exited through the roof. I called Greenslade to tell him about the fire pictures and the bullet holes. Then I made two more calls: one to the Royal Canadian Mounted Police detachment in Kelowna, and another to the city desk of the *Sun*.

I waited for an hour while the tire was replaced and the hole covered, left the evidence and a statement with the RCMP, who had taken a series of photographs of the airplane's damage, and flew back to Vancouver, arriving at the paper after lunch. My in-air adventure was the subject of a wildly inflated, page-one story that implied that the Doukhobors had shot down an unarmed *Sun* aircraft. My protestations that I hadn't even known about the bullet holes until after I landed were taken as modesty on my part.

Buchan meanwhile received a call from an abusive city editor who told him of Greenslade's immediate dismissal and his own demotion. I had been placed on notice for my part in the escapade. When Buchan told Greenslade of his punishment for being the unwitting victim of the prank, he immediately sent a telegram to Koshevoy stating that the policeman from whom I had borrowed his pistol wanted it back. The implication, of course, was that I had shot up the airplane myself. This wire caused a great deal of merriment among the reportorial staff until the police report revealed that two .30-.30 slugs had passed through the plane, one into and out of the tire under my left leg, and the other through the opening on my left side and out through the roof.

Unknown to us at the time, a news team from the *Province*, led by veteran reporter Eddy Ingram, was also in the troubled area and working on a similar story. Ingram had also partaken of one too many and was alleged to have purchased a taxi outright, charging it to his newspaper. The upshot of the day's events was that Greenslade was fired by the *Sun* and immediately hired by the *Province*; Ingram was at the same time fired by the *Province* and hired by the *Sun*. Buchan was reduced to second-in-command of the *Sun*'s photo section, and I was on notice that with one more caper like that I too would be dismissed.

LIFE IN
LOTUS-LAND

EVERY DAY I missed my children, until the thought of them consumed many of my waking hours, and their letters and my telephone calls only sharpened my need to be with them. Knowing that I could not care for them alone responsibly, I invited my parents to cross the country and make a home for us all in Vancouver. They loved the children dearly and in some small measure saw their dead son Roy in young Rob Roy.

We leased a large home in a quiet section of the city and settled into a family way of life. But, by summer's end, my parents' health caused a revision in our plans. I arranged for a housekeeper to come and care for the children and me. Then my parents moved to a tranquil community on Vancouver Island, where the children and I visited them frequently by seaplane.

During this period I started on a three-year course in senior industrial first aid, which brought me into contact with hundreds of city police officers, many of whom I came to know very well. In the trunk of my coupe, I kept a full array of photo equipment, life-jackets, bush clothing, and first-aid requirements.

I also began to offer, as I had in Toronto, sightseeing flights to visitors, especially motion-picture personalities who came to Vancouver. For the more adventurous I used a war-surplus military trainer, and capped the flight along the majestic coast and over the forbidding north shore mountains with an inverted pass between the two great twin peaks called the Lions. I never lost the thrill of rolling the airplane about its axis and watching the snow-covered rocks rotate around me.

When Gary Cooper came to town, he learned that I knew the locations of several of the largest rookeries in lower British Columbia. His great joy was to lie afield at false dawn, cradling a specially crafted .22 Hornet rifle with a telescope at least two feet long attached to the barrel, and snipe crows from branches on trees I could not see. I drove him to an isolated area near Hope over deserted roads, and before the first colour of dawn lifted the night above the trees, he was in position, dressed in woollen breeches and mackinaw over a two-piece set of silk and wool underwear he'd had custom-made for his lanky frame. Before we parted that afternoon he gave me his extra set of red long johns, which he liked because they were "psychologically warmer."

Then came to town a rascal of the first order, Dan Duryea, who was starring in a grade C movie entitled *Johnny Stool Pigeon*, in which Tony Curtis made his debut, playing a deaf and dumb lad. They were in town to attend the première.

On his arrival Duryea somehow wangled an invitation to attend a party at the palatial residence of Mrs. Ronald Graham, where he managed to upset the dignity of the occasion and colour a few cheeks with his unacceptable vulgarities.

Curtis and I met at a civic reception and took to each other immediately. He was a tough kid from the Lower East Side of New York City, who'd been prettied up with a nose job and a decent haircut, then shoved in front of a camera. He was alive to everything around him and ate up each waking hour as though it were his last.

We talked about flying, and I agreed to take him on a flight the next night in the big Stinson. That afternoon, while Duryea was being photographed in the mayor's chair at city hall, Curtis was out scouting a ballet school to which he'd followed four exquisite legs.

Near midnight, after the party following the première, he arrived at the airport in a taxi with two nubile maidens still dressed in their short ballerina skirts and dancing slippers. He escorted them to where I lounged against the cabin door.

"I"—he gestured grandly—"have brought along my two great loves, whose names may escape me for the moment but whose bodies I intend to remember forever. Take us, pilot, to that place beyond the stars." He was perfectly sober, but the girls were drunk on stardust and would have boarded a rowboat with him for an ocean voyage if he'd asked.

"Two in the back and two in the front, in any combination you want." I offered him a choice.

"Three in the back and one in the front," he insisted and lifted one of the giggling Aphrodites into the rear seat by slipping one hand under her crotch and the other around her breasts.

"More, more," she begged laughingly.

"Me next," the other ordered Curtis, who held her aside, climbed in alongside the first girl, then reached back and pulled the panting nymph in.

I slid into the pilot's seat and was about to fire up the engine when suddenly I was smothered in layered swirls of tarlatan, bumped by buttocks, and kicked by tiny feet fighting each other for positions of leverage on the ceiling, the seat back, my shoulders, and my head. The girls were skirmishing with each other to sate their sexual appetites with Curtis, who was trying desperately to complete the impossible task of fornicating with both of them at the same time. Between the great thrashing heaves and animal sounds emanating from the roiling clouds of white tutus, I felt like a swimmer being sucked into a whirlpool while watching a school of piranhas attacking a shark.

I bent double to ease myself from the cockpit into the coolness of the lonesome night and watched, transfixed, as the whole airplane rocked from side to side in ecstatic cadence to the high, wild sounds of a full-blown orgy until finally the craziness ended.

Curtis later apologized profusely for permitting himself to be so weak as to succumb to such a temptation. The girls, exhausted from spending their passions, were silent as I drove them back to the side door of the Vancouver Hotel where they all disembarked.

"Call me in the morning, late. We'll get together for lunch." Curtis squeezed my arm, rolled his eyes, and, with one hand on each of the girls' bottoms, steered them through the door and towards the elevators. I never saw him again. He'd checked out when I called the next morning.

Few of my assignments were quite so light-hearted. In the fall of 1947 I was ordered to fly a reporter, Bill Fletcher, to Little Gunn Lake, up the coast in the mountains, to cover a mine disaster that had trapped the afternoon shift deep underground. The obstacles to the flight were several. It was late afternoon and raining, with a forecast of freezing rain in the high country, and the closest landing site for wheel-equipped aircraft was forty miles from the mine. From there we'd have to go by truck over tortuous mountain roads. Hal Straight left it up to me, and I talked it out with Fletcher.

The proposition was, to beat the opposition, I would fly a seaplane over the mountains at night, land on Little Gunn Lake—if I could find it in the dark—get the story and pictures, and take off again before dawn to arrive at the office by 6:00 A.M. I would then have enough time to process the photos and story and see them spread over page one for the first edition, effectively killing the *Province*'s late-arriving story. There were not only the several flying dangers involved, such as weather, a night landing on a black lake, and a night take-off from the same site, but a double violation of the Air Regulations. The pertinent section prohibited landing a seaplane later than one-half-hour after official sundown and taking off prior to one-half-hour before official sunrise. The challenge was too great. We agreed to go.

Less than half-way into the flight we were overtaken by darkness, but except for some light ice from freezing rain over the higher altitudes, we encountered no problems. There were several lakes in the area of Little Gunn, all unmarked on the aerial map, but from the few dim lights at the mine site and on the workmen's cabins we finally identified our landing place, which from the air looked like a black hole surrounded by high hills. I made three passes, each lower than the previous one, before I dropped the floats onto the black water. After mooring the plane, we walked for an hour along a bush road to the mine.

We arrived at a tragic moment for the families of the trapped men. The mine superintendent and his specially equipped crew had just risen from the depths with a birdcage, in which rested the dead bodies of three canaries. It was then certain that all below had died from methane gas poisoning. I took a number of pictures, and Fletcher gathered the threads of the tragedy together, then we walked soberly back through the great forest an hour before first light. The take-off was scary but uneventful, and we flew back to Vancouver.

Before I had left, I had asked George Young, the chief photographer, to be in the dark-room at 6:00 in the morning to assist me with the photos in time for the first edition.

When I arrived he was not there, and the chemicals were still in their jars and cold. It was therefore after seven before I laid the ten photos on Earl Smith's desk. When Young arrived at eight, I told him how upset I was. He replied that he had no intention of helping me improve my position with the paper. Unfortunately, the door was open when I hit him. He promptly passed through it backwards and fell down half the flight of stairs leading to the twelfth floor.

My wrist, which was swollen from hours on the aircraft's controls during the previous night's flight, was the only reason Young did not require medical treatment.

I was in agony when Straight sent for me, minutes after the chief photographer had staggered bleeding into his office and complained about my attack.

"Did you strike this man?" Straight thundered.

"I did," I responded, "but not in the manner I had intended."

"You mean you hit him but you didn't mean to?" asked Straight incredulously.

"No, I intended to hit him, and I hit him where I intended, but with much less force than I intended," I explained.

"You're suspended for a week without pay, and then we'll see about your future with this newspaper." He pointed towards the door. "And you"—he thumbed Young from the office—"have let the paper down."

I was delighted with the holiday and was about to leave for home when I remembered it was going-away day for Pierre Berton. Berton had been on the *Sun* staff for three years as a reporter and was considered the finest feature writer in Vancouver. After he'd graduated from the University of British Columbia and before he had joined the *Sun*, he had been the youngest managing editor of a daily newspaper in Canada, the morning *Vancouver News-Herald*. On the side he had held sway as a modestly successful radio-show host and had written articles for magazines. He and managing editor Hal Straight were bosom buddies. The party was to be a farewell before he left on a dinnertime train for Toronto, to take up his new post as editor of Canada's prestigious *Maclean's* magazine.

Having been teamed with him on many assignments, I did not wish to miss the party. Before I joined it, however, I made some arrangements to ensure that Berton and his wife had a departure from the *Sun* they would always remember. I telephoned Kingsway Ambulance, where I worked on occasion as a driver on night police calls, and requested an ambulance in front of the *Sun* at five o'clock sharp. The driver and an attendant with a stretcher and a strait-jacket were to rush into the news-room and put Berton into the restraining device and onto the stretcher. With his wife in tow, they were then to load him into the ambulance and, with red lights and siren clearing the way, drive them through the rush-hour traffic to the railway station. Two of the largest men on Kingsway's staff promised to complete the task, despite any verbal or physical protestations from Berton, who was no ninety-eight-pound weakling.

The party started even before the last copy left the news desk for the press room. When I arrived it was well under way. Most of the people whom Berton had worked with over the years were there, as were others from the advertising, circulation, business, and promotion offices who just wanted a good time. I matched the others drink for drink and listened to an increasingly drunken Berton recite some of Service's poems of the Yukon and assorted doggerel.

A few minutes before five, Koshevoy knelt down behind Berton, and Bill Fletcher, the *Sun's* financial editor, shoved him backwards. Pierre lay horizontal for a moment, as though he'd been levitated, then crashed onto his back, slamming his head on the metal corner of a desk and rendering himself unconscious. Janet Berton rushed to his side and cradled his head.

"Jesus Christ, he's hurt!" yelled Straight, who was only an ounce this side of total intoxication.

"Get an ambulance, and hurry!" slurred Koshevoy, ineffectually trying to force himself through the wall of bodies surrounding Berton's stilled form.

"All right, clear aside. Out of the way, please." The huge ambulance attendant shouldered his way through the crowd, while his partner, the driver, scattered drunken bodies like chaff in a wind.

"Christ, but that's quick service," commented a reporter, as he opened another bottle.

"Harry," the attendant called his partner, "get the jacket. We don't want no trouble from this son of a bitch."

They pulled Janet Berton away from him, laughing at what to them was obviously an act. Then, despite the protestations of thirty drunks, they stuffed Pierre's arms into the sleeves, lashed them behind his back, laid him face down on the stretcher, and wheeled him to the elevator. The elevator was too shallow to take Berton's six-foot-four body horizontally, so they propped the stretcher partially upright, crushing his wife into a corner. The party-goers, meanwhile, ran out of the fourth floor news-room and reeled down the stairs, fighting the two ambulance men for possession of Berton's body. But true to their promise they shoved him, still on the stretcher, into the ambulance, the attendant straddling Pierre's back and Janet trying frantically to help him, while the driver swung away from the curb, siren wailing and lights flashing, and disappeared into the traffic.

I had known for some time that my days with the *Sun* were numbered. Another photographer, with whom I had become good friends, was also thinking of leaving the paper. Art Jones was a likeable, cheerful, lanky chap in his early twenties and was by far the best news photographer in Vancouver.

By chance or design all the messy news happenings were assigned to Jones or me to photograph. If a child was crushed under a streetcar, a jumper was splattered on a sidewalk, a fire victim immolated, or someone died in a pool of their own blood from a policeman's bullet, Jones or I got the assignment. It was almost as though a conspiracy existed at management level to seek out our individual failing points. While we had never designed any situation to relieve our tensions, conversely we did nothing to quell any momentum that built up naturally to such conclusions. Straight, unfortunately, took our capers as personal attacks on his authority.

It was becoming increasingly clear to Art and me that our temperaments did not exactly suit the paper's senior management. Moreover, we knew that if we stayed on we would never make the kind of money we both needed.

Finally, on one particularly onerous day, Jones was verbally abused by a female thief he'd photographed stealing some perfume from Eaton's, and I was punched in the face by the husband of a woman taking a driving test. (She had placed his car rather messily inside a grocery store, and I was photographing the resulting destruction.) Later, when Straight raised his stentorian voice to both of us about a complaint he'd received that we'd outrun a motorcycle cop in Jones's car, we decided to part company with the *Sun* and start our own business. As the level of the bottle of rye was lowered, we chose Artray Limited as the name of the new venture and flipped a coin to see who would be president for the first year. I won and immediately suggested that since we were going to quit the *Sun*, it should be with *élan*.

We had no trouble deciding just how to make sure Straight and the Cromie boys remembered us. The pride and joy of the paper was the huge spherical steel framework atop the building's spire.

This great globe, impregnated with 1,000 light bulbs in pale imitation of earth's sun, was visible for at least twenty miles on a clear night, which that night just happened to be.

The plot was drawn. We would reach the uppermost storey by an inside stairwell, then force the trapdoor leading to the cupola. From there we would climb hand over hand upwards within and without the geodesic lattice-work, and commence the operation. Our intent was to unscrew enough light bulbs to leave our names illuminated on both the east and west sides for all to see and wonder at, our first advertisement of ARTRAY.

We made it up to the lattice-work with relative ease and began unscrewing the bulbs, but the cold wind soon took most of the dexterity from my ungloved fingers. While most of the bulbs fell to the roof-top some twenty feet below, some bounced off into space. Jones had unscrewed enough lights to leave the name ART bright against the night sky, and I had just finished the AY of RAY when we heard sirens approaching and saw the red flashes of both police and fire vehicles curving along the street towards the *Sun* building.

Someone must have reported the hundreds of light bulbs that exploded when they hit the street below. We flung ourselves from the globe and through the trapdoor, which we slammed behind us, then raced to the thirteenth floor, where we grabbed our cameras and leaped down the spiral staircase to the lobby. The upgoing elevator passed us midway, crammed with firemen and police.

"You photograph the fire trucks and the police cars," Jones yelled at me on the front steps, for the benefit of the few uniformed men still in view, "and I'll try to photograph the monkey from across the street."

"Monkey?" asked an incredulous fireman.

"Yeah," I enlarged on the fantasy, "some guy took his pet monkey inside to get a story in the paper about how it could spell as well as third graders, but the bloody thing got loose and made for the roof. When it started unscrewing bulbs and tossing them into the street, Jones over there called the cops. Crazy, eh?"

We left then to let the lie disseminate, and refused to answer our home telephones for several days. The matter blew over, but everyone in the business knew that Art and I had left in style.

In February 1948 Artray was launched. Our reduced financial straits compelled us to rent space in a run-down building in a less than savoury district near the police station and above Big Three

Tailors, whose steam pressers helped warm our draughty room. We divided the space in two, transforming one side into a professional dark-room and the other into an office/work-room. Operation of the Airvue Division, as we advertised our aerial photography expertise, fell to me, as did the less technical picture taking, such as weddings and christenings. Art concentrated on more specialized advertising photographs and all colour work, which was still in its infancy. We shared the morning *News-Herald* contract, which called upon us to take all their sports pictures and, when required, handle major news breaks.

The only diversion we had from 100-hour work weeks was in photographing the numerous drunks who collapsed on our doorstep. We'd make a quick contact print and slip the picture into an inside pocket, so that when they recovered they'd see themselves as others saw them.

When the mighty Fraser River went on the worst rampage in recorded history in May of 1948 and flooded the Fraser Valley from Hope westward to the Pacific Ocean, 16,000 people were left homeless. Had it not been for the courage and steadfastness of some 30,000 civilians and members of the armed forces who battled it around the clock for twenty days, the death toll would have been frightening. In the interior of the province, the Columbia and Kettle rivers wrought similar havoc, and the government of Canada proclaimed British Columbia a national disaster area.

The *Daily Province* offered us a contract to cover the floods from the air. The fee they promised was enough to allow me to put aside all other business for the duration of the catastrophe. Instead I spent an average of sixteen hours a day flying the paper's airplane. I landed in flooded fields and on top of submerged railway tracks and transported dozens of adults, children, and farmyard animals from floating houses and roof-tops to hospitals and places of safety. Once I used the plane to tow refugees on a raft through swirling flood waters, pregnant with floating debris. At night I flew the Coast and Cascade mountain ranges taking medical supplies to isolated communities, calling on all my skills to land on moving water after nightfall and take off from deep valleys and trembling canyons.

Suddenly it was over, and our young business was in the black financially.

The *Province* had first choice of the more than 600 photographs I took. The rejects were sold to several wire services and used around the world. More than fifty Canadian newspapers published our pictures, each of which was given an Artray byline.

Artray soon became the best-known picture-taking company in the west, and the Airvue Division had trouble filling its contracts. Jones meanwhile had pioneered new colour techniques with film, and could not keep pace with the assignments offered him.

The management of the *Province* had made several overtures to me, asking me to join the paper as staff pilot and reporter/photographer at a fair wage with an assured forty-hour work week. Jones and I talked it all out, and I finally sold my half of the company to him and took the job. He floated a major bank loan and set up the finest commercial studio in Vancouver and within two years became the foremost photographer in the city. He eventually sold out when he obtained the first commercial TV station licence for the area.

While the *Province* job was less remunerative than Artray, and the management was less colourful than that at the rival *Sun*, they did want to rebuild the circulation they had lost during the strike. They hoped that their superlative airborne coverage would become a major selling point of the new look. Previously, they had used only chartered aircraft and disinterested pilots. My job would be to bring a new enthusiasm and competence to the news coverage, which was exactly what I set out to do.

THE PERILOUS
SKIES

IT WAS THE OWNERSHIP at the *Province*, as at the *Sun*, that set the tone for the contents of the paper. The *Sun* under the Cromie brothers and Hal Straight was loud, brash, uninhibited, and given to the spectacular. The *Province*, once the dominant paper in Vancouver, was more discreet, but still game to print exposés that were truly *pro bono publico*.

At the helm when I joined the paper in March 1949 was the publisher, a former newspaperman named Pete Galbraith, who had the respect of all those who worked under him. He was firm, fair, and tough-minded when the need arose, drank like hell, liked me and the idea of the newspaper having a staff pilot. He died a couple of years after I started, and disaster struck with the appointment of A.W. Moscarella. Moscarella was an accountant who looked only at the balance sheets.

Torchy Anderson, as editor, was below Galbraith on the totem-pole, but he retired shortly after Galbraith died and was replaced by Ross Munro, a lanky, bespectacled, charming man with great compassion and an incisive wit. He was a former Canadian Press war correspondent and distinguished author. In Ross I found a companion-at-arms; he could smell the making of a great story, and he went after each one in the same manner that Grant attacked Richmond.

Perhaps the single most powerful post on the paper was that of managing editor. He was the person who hired, fired, and made the daily judgements about who went where and why, and about what news and photos appeared in any particular edition. Bill Forst took over that job shortly after I joined the paper from a fine old gentleman of the press, Syd Scott. Forst was a huge, athletic man, and a great toper. He had a magnificent baritone voice, charm, news sense, and the ability to get the very best from every member of his staff. With Don Mason, a small tough streetfighter as city editor, it was a powerful command unit.

Most newspaper assignments are boring; only occasionally is the routine altered by a dramatic occurrence. In my case, however, drama was the rule rather than the exception. I was looked upon with some awe by other staff members, who thought I couldn't have a coffee without a truck crashing out of control into the lunch counter. The others engaged in news gathering as a livelihood only; they took away from each day no more and no less than they gave to it, and for reasons I have never been able to define, they were seldom on the scene of a major story when one broke.

Shortly after I began working for the *Province*, a small aircraft went missing in a major snowstorm that swept the Rocky Mountains. I was ordered into the air immediately, since the prompt location of a missing airplane can save lives. I also had a personal interest in this rescue attempt. I knew the pilot.

Bill Grant, a draughtsman at Vancouver's city hall, was an amateur pilot with something over 100 hours of flight time as pilot in command. Weather had delayed his take-off from Cardston, Alberta, but he was still scheduled to arrive in Vancouver before dark, and his plane had no instrument flight equipment.

At 3:04 on the afternoon of May 2, the Carmi radio range operator sitting in his heated cabin in the thin air atop Goat Mountain, 190 miles east of Vancouver, acknowledged the pilot's call for flight information. With the weather ahead failing fast over the snaggled chest of the Cascade Range, he advised the pilot to land forthwith, at Princeton perhaps, or even to return to Cardston, 210 miles behind him. But Bill Grant had three personal problems on his mind that dangerously altered his perception, and that ultimately would trigger the largest air search in Rocky Mountain history. His wife had been admitted to Vancouver General Hospital; he was returning from a weekend stay in Cardston with his companion, Sheila Curé, a nurse who worked at the same hospital in which his wife lay, and he knew his skills were adequate only in clear weather. Bill Grant accepted the radio operator's weather advisory and opinions without comment and went off the air.

Trapped in the fury, powerless against the roaring turbulence that made the compass dance in front of his eyes and that threatened repeatedly to seize control of the airplane and dash it to earth, Bill flew the plane for fifty-six minutes past unseen crags and towering, invisible forests. Below, for the briefest moment—as though God were inviting them to live—a road unfolded and just as quickly disappeared.

Abruptly, a savage blast of wind smashed the plane down 1,000 feet and then up again as the airscrew whined in a void of frozen air. Another sledge-hammer blow hurled Bill and Sheila's belted bodies forward. The sudden silence that followed was broken only by the final throbbing of their bludgeoned eardrums and the crackling sounds of ice on the hot exhaust stacks. High on the eastern flank of a mountain peak 9,070 feet above the level of the gale-lashed ocean to the west, the yellow back of the broken plane turned white as darkness swallowed it. At six o'clock that Monday night Bill Grant and Sheila Curé were officially presumed down, their fuel exhausted, somewhere in the vastness of the Rocky Mountains in the worst blizzard in living memory.

The Royal Canadian Air Force Search and Rescue Centre in Vancouver went to work. They checked with the Calgary airport and other fuelling points between to compute the missing plane's endurance, based on the amount of gas it had aboard and the winds aloft. Transforming this into distance flown, they inscribed on a wall-sized map a great circle that included 80,000 square miles of whitened, alien earth. They contacted every pilot known to be airborne over the Rockies during that time frame, and asked if they had heard even a whisper on their radios that could have come from the missing airplane.

In charge of the search was Group Captain Zebulon Lewis Leigh of the RCAF, an airman with awesome credentials. He was a first-generation arctic bush pilot, the first Canadian airman to be licensed to fly on instruments, the country's first national airline pilot hired by Trans-Canada Air Lines, back in 1937, and possessor of a distinguished war record as well. He ordered his staff to call each cell of human habitation within the zone large enough to boast a constable and ask if anyone had heard or seen anything of the missing flight. And lonesome trappers, white-walled into mountain cabins, were called by radio and asked for help.

At dawn on May 3, when the weather eased, twenty-eight multi-engined military planes, whose crews would scan the earth from 11,000 feet, were in the air along with single-engined air force craft and selected civil pilots who would fly designated smaller patterns 1,000 feet above the land.

As staff pilot of the *Province* I had free rein to choose my own course and the type of aircraft I would pilot. I chose to fly the sister ship to the missing craft because it would enable me to judge the range that Grant's plane had, approximate the speed over his known route, and permit me to fly just above the tree-tops if I desired. Speed was not essential to my plan; thoroughness was.

With two reporters aboard I flew eastward from Vancouver to the mountains' face and refuelled at the flare-lighted field at Hope. As the first faint light of dawn pushed back the shadows, we entered the south canyon, scoured by flailing winds. I was en route to the starting point I had chosen, the place from which Grant had radioed the Carmi range.

The air was whipped by vagrant squalls of dry snow that scratched eerily along the plane's tight skin and pushed us perilously close at times to narrowing canyon walls or to the carpet of trees. In a weird half-glow, with the crew scanning every sidehill for a trace of alien colour, newly splintered trees, or a fresh burn, we plunged unspeaking onto the trail of the Sumallo River. We rose with it, ever closer to the shimmering mist above, following the rushing water from its mouth at the Fraser River to its birthplace 7,000 feet up the sidehill of Chuwanten Mountain. We somehow blundered past the crest and flew our way downhill through the Similkameen's vaulted canyons to the Princeton Plateau, where we landed for gas and a phone to file a story. The route from there unfolded through sculptured sandstone canyons mad with twisting winds, and over whitened mountain sage-brush to the broad valley of the Okanagan, then high over the Beaverdell Range where Grant could have met his challenge.

The night before I'd spent with my aerial charts, which I knew like old friends. On one, I drew a 270-mile-long arc westward from the point we were then orbiting. I divided the half-circle into thirty equal segments, each about eight miles apart at their outer extremity of ninety miles. It looked like a half wagon wheel. I planned to fly the length of each of the thirty-one spokes like walking a tightrope, my eyes keeping the course and searching ahead and below and the crew's eyes scanning either side and below.

An hour north on the first spoke, we passed the shoreline of

Okanagan Lake. From there we went on to the Spa Hills and across the Salmon River to looming Tuktakamin Mountain, whose crest was wrapped in thick vapours. I black-circled the beast on the map for a second look when the weather cleared, then flew south across the green-white timberlands to Goat Mountain. We'd chalked up two more hours with no more to show for the effort than frayed nerves and a deeper compassion for the lost couple and their waiting families.

Northward we flew on the third spoke into gradually worsening weather, searching the small lakes of the Douglas Plateau, always out of radio range and never knowing until we were able to make contact with the Carmi station if the missing plane had been found. Grudgingly, I landed at Princeton for food and fuel, and to transmit another negative report to Search and Rescue and to the waiting news-room.

We were airborne again at one o'clock in the afternoon, riding the fifth spoke over Stump Lake and the wild back country. At low level we arced around Nicola Lake and the Quilchena River, followed by a full loop around the near-shrouded peak of Pennask Mountain, which rose 6,500 feet into the mist. With this foul weather nipping at our rudder, we scrambled back on spoke six for another load of fuel, a storm-dodging flight to Vancouver, and a night landing. Our hopes had been raised many times by newly shattered timber, a fresh scar on a mountain's face, landslides, snowslides, the sun glinting from broken ice or sleet-glazed rocks, or chimney smoke from trappers' cabins. All had been checked. All had proven wrong.

Thirty-three pilots had ventured out and thirty-three had failed. Day two of the search had ended.

At dawn we bucked the scud of the Coquihalla Pass to fly inbound on spoke seven, fighting the urge to break away and avoid sharing the same fate as those we sought. During the day my anger built slowly as my body grew more weary. I'd spent two sleepless nights plotting and dissecting all of Grant's possible actions and reactions. That his passenger might have felt a nameless terror caused me no concern; I needed to know only Grant's feelings at the time and his subsequent actions. They alone could affect my search pattern.

If he was alive, I asked myself, then why in hell didn't he reach out just one good arm and light a fire? Torch a dried tree? Set fire to

a mountaintop? Drain some engine oil and make black smoke with
rags? Do the same with the tires from the plane? Why in God's
name didn't he twist off the inside mirror and signal? And, lastly,
why was I out looking for a stupid son of a bitch who'd fly into the
face of a mountain blizzard?

Ashamed of my mental outburst, I damned myself for being so
smug in the warm safety of my airborne office, and vowed then and
there to fly until I found them dead or alive, or until someone else
found them before me. When I finished flying the last spoke of my
self-assigned 3,000-mile tightrope I'd halve the distance between
them and start all over again. They had to be in my pencilled area!

We flew the Trepanege Plateau in ordered lines from Iron
Mountain's tip on the Columbia to the broken rock top of Coquihalla Peak at 7,000 feet, until finally the winking lights of Hope
signalled day's end. At night we flew back to base.

Seventeen pilots had ventured forth and seventeen had returned.
Day three had ended.

Dawn broke cloudy-clear over the Rocky Mountain Range from
Alaska to the Great Divide. Cold winds blew inbound from a white-
capped sea forming mares' tails of blowing snow along the lordly
summits. Tom Hazlitt was the only crew aboard. No one else would
volunteer for what was now called the White Knuckle Patrol. Those
newspapermen who had served and survived felt they'd earned a
badge of honour. But Hazlitt's courage was as formidable as the
accuracy of his reporting skills.

One cloud hugged the top of big Mount Tulameen, flowing down
the lee side like a giant waterfall into the valley's gut then rising up
again sharply, higher than the peak itself. This was the deadly
mountain wave, which in one capricious instant could sweep us up
to stratospheric heights with its unbelievable power. We jousted
mildly with its sucking edge and darted just as swiftly off to search
the peak again when it died.

Old familiar granite faces, new and nameless hidden valleys, all
felt the breath of our searching wings. Against the beating currents
of air we flew southbound on spoke nineteen to sweep Three
Brothers Mountain at 8,000 feet, then deep into the Sumallo Valley
to the Skagit and low along the Silverhope River with near-empty
gas tanks to the welcome sight of Flood Field at Hope. And then
home.

Nine pilots had tested the mountains that day and all had returned to base. Night four was upon the face of the land and the bodies of Grant and Curé. The military had curtailed the search on orders from Ottawa, leaving only a token three-plane flight while the clear weather lasted.

Arguing with Bill Forst was as ridiculous as a flea climbing an elephant's tail with rape on its mind. As managing editor of the *Province* he was boss of the news-room and my immediate superior.

"You're grounded," he telephoned. "You're overtired and taking chances. The air force has called it off and it's over for you too. Besides, you've run out of crew. Take the long weekend off."

His decision was as immovable as his 250-pound frame. I went for a drink, the first in a week.

"Lease any plane you want for as long as you want and send us the bill," offered the manager of Vancouver's Arctic Club. "Bill Grant's a member. Find him."

Flying Officer Dennis Caldecott of the RCAF was a navigator by profession, and he jumped at the chance to join me as crew. By night we flew to Hope, and in the rainy half-light of false dawn we plunged into the muck of the Silverhope Canyon. We cheated our way for forty miles until our wheels brushed the swaying tree-tops. Then, chastened by the stark brutality of nature, we soberly found our way back to Hope and tried a wider pass along the Sumallo River.

Fat with fuel from Princeton we sped along with a tailing wind. Spoke twenty-one on the much-abused map took us past Crater Mountain and deep into Washington State after searching the peak of the now-clear Mount Hozomeen. Under clearing skies we doubled back to Princeton for fuel, then tracked outbound again on pencilled line twenty-three.

"There, there!" I heard Caldecott shout above the engine's noise. "Look!" He punched my arm excitedly as he pointed past my face to a twinkling light on the snow-filled floor of a deep, blind canyon. "Christ, it's them," he almost screamed as I steep-banked the plane for a double-check of the flickering point of light.

"Yeaaaahh!" I heard a boyish shout well out of me as the chill of discovery swept over my skin. We dived at redline speed into the shadowed canyon's trap and vertically up the mountain's sheer face, falling off sideways in a wingover, downwards again into the black shadows where sunlight seldom dwelt, and out of the jaws into the daylight from whence we had come.

It was them, one standing and one kneeling in the snow by a weak fire in a crevasse-like blind canyon 4,000 feet in the air, and 5,000 feet below the sinister peak of Jack Mountain, eighty-five miles outbound from the hub of my pencilled arc.

Three times more we challenged that granite wall, Caldecott tossing out one emergency pack on each run before the G force pinned him to his seat as the plane clawed its way upwards to reverse its course. We left with a dwindling fuel supply and a mark on the map to show their place. The engine quit on the approach to the strip at Princeton, and the tail wheel ripped the top cedar rail from the boundary fence.

Caldecott handled the advisory details and Flying Officer J.H. "Shorty" McLeod took his big plane in low enough over the hidden canyon to circle the couple and give them hope. Then he found their plane stuck into the snow cornice of Lone Mountain's peak. Grant and Curé had fallen down a sheer mountainside and then stumbled fifteen brutal, frozen miles to where we found them, six days after they had crashed.

I flew home and slept through Sunday morning.

It took three days to get them out. Lewie Leigh authorized Flight Lieutenant Lyle Harling to pilot a DC-3 aircraft bearing a trio of expert RCAF para-rescue specialists, to penetrate the infamous blind canyon. Led by Sergeant G.B. Leckie, Corporal L.H. Binette and LAC R.B. Braidner launched themselves from the low-flying aircraft onto the heavily-treed canyon wall above Grant and Curé's position. Despite enormous odds, they survived their landings and reached the stranded couple to care for their immediate needs.

Bill Grant's woodsman brother Cyril, waiting at Hope for news of any sighting, learned of their location from my report to the *Province* newsroom and was flown to a tiny border lake ten miles south of it. He started walking to them on Friday night through the dark mountains, intercepting the party at dawn. A US Coast Guard helicopter flew them all back to Flood Field and then to Vancouver and a tumultuous reception.

The fact that I had stuck to my conviction that Grant and Curé's plane would be on one of the spokes I had drawn on my map, and the fact that I had refused to quit searching until they were found, had given me a special stature with the newspaper. I was not lionized by any means, nor was my friendship sought after, but when any flying job came up I was simply asked to take care of it.

Thus, when a great storm attacked the British Columbia coast with winds gusting to sixty-eight miles an hour, I was sought out by Torchy Anderson and Bill Forst with an unusual problem.

"The hospital at Powell River needs a rare type of blood and plasma quickly or a patient will die," Forst explained. "There is a case of each at the Red Cross blood bank here in the city, but in this storm there is no way of getting it there."

"Air force?" I ventured.

"We've enquired. They don't have a plane small enough to land on the closest strip, which is fourteen miles from the hospital. The sea is too heavy to land a flying boat, and the only helicopter available would lose its rotors in the wind. There is a chance of getting a U.S. Coast Guard helicopter up from Seattle, but it too would have enormous difficulty, and Ottawa would likely have to get into the act. And a parachute expert has advised us that the plasma would not survive a drop in this wind, even if it landed near the target." Forst shook his head.

"Have you taken off and landed in winds like this?" asked Anderson.

"If you're asking me if I'll fly the stuff up there, of course. I'll need a goddamn good man with me, an ambulance at the door right away to take us to Shaughnessy Hospital and pick up the blood, and someone to call the airport and have the big Stinson warmed up and ready in twenty minutes. Then I'll need some people at the airstrip in Powell River to grab the wings when I land and a fast car to take the blood and plasma to the hospital."

While a Kingsway ambulance was en route to the *Province* and the Red Cross was packing the twenty-four bottles into two padded crates, I approached a reporter named Bruce Larsen, who was said to be tough and cool—a good man to have along when trouble loomed. His excuse for not going was just that, a desire to remain earth-bound.

"Forst told me about the Powell River trip. I'd like to go," intruded Gordon Dickson, a slight senior reporter who had served overseas with the military as an intelligence officer.

"You could get hurt," I told him, "and we could go down in the bush or the water. Or we might just make it, with a little bit of luck."

"I'd like to go," he said again.

Twenty-seven minutes later, four men released their grips on the

Stinson's wings, and with throttle full on we ascended almost vertically through heavy rain in a northwesterly direction almost dead into wind, fat with fuel and carrying the two crates. Our flight, measured on an aerial chart as the crow flies, was to be eighty-seven miles. Yet our route would take us more than 130 miles, often at wave-top height and seldom above 500 feet, to Horseshoe Bay and across Howe Sound to Gibsons, up the Sechelt Peninsula to Bargain Bay, where we almost lost it all when a savage gust slammed us sideways towards a rock face, then suddenly downwards to the very tops of the great firs. The weather was so bad at Nelson Island that we lost another twenty miles when we were forced to take the inland passage away from Powell River, then cut back northwest again along the thunderous stretch of Jervis Inlet. Twice more the airplane was so savaged by the turbulence that I had to call on Dickson to hold the controls with me. Had the crates not been secured, they would have smashed us both into the instrument panel and plunged the airplane to earth.

We passed Grief Point after seventy-two minutes into the contest. At 2:40 on the dash clock we touched down on the Powell River strip, where four men waited to hold the wings until the airplane could be lashed down against the howling force. The crates were loaded into the back seat of a waiting sedan. I got in beside them while Dickson eased himself in next to Pearson, the driver. A large man with ham-like hands, he coaxed the big car along the mountain road. At times the car was propelled by the violent winds and other times it was held almost to a crawl.

It happened so fast the driver could not be faulted. On a mountain curve, exposed to the elements on three sides, the car was flipped over like a tossed coin. It rolled several times and came to rest upside-down against a log. The crates smashed onto me during each revolution, and Dickson, with nothing to grab, was thrown about like a rag doll.

It was over in a moment. I remained conscious despite a severe crack across the face that immediately closed one eye, and I managed to kick a door open while sitting on the inside of the roof. Then I yelled to Dickson and the driver but got no answer. With my omnipresent fear of fire spurring me on, I managed to wrench open the passenger door and pull Dickson out, then the crates of blood and plasma, which were fortunately unbroken. Dickson was semiconscious and bloodied about the face and head. I held him for a moment. He came gradually alert, fought me off, and rose to his feet, then fell down again. Between us we managed to reach the driver, who was unconscious, and pull him gently from the wreck.

His back was badly injured, and because his legs were totally numb we hesitated to move him, except to take him a safe distance from the car and lay him flat. Then Dickson heard a motor in the distance. I sprinted back to the road and stopped a flat-bed truck, whose driver was also having difficulty navigating the wind-swept road. Between the three of us we placed Pearson on the rear deck, lashed the crates down on either side of him, and crawled slowly to the hospital, where a medical team was waiting. Within minutes they had the life-saving liquids flowing into the patient's arms and our driver on a table in the operating room.

Dickson and I hired the truck driver to take us back to the airplane, which, thanks to the attention of the four volunteers, was still intact. Since both my feet and legs were operable, and since each of us had one good eye and one good arm with which to navigate and operate the controls, there was no reason not to fly back to Vancouver. The flight, with a roaring wind at our side, was uneventful. We returned to find that the news of our success had preceded us by radiotelephone. The patient to whom we had taken the life-saving fluids lived, and our driver eventually recovered. The Canadian Red Cross Society then honoured us, which was not at all necessary.

THE
STANLEY PARK
CAPER

IF, on a warm and sultry August night in 1949 you happened to be spooning in the cosy lovers' nook called, prosaically, Pipeline Road, in Vancouver's Stanley Park, you might have seen the following:

Me, low in the driver's seat of a fast coupe, a Colt .45 under one armpit and the other across the shoulders of a red-headed dish equipped with two huge bosoms punching their nipples out of a tight sweater, worn above a grosgrain silk summer skirt and below a five o'clock shadow. And you might have gotten your head knocked in. Either by me, the babe, whose tresses hid the muscular frame of a superbly conditioned body, or by a gang of rapists who were lurking in the shadows. For this was the climax to what has ever since been known as the Stanley Park Caper, an escapade that could have been entitled, "Don't mess with the press."

It all started soon after I was assigned by the *Province* to cover the city police beat in the main headquarters building. I had come to be fairly well known and trusted by members of the detective squad over the past couple of years, almost a fixture in fact. And I had learned in Toronto, as a police photographer for the *Globe and Mail*, that looking like a chair could get you on the inside of conversations that you'd otherwise never hear.

One day, a team of detectives were talking in the interrogation room when one remarked casually about "another rape in Stanley Park last night." I didn't catch the whole of his partner's response, but the gist of it was "so what's new?" The exchange struck me as odd, because I had seen nothing about any Stanley Park rapes in the overnight reports. The only way they could have been left off would be on orders from the superintendent of detectives. Such an action would, in turn, mean that the information was being kept from the public. And if that was happening, I argued to myself, what the hell could the reason be? It was this kind of deductive logic that frequently made me the subject of news stories, rather than the author. Another reporter would have rushed in to Detective Inspector Fred Fish's office and demanded, in the name of the press as the lawful eyes and ears of the public, to know just what was going on after dark in that wild and forbidding pastoral retreat. Duly alerted, Chief Constable Walter Mulligan would then have clamped such a lid of secrecy on the happenings that even the victims would believe they had only dreamed of the sexual attacks.

Instead I set about getting information concerning the discussed rape and any others prior to it. But how? To ask the head of the Criminal Investigation Branch might result in a total news black-out, followed by a snow job from the public relations officer and a series of restrictive measures being placed on all police reporters. To seek information directly from the officers who mentioned the crime in my presence would place me in Coventry for all time with them. There was only one place to get the facts: from the document vault of the department, beneath the main stairs in the headquarters building. And while the double-locked steel door was not impregnable, the chances of my getting in, finding and reviewing the files, and escaping undetected were miniscule.

I explained the situation to Bill Forst, omitting only my plan of entering the document vault. My reasoning was that if I did gain entry and was caught, he would not be involved.

"Keep your ear to the ground. Use whatever contacts you have on the force without asking any direct questions, and I'll call a couple of doctors I know at Vancouver General and ask if any rape victims have been treated there recently." He buoyed me up with his personal involvement. "And we'll keep this between us, so there's no possibility of a leak."

I tried to engage several detectives from homicide in conversations touching close to the subject, but I got nowhere. They either diverted me from my course or they had no information to impart. Then I got lucky. Just after seven in the morning the following week I answered a long-ringing telephone in the *Province* news-room. A voice I could not identify called me by name.

"Munro?"

"Yes. Who's this?"

"I'm the car man from the north shore and you know who that is. Don't mention my name. Just listen carefully and give me your word that you won't involve me at any time." The clues narrowed down the man's identity. He was the owner of a large automobile dealership in West Vancouver, with whom I had had a drink or two when I worked for the *Sun*.

Whenever anyone asked me to keep their name secret, I did so with a proviso. "Okay. But if I hear this story from anyone else and your name is mentioned, I'll have to give whatever you tell me to the managing editor. Otherwise, it stays with me." He agreed and then told me the story of what had happened to him between ten o'clock and midnight the previous night. His strangled voice revealed his inner torment. Choked with fear for his own physical safety and for his standing in the community, he clearly also loathed himself for being a coward.

He was unhappily married and had entered into a sexual liaison with another woman. To secure a private location for a romantic interlude, he had driven with her to a small side-road deep in Stanley Park and half-hidden the car under huge fir trees. Feeling safe in their darkened retreat, they had settled into a hugging and squeezing routine that generated enough heat to require the shedding of their outer garments. Lost in desire, neither of them heard a sound from the three rubber-shod stalkers who listened unseen through the partly opened windows.

Both doors were suddenly ripped open. Flashlights shone directly into their eyes, blinding them.

"This is the morality squad! Both of you get out of the car, now!" a stern voice shouted. "I said now!"

The lovers tried to pull some clothing around their near-naked bodies. And because he was too slow for their demands, my informant was hit savagely in the face, then in the genitals. As he writhed on the ground, he was kicked repeatedly.

"Grab the woman," he heard the tallest of the three men shout. "I'm fucking her first."

And as he lay on the floor of the dark forest, trying to pull himself upright and go to her aid, my informant was kicked again and told to stay down or die.

"I heard her pleading for mercy and then her terrible screams," he haltingly related the first of the many sexual torments his twenty-five-year-old lover would suffer at the hands of the three men. "They took her a few yards away and the tall one punched her to her knees and filled her mouth with his sex and then raped her. I heard one of the other men claim it was his turn. By this time her screams had turned to choking, sobbing prayers.

"I pleaded with the man standing over me to let her go and then do what they wanted to me. I was kicked again in the stomach and heard my assailant say he was one of a team of special Stanley Park police ordered to keep the park safe for decent folks."

Half-sobbing, he then went on to relate how he heard the two men in the bushes talk about stuffing her mouth with sand so she couldn't scream. Then she broke loose and ran through the darkness towards the car and directly into the arms of the third man, who punched her to the ground, twisted one of her legs until it went completely out of shape, and then raped and sodomized her. "When he had finished, he and the tall man dragged her naked and bleeding back up the path, and spread-eagled her so their partner could satisfy his lust again. I heard them all laughing. Then I heard them leaving through the heavy underbrush, and after a while, when I could stand, I called out to her. When there was no answer I went to find her. I didn't know it at the time, but she had regained consciousness and crawled for some time, until she reached a paved road where a car's headlights picked her out. That driver had taken her to the police," he related.

After a fruitless search of the forested area, he forced himself into his car and drove to the hospital for treatment. From there he called the police and gave them his story on the understanding that both his name and the name of his raped companion would not be made public. It was from his hospital room that he called me.

I gave Forst the information immediately, omitting my informant's name as I had agreed, but assuring Forst that the man was known to me personally. In my view, I explained, his act was both courageous and public-spirited.

Forst then learned from a friend, a doctor at Vancouver General Hospital, that a woman had been brought to the emergency ward shortly after one o'clock that morning by police car. She had been sexually assaulted in several ways, badly beaten about the face and body, and her legs had been severely injured. She was in serious condition and would shortly undergo surgery. Of greater concern to the doctor was the victim's mental condition, which he described as "in fragile balance." A brief report on her companion's condition confirmed his claim that he had been savagely kicked in the genitals and about his body and head. He would be released the following day.

Forst was visibly shaken by this news. We agreed to meet after the final edition had gone to press for a quiet drink and a thorough review of the whole matter, before determining a course of action that the newspaper might responsibly take. In the meantime I checked the overnight reports at the police station, taking great pains not to attract attention. Nothing was on file concerning Stanley Park, rape, attempted rape, or the name of my informant. As I passed into the hall I met Harry Whelan, superintendent in charge of the uniformed patrol officers. He and I had recently fished for salmon. We chatted for a moment about inconsequentials. Then on the spur of the moment I asked if I could see him on a private matter later in the day.

Harry Whelan was a Bostonian with a seafaring background and a master mariner's ticket for inland waters. During his twenty-two-year police career he had served with distinction for seventeen years in the detective branch, and been decorated for saving the life of a drowning man. When his name cropped up in conversation, it was spoken with respect for his firm conviction that a policeman's prime responsibility was the protection of the public. He was a man's man in every respect.

I rapped on his office door in mid-afternoon.

"What can I do for you?" he asked pleasantly.

I had considered the tack I would take so carefully that I had even memorized my first statement, but threw it all out the window as he looked at me with his piercing eyes.

"First, I have to know if you will accept this conversation as private," I said.

"A conversation requires more than one person to speak," he replied easily, "and I cannot give my word while I am a police officer. But if you care to talk, without causing me to respond, then of course I shall listen," he added, giving me the opening I needed. "But, by the same token, I must trust you to refrain from mentioning my name at any time concerning the matter."

"And what I say will stop here too?" I asked.

"Unless you are in some manner party to a criminal act."

Emboldened by his candour, I told him about the conversation I had overheard about rapes in the park, about my informant's phone call and Forst's information from the doctor, and about our meeting that afternoon. He said nothing, merely made a few pencil marks on a pad he held in his lap. Before I had finished speaking he made circular motions with his hand at his mouth, indicating that I should not pause, but continue talking. I was further intrigued when he slid a note to the centre of the desk which read, "Keep talking and watch me."

As I related in finer detail the events that the rapists' male victim had relived for me over the telephone, Whelan placed an empty file folder on his desk, inserted a single sheet of paper in it, and opened and closed it while pointing a finger at me, as if telling me to do the same. He moved it to the centre of his desk, and then scribbled another note which read: "2 sharp tomorrow aft, five minutes alone, read and leave."

"I cannot help you," Whelan spoke for the first time since I'd started my presentation, as he pocketed the two messages. "I am not privy to all reports on these matters. In any case, I have no authority to discuss situations that are not approved in advance by the chief constable." He stood up abruptly. The meeting was terminated.

My head was spinning when I met Forst at the Irish-Canadian Club and related to him over a drink the events of the preceding hour, omitting only the name of my contact, which he asked me for only once.

"We'll wait until after you come back from the station tomorrow before we work out a course of action," he concluded.

I began checking the night's occurrence reports at six the next morning, without finding any reference to Stanley Park or a sexual assault of any description. I watched the clock through the long forenoon, safe in the knowledge that no news break, however large, would keep me from my two o'clock appointment. Dead on time I rapped lightly on Whelan's office door, pad and pencil readied to take notes, then entered the empty office. In the middle of his desk was a lone file folder, which I opened to disclose one single sheet of paper with typed notations on it. The words had obviously been picked out on a portable typewriter with no regard for neatness.

It was headed "SP rape reports," and the several typed lines revealed that 113 sexual assaults on women in the park had been reported to police during the previous twenty months. On all but a handful of occasions, either three or four men had been involved in the assault. Posing as police morality squad officers, the men had pulled escorts and victims from cars and abused them before disappearing into the forest on foot. Several mentions were made of a dilapidated green panel truck being seen in the vicinity before the attacks. The apparent leader of the group was in his early thirties, tall, ill-dressed, and uncouth, with longish blond hair falling over his forehead.

A second sense urged me to quit the room immediately. After replacing the paper in the folder, I left, entering the main lobby just as Harry Whelan came down the central staircase towards me.

"Afternoon." I nodded to him.

"Afternoon," he responded as he walked to his office.

Within minutes Forst and I were stunning each other with variations on a theme, as we tried to figure out how and why such an enormous crime would be withheld from the public. As newspapermen, we knew it to be by far the largest story of our combined careers.

"Bill," I laid my proposition out for him, "before we blow the whistle I want a shot at getting a first-person story on how these bastards operate. I want to stay in the park all night, alone in my car with the doors unlocked, waiting for them to strike. If they do, I'll take care of myself—and maybe them—and break the whole ugly mess to the public. In my story I'll detail the small rumours at the police station and the call from the man we'll identify only as our 'hidden witness.' I'll use his horror story, then say that I gained all the background information on the rapes from the files in the police vault."

"You're crazy," said Forst. "First off, you could get your head stove in if they target your car. Or you could frighten them off and the police might never catch them. Worst of all, they could see you as a sexual object and leave you talking in a high voice and with a very low esteem for yourself. Then, after the fact, the police might lay charges against you for breaking and entering, theft, public mischief, and obstruction. All of that would involve the paper, and I can't permit that to happen. Nope, that's out of the question."

"If you'll wait here for a minute," I said, undeterred by his refusal, "I'll hand you my written resignation from the *Province*. Then I'll take those guys on as a private citizen. I'll give the story to the *Sun* as a public service, and explain in it that somewhere along the way you lost the first requirement of a great newspaperman—courage." I stood up to leave.

"Jesus," he said. "You would do it, wouldn't you?"

"Right now."

"Why don't you take three days off and think this whole matter through very carefully," he offered me a compromise. "Give me a note requesting it, and I'll agree. What you do on your own time is your business. And you know I'll stay close to a telephone."

"With or without pay?" I asked. My mind was already racing ahead forming a plot.

"With, of course," he sighed. "And watch yourself."

My plan was simple. I waited until dark, put on a shoulder holster carrying the .45 Colt automatic I was licensed to carry, and strapped a sharp hunting knife in its sheath upside-down to my left calf. Then I drove into Stanley Park to the same area where my informant and the woman had been terrorized. It was on a section of the old Pipeline Road, lonely, generally untravelled, and overhung with huge tree branches. The radiumed hands on my watch stood at 10:30 when I rolled down the windows and settled my body into the seat. I let my mind wander freely over every aspect of the operation, even to plotting the opening lead for the story I'd write after meeting my fate with the unholy group, and exposing the police department for failing the public.

By three o'clock, I knew my plan had failed. I checked in with Forst by telephone before breakfast to learn that no overnight rapes had shown up on the occurrence sheets; then I slept fitfully through the day. That night I went through the same routine again in the same location. Instinct told me that sooner or later they would return to the scene of their gang rape, seeking another victim. They did just that near two o'clock on the third morning. I didn't see them, but suddenly all my senses keyed themselves to the pitch of an over-taut piano string. Even the short hairs on my neck stood stiff as fear of the unknown tightened my skin. Almost as suddenly the feeling was gone, replaced by the lousy reaction of the unused adrenalin invading my tissues.

I realized then that they wouldn't attack unless a woman was present. I knew also what they wanted: the feel of a woman's body in sexual torment, the sound of their own fists hammering into defenceless flesh as though they were punching a side of beef in a slaughterhouse. Above all, I knew they needed to experience again and again the insane excitement of mental and physical dominance over a terrified human being.

On the way home I promised myself that until they were caught, I would not fail to keep my vigil, even at the expense of my position with the paper.

Forst's concern for the public's safety grew. He was all for laying the matter before both the editor and the publisher at an immediate private meeting.

"It's too big for us to handle," he stated. "I cannot accept further responsibility."

"They were there, right near the car, and they wouldn't attack," I explained again. "They want a woman but I can't take one on such an assignment. I wouldn't even hire a lady wrestler for the decoy, because no matter the result, both I and the paper would be condemned for risking a woman's life."

"You could take a man—dressed as a woman, of course," suggested Forst.

"Splendid," I retorted, "and what size clothes do I buy for you?"

"Not me," he laughed grimly, patting his ample girth and shrugging his massive shoulders. "How about a reporter?"

"Who is there on staff who could pass for a female and still have guts enough and the rough-house talent to survive a brawl? I wouldn't want to have to look after him while defending myself."

"McLean. Young Don McLean. He's small enough, has soft features that could pass in the dark if he wore a wig, and the kid had a couple of years of hand-to-hand combat training with the RCAF at war's end."

"Could he be trusted with the information as to why he'd be there?" I asked.

"I'll leave it up to you what to tell him, providing he knows he can get hurt, but it's him or no one, and if it's no one, then it's all over for your dawn patrol. Tonight's your last chance. If nothing happens, I'm taking it to the top tomorrow afternoon, and you're going to be there."

"Okay. Tell McLean to see me right away." I reminded myself I was agreeing only to the meeting if we failed, not to the cessation of my nocturnal activities.

I bought McLean a drink and explained simply that I wanted him to join me on an assignment involving absolute security, that we were going to play decoy to attract a gang of rapists, and that if they struck we were going to have to fight our way out. I added that he had the option to refuse without staining his character.

"What protection will we have?" he asked.

"I'll have my gun and you will have a policeman's weighted nightstick—and me," I explained. "Also, you will wear a female wig and a sweater with big boobies inside that they can see in profile from a distance. Now, are you in or out of this operation?"

"I'm in," he said.

I picked him up outside the *Province* at 9:30 that night, and he slipped into costume in the car en route to the park. It was a very black night, and only after we had sat in the car for half an hour or so could our eyes make out the shapes of the giant fir trees silhouetted against the darkened sky. I kept the radio off and our conversation to a whispered minimum so that any outside sound would reach us.

Near two o'clock we heard a car's motor in the distance. It suddenly stopped. The forest pressed tighter around our metal shell, and one lonely owl hooted eerily.

"Stay where you are! This is the morality squad!" The shouted command startled us into action, just as flashlights were shone into our faces through the open windows.

"Get the bastard!" I yelled as I pulled down the release handle and kicked the driver's door into the man standing outside. The flashlight disappeared, and a figure crashed through the underbrush in his panic to escape.

"Munro! Munro!" I heard McLean shout from the other side of the car as the sounds of a violent struggle diverted me from chasing the fleeing man. I rounded the front of the car to see McLean being struck savagely in the face by a flailing attacker, who then sprinted for the tall timber.

I didn't waste time yelling at him to stop, I just pulled out the .45 and thumbed off one shot at his legs, just as his fleeing form melded with the ebony night. I heard the bullet strike something solid and saw the almost invisible form rear upright, clutch one leg, and fall to the ground. I was on him in a moment, bent on smashing his face in with my gun barrel if he moved.

"Don't kill him, for God's sake!" I heard McLean's shout through my rage. Then I heard great crashing sounds as he took off courageously after the two other fleeing assailants.

What I did not know was that the single bullet I fired had hit the side of a tree as the fleeing man passed it, and sheared off a large piece of bark. The bark had struck him in the leg just as he heard the report of the gun. Thinking he'd been hit, he fell to the ground.

As I reached for him, he sprang, smashing me in the body and the gun hand, causing me to drop the weapon. I felt the blows on my face and body, but not the pain. My whole being was intent on reducing the attacker to an inert mass. Each time I connected with a solid blow I felt uplifted. It must have been only a minute or so that we fought. Then I found that I was on my knees and unable to raise another fist, and my enemy was slumped over, inert. I shouted for McLean to get back from his fruitless chase of the other attackers, then knotted handfuls of the man's long hair into my fists and, with the last of my ebbing strength, dragged his body back through the brush to the car.

"You all right?" McLean called out as he emerged noisily from the underbrush. When he saw the man I was dragging, he asked, "Is he dead?"

"I hope not," I replied with sincerity, "because the son of a bitch is going to wish he was a thousand times over. Look at him. He's the bastard who's been leading the pack. Put your foot on his throat while I get the keys."

I opened the trunk and pulled out my Speed Graphic press camera, and ordered McLean to haul the bloodied man to his feet in a hammer-lock and pose beside him, the heavy policeman's club ready for action. Then I took one flash picture and stuffed the moaning animal into the trunk, locking it securely from the outside.

Next I used the car's radiotelephone to call the police radio station on Cambie Street. I identified myself and my position, and asked for immediate assistance from detectives without specifying the need. I didn't wish to alert any other press people. Then I went looking by flashlight for my gun, and found it along with a cheap black notebook.

In less than ten minutes an unmarked car with two detectives arrived on the scene. I briefly explained the situation and handed over the prisoner and the notebook. I told them that McLean and I had made a citizen's arrest of the subject for posing as a police officer, and I requested that he be charged with the offence. The detectives radioed for more assistance to search the area and cordon off the park, and for additional help to search the underbrush for clues to the identity of the other three men. They found a military tank beret belonging to our impersonator, and a green truck parked down the road that was proven to be his also. The notebook was the attacker's too, and penned on its pages in his handwriting were the licence numbers of many cars whose occupants he had violated, and in some cases descriptions of what he had done to them.

Within the hour I had developed and printed the photograph of McLean and the prisoner, identified by police as John Kenneth Clark, a thirty-two-year-old labourer from the nearby community of Port Coquitlam. McLean typed the story as Forst clambered out of bed to prepare a special front page for the first edition, due on the street in six hours. And I went home to bed.

PROVINCE MEN TRAP SUSPECT. The eight-column headline screamed across page one of all editions that day, with a subheading, "Camera Ace, Writer Nab Park Prowler," together with my large photograph of McLean holding the bloodied Clark. The *Sun*, to their discredit, carried a simple one-inch item about "two citizens" capturing a rape suspect in Stanley Park overnight. Canadian Press picked up the story, and it ran in most daily newspapers in North America. Later, several international detective magazines enlarged and distorted it out of all proportion.

That morning Clark was placed in a line-up and picked out as the leader of the rape ring by each of the three victims called to attend. Separate charges of impersonating a police officer were filed by the man and the two women who identified Clark. These charges gave the various teams of detectives assigned to the case ample time to investigate the numerous complaints lodged against the gang of rapists in the preceding year and eight months.

Chief of Police Walter Mulligan studied the matter carefully with his public-relations officer and the head of the Criminal Investigation Bureau. He then issued a public statement praising McLean and me for our efforts as citizens, while hinting that just as we came on the scene, the case was about to be broken after extensive investigation by specialized teams of detectives.

LOVER'S LANE PROWLER MAY FACE NEW COUNTS. That was the second day's headline. It ran above a story detailing the new charges of impersonating a police officer that had been laid by Clark's other victims, two of them women who claimed they were raped by him. The story stayed on page one all week in varying forms, until the seventh day when another double headline appeared: LABORER FACES ATTACK CHARGE AS "LOVER'S LANE MARAUDER." The story told of a twenty-five-year-old woman from Courtenay on Vancouver Island, who identified Clark from a series of pictures and gave her account of the night she was raped by the gang. They had said they were park police, allowed her companion to drive away, and told her they would take her home in a police car. Instead, she was beaten and raped repeatedly, her body openings stuffed with mud, and she was left naked in the forest. Her companion, sensing something amiss, returned to the park and located her from her cries, took her to the hospital, and called police.

GIRL SOBS STORY OF PARK ATTACKS ran another full-page headline over the subheading, "Identifies Man As Police Imposter." That story came out of a preliminary court hearing from the same woman, one of many to come forward when the news story broke. She described on the stand how Clark had raped her, then how he and another man held her down while they did it again and again, taking turns after they filled her mouth with sand to stop her from screaming.

Clark pleaded not guilty to all accusations and was remanded for trial on a charge of raping the Vancouver Island woman. Meanwhile, *Time* magazine, on September 26, 1949, devoted most of a page to a picture of me and the photograph I had taken of McLean and Clark. In its story it referred to the *Sun*'s miniscule reporting of the event.

LOVER'S LANE MARAUDER GUILTY ON FOUR COUNTS: This headline preceded Clark's trial on the first rape charge, which resulted in his conviction and sentence:

LASH, JAIL FOR PARK ATTACKER
   "15 Years, 10 Lashes For Park Marauder."
One of the heaviest sentences ever given in Canada for rape, 15 years in jail and 10 lashes, was meted out Wednesday by Chief Justice Wendell B. Farris to John Kenneth Clark, 32, of Port Coquitlam.

That was the first paragraph of the story, which went on to rehash the part McLean and I had played, the subsequent police investigations, and the trial, which was a standing-room-only affair. Through it all, Clark refused to name his three companions. All of them were known to the police, but there was insufficient evidence to charge them. Instead of fingering them as his accomplices, Clark had struck a deal with them to care for his wife and children as long as he was in jail. If they failed to do so, he would name them as accomplices, and each of them would serve sixteen years in prison and receive ten lashes as Clark did, five when he entered prison and five before he would be released, in 1965.

I knew who two of his three partners were and where they worked, and once in a while I would park within sight of them as they loaded their trucks. Then I'd honk my car horn to attract their attention and just stare at them for awhile.

The reason for the police cover-up, I eventually learned, was that the first dozen rapes were deemed to be spasmodic and unorganized. But when they began occurring with alarming frequency, Chief Walter Mulligan was afraid of being accused of failing to advise the public in the first instance. He then put a lid on the whole matter, hoping that the rapists would either stop or be caught. If the latter had happened, he could have argued that the secrecy of his operation resulted in the successful break-up of the rape ring.

Eventually I received a cheque for $16 from the Province of British Columbia as witness fees for the days of October 27 and 31, and November 1 of 1949. I endorsed it and mailed it to Clark's wife, then pasted the stub inside the cover of a book entitled *Stanley Park, 1000 Acres Of Unspoiled Beauty*.

THE DISAPPEARING
LAUNDRY MARK

I WORKED part-time as a driver of an ambulance on police calls in those days, to make a little extra money. I was on duty one Sunday afternoon when a call came through from the Criminal Investigation Branch to go to an address in the east end of the city and see the detectives on the scene. Detective Ken McLean answered my insistent knocking at the cottage's rear door. He asked the attendant and me to step inside, where a nauseating odour of putrefying flesh hung heavy in the stagnant air. On the floor of the bedroom lay two near-naked bodies, brown-black with rot and swelled to bursting with expanding body fluids and maggots. They were identified as Mr. and Mrs. Michael Geluch, an elderly couple, and they had both been strangled a week previously, then locked into the house. It was a double murder.

The print and picture boys had finished their work, and we were told to take the bodies to the city morgue, situated beside the main police station. Not wanting to be scooped by the *Sun*, I arranged by telephone for another driver to be there in ten minutes to take my place, and I agreed to return his car to the dispatch office. I took a number of pictures of the bodies, the interior scene, and the outside of the house. I also photographed the stack of daily papers and the row of soured bottles of milk on the porch, which were guarded by a lonesome cat that appeared to reside there.

McLean and his partner began a methodical search of the cellar, and I joined them. It was dark in the basement, and the light would not work. As a result I tripped over a small pile of lumber and fell forwards against the cast-iron clean-out flue of the chimney, knocking it to the floor. Some ash spilled out, and as I tried to fit the cover back into place, apologizing to the detectives for my clumsiness, I noticed a piece of blue cloth protruding from the flue.

McLean pulled it out carefully and unrolled it to reveal a man's shirt, stained with blood. A quick examination of it showed a numerical laundry mark in indelible ink inside the collar, which he copied into his notebook. The exhibit was placed in a clean bag, and a police car was summoned to whisk it away to the science lab. I left shortly after to process the photos and write the story for the night editor's follow-up.

The next day I learned that two men, William Worobec and Walter Prestyko, had been arrested and charged with the double murder. A quick check revealed that Worobec had run the tailoring shop beneath Artray's dark-room, and the blue shirt was traced to him. He had cleaned and pressed my clothes for a year. At the trial, when the shirt was produced in evidence, the laundry mark had disappeared, and no technical reason could be given for its absence. The affair would later become known in the pulp detective magazines as "The Case of the Disappearing Laundry Mark." Despite this problem, the prosecutor was able to prove that the two men had killed Mr. and Mrs. Geluch by strangulation. They had hoped to gain $40,000 they thought was secreted in the house, when in fact they found and stole no more than $40 and some War Savings Bonds. These they placed in a coffee can and hid in a hole dug in Prestyko's backyard.

Worobec and Prestyko were sentenced to death by hanging, and by random choice I was named to the jury required to witness their execution, and then chosen by the other members to be their foreman. As foreman, I was required to be present with the prison doctor when the two bodies were cut down. I had to witness his examination of them, have him verbally certify to me that they were indeed dead. After that I had to sign the death certificate.

Each succeeding federally appointed hangman used the alias "Arthur Ellis," the name of Canada's first fully professional hangman, who in 1913 assumed the title of Official Executioner to the Dominion of Canada. The Arthur Ellis who would execute Worobec and Prestyko was a fruit farmer from the Niagara district of Ontario. He was slight, hunched-over, bland, addicted to alcohol, and an inveterate poker player. He refused to use anything but a new rope for each execution. Such sisal rope was known on previous occasions in other countries to have slipped from behind the condemned person's ear, causing strangulation rather than breaking the person's neck on the fall. That Arthur Ellis should have spent more time stretching the ropes, weighing the accused, and figuring the drop distance/weight factors involved in the taking of their lives would become evident to me before 6:30 A.M. of the murderers' last day on earth.

It was an unusual execution in that both men were to be hanged at the same time. The trap was set in the wooden floor at the top of an old elevator shaft in Oakalla Prison in Burnaby, on Vancouver's eastern outskirts. I was required to stand in the centre of a group of eight others. Facing me, some six feet away, stood Worobec, his ankles belted together, his hands lashed behind his back with a leather strap, and clad in prison shirt, trousers, and slippers. Behind him, facing the other way, was Prestyko, similarly restrained and clad. Worobec's last sight through the barred window above my head would be of the sunrise touching its orange brush to the snow-clad north shore mountains. Prestyko would have only seen the bricks in the wall facing him, and the hairs on the back of a guard's neck.

Two efficient prison guards pulled long black hoods swiftly over the condemned men's heads, and two others worked efficiently on each of them to set the nooses of the heavy ropes over the hoods and cinch the large knots tight behind their left ears. The hangman gave the knots a final adjustment, then all turned their backs on the doomed man.

Suddenly they were gone from us, as the trap fell away beneath their feet. Only the two trembling, swaying ropes bore witness to their having been alive and visible one breath before. I turned away to see with my own eyes the vision Worobec took with him, to wherever he went, then soberly, as though God were watching my every step, I made my way down the narrow private stairwell into an ante-room next to the bottom of the elevator shaft, where I was barred admittance by a heavy door, locked from the inside.

From the other side of the door I could hear an excited, unintelligible conversation and what sounded like the scraping of wood on cement, followed by several heavy thumps. I waited a few minutes while the noises continued, then rapped smartly on the door. When I got no response, I rushed back up the stairs to see if I could look down through the trap, but that was also locked. Swiftly I ran back down the stairs in time to see the bottom doorway start to open. I grabbed the handle and shoved my foot in the opening.

As the guard pushed his way past me I could smell his fear. I stepped into the small shaft. Only the doctor was there, looking strange and dishevelled. He quickly placed his body in front of mine, barring my route to the two army stretchers set against the far wall, each bearing the outline of a body covered by a grey blanket.

"What the hell's going on?" I was amazed at my anger as I pushed him aside, strode to the first stretcher, and flipped back the covering.

It was Worobec, and he had not died easily. The rope had been removed and his neck was a mass of peeled-back skin, which exposed the muscles and ligaments underneath. His face was frozen in anguish. As the doctor pulled my arm, I threw the second blanket back. Prestyko's neck was stretched to an enormous length, and his face was a picture of indescribable torment.

"You bastards!" I heard myself shouting, as two guards came in and urged me physically through the door and out into a great hallway, where a senior prison officer escorted me to his office.

"I want a telephone and now!" I demanded.

"There are no telephones available to the press," he stated firmly. "And you had no authority to enter the shaft. You were to wait outside until the doctor finished his examination, then sign a form and leave."

I pushed past him, hurried through the prison gate, and got sick twice before I gained the sanctuary of my car. Then, looking through the windscreen at the now-fiery mountains, I set the tone for the story in my mind.

Back at the *Province*, I wrote it the way it happened, and Forst slashed it across page one. I later learned Ellis had been drunk when he weighed the men and stretched the ropes, and he had stayed up all night playing poker with the guards. The condemned men had not died from the drop, but had hung, semi-conscious — or at least still alive to some degree — at the end of their ropes. The prison guard, on the doctor's orders, had dragged a chair beneath the hanging men, grasped each in turn about the waist with his locked arms, and jumped into space again and again, until the doomed men stopped breathing. After cutting them down, the doctor pronounced them dead, then tried to prevent me from seeing the bodies.

Such was the displeasure of the warden of the prison, and the doctor, that several years would pass before any member of the press was allowed within Oakalla's walls.

CALM BEFORE
THE STORM

IT WAS on a Friday, after the noon edition had gone to press, that a wealthy Vancouver furrier was in the lounge of the *Province* newsroom, pouring drinks from a bottle of decent rye he had brought with him. The subject turned to religion, of a non-denominational nature, and how the richer churches of the world could display such pomp and pageantry in the face of near-universal human need.

"For instance," said the furrier, "I know of a small order of nuns who run a little orphanage on a back road up on top of Burnaby Mountain, less than an hour's drive from here. They are pitifully poor and look after the kids in their care with a very special love. No government supports them, and whatever the children have to eat and wear is provided by the nuns' labours, and by those few people who know what good they do by helping in their own way."

"Do you give them money?" asked Tom Hazlitt.

"I don't discuss my charitable activities," the furrier answered. "But I do know that they are very proud and will not permit others to give them just food, clothing, or money. No, the donor must give of himself."

"When I was a kid, I was in a foster home for awhile," interjected Ed Moyer, another reporter, "and what made me feel better than anything else was knowing that someone cared about me. The other thing that made me feel good was getting a chocolate bar all to myself. Man, that was a special moment."

"That's what the kids on the mountain are like," the furrier explained. "A hug and a chocolate bar and they forget their daily pains."

"Well then, why don't we all chip in and buy them a batch of candy bars?" asked Hazlitt. "How many kids are there anyway?"

"Twenty-two at last count, ranging in age from seven to fifteen," he replied, pouring another round. "Tell you what I'll do. I'll toss in twenty bucks and you guys put in five each, and we'll buy a whole mess of chocolate bars of every description. One of you can drive up there and leave them on the doorstep."

"Great idea," said Moyer, and pulled out a five-dollar bill, which was instantly matched by Hazlitt.

"Better yet," I suggested to the furrier, "you've got all the money in the world. You put $50 to our $15. Then we'll buy the bars wholesale, and I'll deliver them to the orphanage tomorrow morning by airplane."

"Jesus," breathed Moyer, "can I go?"

"Most certainly," I agreed. "We'll drop the goodies to them by parachute."

"Marvellous," said the furrier, "but have you any idea how many chocolate bars you'll get wholesale for $65?"

"At least 1,500," Hazlitt reasoned. "Can you get a box that size out the door of the plane in flight?"

"We'll remove the passenger door, as well as the passenger seat. Moyer can sit in the back, and when I give him the word he'll just shove the box and the large paper parachute out the door. If I go in low and slow we'll drop it right on their lawn. But first we'll buzz the place and get them all out looking at the airplane."

"It'll be like Christmas. And they'll think you're Santa Claus!" Hazlitt finished off the last of the bottle.

"How are thirty people—that's the nuns and the kids—going to eat 1,500 chocolate bars? That's fifty each!" the furrier muttered to himself as he gave Moyer his money, who then took Hazlitt's and mine and sat down to call some wholesalers for the best deal. I drew a map of the route to the orphanage and arranged with Moyer to meet me at eight o'clock in the morning at the airplane. I told him to have the chocolate bars packed inside a tough box and that box packed inside another.

I still had a new 28-foot paper parachute of a kind used during the war for dropping light items when the chute couldn't be recovered. They were good for one drop only, and were even weather-proofed against light rain. That evening I reefed some nylon parachute cord into a sling for the box and folded the parachute into its sack. Then I attached a static line to the apex of the canopy, which I would tie off under my seat. When the box went out the door, it would fall about twenty feet, then the static line would pull out the canopy. Then the line would break, allowing the parachute to deploy and drift the box down light as a feather.

I arose at six to a slanting rain which the airport weather office said would clear within two hours, then phoned Moyer to make sure he was up and aware that we were flying, weather or no. There was no answer, so I headed for the airport and found him waiting for me. We had the right-hand door and seat removed and stored in his car within minutes, as the rain eased off to a vagrant mist. The box just fit through the door opening. We set it inside on the floor, lashed securely into its harness. As Moyer worked his way across it to the back seat, I tied the loose end of the static line to the cross-bracing under the pilot's seat. Then I started the engine, warmed it up as we taxied out, and gained clearance for a special VFR local flight.

The top of Burnaby Mountain, only twenty minutes by air at slow speed from the airport, was lost to us intermittently in the dissipating clouds that dropped only a light mist. We were right on target, and the old sprawling three-storeyed house set in the great cleared area surrounded by trees was just as the furrier had described it. On the first pass I put the prop into full fine pitch, and gave the engine some extra throttle to wake up those still abed. Sure enough, before I had started our second run there were kids running all over the grass, together with black-robed figures, all jumping up and down and waving.

"We'll drop it on the next pass at 300 feet. I'll hit the box as the signal for you to shove it out the door," I shouted at Moyer, who gave me a thumbs-up sign. Then I busied myself with the target run. I slowed the plane down with full flap and pulled the nose up with extra power to give us a stable platform. Then, looking out the pilot's window, I waited for the perfect horizontal distance from the lawn, and then banged the box with my right fist.

The box was gone in a second. I banked the plane hard right so we could both watch its descent. Horror-struck, we saw it rotate slowly and fall directly onto the roof of the house and disappear completely through it.

"Jesus Christ, what happened?" I heard Moyer shout as I banked the plane closer to see all the people running into the house.

"It went right through the roof because the parachute didn't open," I said, pulling Moyer's head close to my mouth so he could hear me. I felt under my seat for the static line's knot. It wasn't there. For a moment I took my eyes away from the instruments and looked at the crossbar to which I had knotted it with a bowline. The rope was gone.

"Where's the static line?" I yelled at Moyer.

"I undid it so the box would fall out of the plane," he yelled back at me, with some show of pride that he had done the job properly.

"You stupid so—" I gave up shouting at him and flew the airplane back to the field as fast as it would go, then raced to a phone and called Hazlitt and the furrier, telling them what had happened and asking the furrier to telephone the nuns, pick up Hazlitt, and hurry out to the orphanage.

It wasn't until mid-afternoon that Hazlitt telephoned me to explain what had transpired.

"The kids and the nuns knew the plane was coming because the furrier had phoned and told the nuns some presents were being dropped to them after breakfast. Fortunately no one was left in the house when the parachute failed to open. The box went through the roof into a hallway of the third floor," he related in great detail, admirable reporter that he was.

"The double boxes on the outside and the nylon cord wrapped around it held the whole issue together remarkably well, and the fact that the chocolate bars were packed in separate boxes inside saved most of them from being broken. The only damage was to the roof, which our friend the furrier will have repaired before nightfall," Hazlitt ended his narrative.

The *Province* news bureau in New Westminster filed a one-paragraph item on Monday to the effect that a resident of Burnaby Mountain had heard a very low-flying aircraft on Saturday morning in light fog. The plane sounded as though it was in trouble and had crashed not too far distant. The police had investigated, but found nothing to warrant a further search, and the Department of Transport in Vancouver reported no aircraft missing or known to have flown over the area.

Later that week, I was at the airport to say goodbye to Ramon Novarro, the silent film star, whom I had just interviewed. Just as Novarro was about to board his flight, I noticed a tall, dishevelled woman emerging from the customs door among the incoming passengers. I had to look twice before I realized it was Eleanor Roosevelt, widow of Franklin Delano, thirty-second president of the United States. I looked quickly around to see who was meeting her. I had heard that she was not due in until six, four hours hence, and that she was to be greeted by the mayor and the ubiquitous police chief, Walter Mulligan. From the airport she was going downtown to a special evening function at the Hotel Vancouver.

No one seemed to be meeting her so I scanned those persons near her to see if she was travelling with a companion or a Secret Service agent. No one. Improbably, she was alone.

"Mrs. Roosevelt, good afternoon and welcome to Vancouver. My name is Munro, Raymond Munro." I doffed my fedora and enquired if she'd had an enjoyable trip, knowing only that she had arrived on the flight from Los Angeles.

"How nice of you to meet me, Mr. Munro, and I did indeed have a most enjoyable journey." She offered her hand after setting down the small case she was carrying.

"Do you have any other luggage?" I asked, my heart quickening to the adventure.

"Only one bag. Here's the claim check." She fumbled in her purse, then passed it to me.

"Please, permit me." I rushed to get her bag and was beside her again in moments, steering her through the lobby and into the parking lot, where my coupe was parked. I opened the passenger door and assisted her in, then placed her bags in the trunk and got in beside her.

"If you want to telephone, there's one right here," I patted the receiver, which was on the dashboard.

"This is a strange car," she remarked, turning to look in the back and seeing no rear seat. In its place was a folding stretcher, emergency gear, and inhalator.

"Yes, ma'am, it is," I responded while jockeying the car out to the main roadway. "I'll just make a call while we're driving, if you don't mind," I said, then gave the *Province*'s city-desk number to the operator.

"Forst here," he answered crisply.

"Bill? Munro. Listen carefully and don't respond. I am now leaving the airport for the office. I have with me Mrs. Eleanor Roosevelt, who has just arrived from Los Angeles. I will bring her directly into the news-room." I hung up the telephone and turned to my distinguished passenger.

"Now, Mrs. Roosevelt, let me try to explain the situation to you. Do you know that you are four hours early?" I asked respectfully.

"Early? I don't understand. Someone with UNESCO in Los

Angeles arranged the flight and drove me to the airport there. I'm speaking tonight at your big hotel. I was to be picked up at the airport here and driven in."

"Well, Mrs. Roosevelt, I can only assume that someone here has fouled up." Then I told her about Ramon Novarro and explained that it was only by accident that I had seen her.

She grinned broadly, to my relief.

"Since you're here for UNESCO," I went on, "you'll want all the publicity you can get. The top writers in Vancouver are waiting for you now, as a result of that telephone call I just made. After you talk to them, I'll take you to your hotel, and you'll have time for a rest before tonight's affair."

"That's delightful, Mr. Munro, just delightful." She laughed heartily and touched my shoulder in a grandmotherly way.

The airport and the city of Vancouver were connected by a two-lane paved road, which crossed over a narrow arm of the Fraser River by means of an ancient, low bridge. To permit ships to pass underneath, the bridge pivoted lengthways to the river. Weekday afternoons were the busiest times for river traffic, because tugs towing log booms to the river's mills and barges loaded with sawdust from the same operations ran the narrow stretch every few minutes. It was quite normal to have to wait up to twenty minutes to reach the other side.

I explained this problem to Mrs. Roosevelt as we rounded the curve leading to the span and saw two vessels approaching the bridge, towing several huge barges of sawdust. A quarter-mile before we reached it the bridge closed, so I shut off the police radio and chatted with my passenger. Mrs. Roosevelt was interested in crime, narcotics, divorce, child welfare, and nutrition. Not once did she mention politics. I explained that Vancouver was the heroin-using capital of Canada, a tough seaport community with a high divorce rate and a large percentage of the population living on the poverty line. After sixteen minutes the bridge opened.

As I eased onto the south ramp I noticed four vehicles starting across from the far side. There was a police car followed by a limousine and two other police cars, their red roof lights flashing.

"My God," I heard myself exclaim to Mrs. Roosevelt, "that's the mayor's limousine, and he's got three police cars with him. They're on their way to the airport to meet you!"

My first thought, which bordered on the ridiculous, was to ask her to scrunch down as we passed the convoy. Instead, I rolled down my window and waved my arm wildly. The police car carrying the chief pulled to a halt, but I passed it by, and stopped instead only a foot away from the open window of the mayor's car.

"Roll down the mayor's window, constable," I said to the chauffeur. "I'd like His Worship to meet Mrs. Roosevelt." There was a look of stunned disbelief on the mayor's face as I eased the coupe ahead three feet and leaned towards him.

"Mrs. Roosevelt," I said loudly, "allow me to present His Worship Mayor Charles Thompson of the city of Vancouver. Charlie, meet Mrs. Roosevelt."

His face was a study in slack-jawed surprise as he stammered, "How do you do."

"Good aft—" was all he heard Mrs. Roosevelt say. Seeing the driver of the chief's car approaching me, I put the accelerator down and roared across the bridge. In the rear-view mirror I could see the start of a terrible traffic jam. The chief's driver had got back in his car and attempted to turn it around. The car had got caught crosswise on the other side of the bridge, jamming the other three cars behind it. Just then, the bridge signal sounded for another tug to pass through. The bridge swung around again with them on the far side, effectively cutting off pursuit.

I flipped on my police radio, expecting to hear an all-points bulletin out for Munro the kidnapper, but there was no mention of me or the incident. I apologized to Mrs. Roosevelt, hoping she hadn't taken umbrage at my actions, but she insisted that it would make a most amusing story when she arrived home.

We arrived at the *Province* news-room in twelve minutes, and I introduced her to all present. A senior reporter was interviewing her for the paper when Moscarella, the publisher, arrived, red-faced and breathing hard. He insisted that Mrs. Roosevelt come to his office so he could properly welcome her to the *Province*. The mayor's chauffeur picked up her bags from the news-room, then waited in the publisher's ante-room for them to finish so he could drive her to the hotel.

I wrote the story of our meeting and the events that occurred during our drive, but I never saw or heard from her again. But I did hear from the mayor, who suggested obliquely that I avoid visiting his office in the future, which was no loss to me. His male secretary called the following week to advise me that His Honour was again upset, this time because I had removed the film star Gabby Hayes from the airport terminal before the city's car could pick him up. I told him to tell the mayor to stick his problems in his ear. But the *Province*'s news editor was a son of the secretary and the complaint wound up on Forst's desk, who opined that if he didn't get such static I wouldn't be doing my job.

Hayes, the lively, bearded cowboy actor who played second lead in Hollywood westerns for several decades, was a real character. I saw him deplaning from an airliner as I taxied the *Province* plane into a hangar. I had him in tow before he got to the terminal entrance and steered him right into the emergency car. We hit it off right away, and for three nights I flew him around the Vancouver area and taught him the rudiments of flight.

My next night-time passenger was Rory Calhoun, a highly rated screen draw who only a few years earlier had been classed as the top automobile thief in America. He had served time in jail before he was discovered by a talent scout. He had married Lita Barron, a Hollywood dancer, and was in Vancouver with her, Marilyn Monroe, and Robert Mitchum, en route to Alberta to make the movie *River of No Return*.

At dawn, on the second morning of their stopover, I flew Marilyn and Calhoun over the north shore mountains and across glaciers and back through the Lions. That night I was invited to escort Marilyn to dinner with the Calhouns and her travelling Music Corporation of America agent, who became quite upset when he learned of Marilyn's flight. He complained that she had violated a section of her contract by flying aboard a non-scheduled aircraft.

The dinner was a pleasant and friendly affair. Marilyn was delightful company. When she asked if I was going to write about the flight and dinner, I asked her preference. She said she wouldn't have any trouble with MCA if the story wasn't made public, and I agreed to leave the day in my memory bank. She was a most intelligent and feminine woman, bored with bright lights, tinsel, and publicity. When I told her of the pleasure I received from scanning pawnshop windows, she came alive and told me how much she enjoyed dressing in loose clothes and running shoes, and window-shopping incognito for hours on end. We parted in the lobby.

Suddenly the weather changed, as did the temper of the times, and a violence descended upon the city, the like of which had never before been known.

A GANGLAND MURDER

IT WAS near midnight when I entered the Press Club, a drinking establishment only two blocks from the newspaper, but which had no connection with the fourth estate. I had gone there for the sole purpose of questioning the head waiter, one Daniel Brent, better known to his associates as Danny. Brent, a hard case with a lengthy police record, was well known to both city police and RCMP drug squad detectives as a pusher of narcotics in bulk amounts. My informant claimed that one of the two local drug tsars was "close" to Chief Mulligan, and that Brent knew about the circumstances surrounding their liaison.

It was the first time anyone had suggested that the chief had any connection with narcotics, except in his official capacity as an enforcer of the law. I knew this allegation was not true, but I felt obligated at least to talk to Brent and to explore the story.

Brent was there all right, walking towards me between the tables. He knew me and why I was there, but from the look that crossed his face, he was not pleased.

"Brent, I'd like a word with you," I spoke quietly as he passed in front of me.

"Not now. Tomorrow night, same time, out back," he spoke without looking at me and walked right on past.

I kept the appointment, but he didn't. After waiting until midnight I eased into the club. The bartender said Brent was out for awhile and would be back later. It had been a long day and the need for sleep overcame my desire to face Brent, so I went home. But someone else wanted me to meet Brent; they wanted it so badly that they rang me up at 6:20 the same morning with a message.

"Munro? You want to see Brent, get out to the University Golf Course near the tenth green. He'll wait for you." The phone went dead.

I needed no urging, but by the time I got up and dressed and made my way through the fog clinging to the North Vancouver shoreline and the Lion's Gate Bridge, and then eased past the beginning of the weekday traffic to the far west end of the city, it was 7:45.

The tenth hole was only a minute's walk from the roadway. I pulled in behind what I knew to be a detective car, then walked through the fog to some shadowy figures moving near the green.

Two detectives and three groundsmen were there, and so was Danny Brent—dead, with three bullet holes in his body, which was twisted up like a discarded rag doll. Whoever did it was a professional; they'd left his wrist-watch and rings on his body, and had taken away the murder weapon. And whoever pulled the trigger wanted to leave a highly visible message that whatever Brent had done to deserve such an end would not be tolerated.

I called Forst from a pay phone, then drove back to the *Province* to process the photos I'd taken of Brent's body and to write my part of the story. I omitted any mention of seeing Brent, making an appointment with him, and receiving the dawn telephone call.

The murder eventually had all the ingredients of a Mike Hammer story: a gut-shot gangster, narcotics, gangland revenge, the Mafia, frightened witnesses, big money, and the cops. I never saw myself as a Mike Hammer, although I would square off with anyone who provoked me enough. I was known to have put my foot through a car window and pulled the driver out after he attempted to emasculate me with his sedan's scimitar-like hood ornament. I packed a gun, drove a mustard-coloured 1936 Packard convertible, and wore a snap-brim fedora and a trench coat, because it was generally raining or cold and they were the only outer coverings I owned. At the time I was head of the police press bureau for the *Province*, I had a desk in the station across from the *Sun*'s Yorke Vickers, a decent chap and a fine reporter who also carried a permitted gun.

Since Brent's murder was good for newspaper street sales, it was sure to be milked for all it could produce, at least six consecutive headlines. The *Sun* and *Province* assigned their best investigative talents to it. I requested and was given additional help, in the form of Ed Moyer. I assigned him the task of keeping pace with Vickers, while I left the station to talk to some people on the street.

In my next story, I reported Brent's known involvement in the local narcotics scene, and his current link with the Vancouver underworld. I also described the three bullet holes: one slug passing through his back and liver and out his navel; a second going into his head and not emerging; and a third through both cheeks. And they were big slugs, too. From morgue attendant Dave Quigley I learned unofficially that the first bullet through his back had killed him, but not until he'd suffered the torments of hell. After that, two more shots were pumped into his lifeless body, just to make sure he was dead.

I was plotting my next move over a coffee in a local restaurant when the owner passed me the telephone.

"Munro?" the soft voice asked.

"Yep."

"McGann." It had been a long time, nine years in fact, since I had seen him or heard his name. I had been dining with Gene Autry, the singing cowboy movie star, who was presenting his own rodeo at Maple Leaf Gardens in Toronto. We'd been talking, got hungry, and slipped down to Frank Ciccone's Italian Restaurant. I had gone outside to double-check the security of my car when I heard violent scuffling in the vacant lot behind me. In the darkness I saw two men pounding a third. As an exercise in sporting behaviour, I took a flying leap into the fray, landing on the shoulders of one overcoated chap, who promptly threw me off, then lifted me up by the hair.

"Police," he shouted, going for his blackjack.

"*Toronto Star* reporter." I twisted his hand away, reaching for my plastic I.D.

The other plain-clothes officer was kneeling on a slight man's chest. He had several fingers in the man's mouth and was smashing him repeatedly in the stomach with his other fist, trying without success to retrieve a hastily swallowed condom containing nasty little capsules, or so I was told later.

They stopped very quickly after I told them coldly that their actions would be revealed to all on the morrow, when I would pick them out of a line-up and prefer brutality charges.

"What's your name?" I asked the pitiful, bloodied figure.

"Jim McGann," he gasped. "Thanks."

They took him away in a police car, and when I checked on him the next morning he was already out on bail. Now he was across the street, looking at me from a barber-shop window, telephone in hand.

We met in the barber-shop's back room, and he told me about his conviction following our first meeting. He had always been a thief and a small-time narcotics distributor, he said. For the past year, he had been in Vancouver, making a living pushing heroin and trying to beat his own deadly habit, without success. He'd recognized my picture in the paper, saw me entering the café, and wanted to repay me for going to his rescue.

Within the hour he'd laid out the whole scenario of the killing for me, save who did it. He had worked for Brent until two days before Brent's death. Brent was second from the top in a drug combine, he told me, wholesaling already well-diluted heroin to distributors, who cut it again and sold it to street pushers, who doubled the amount by adding milk sugar, and sold it to addicts. McGann claimed his status to be that of a small distributor. Brent had been told twice to refrain from operating west of Granville Street, a north-south thoroughfare that effectively divided the city in two, by one Jacob Leonhard, who fronted for the branch of the Mafia that smuggled the stuff into the city in the first place. Leonhard claimed that territory was his own. He was also beginning to have serious problems with another major narcotics mover, William Semenick.

Brent had twice passed the word that he wouldn't leave town. He even had the temerity to suggest that Leonhard should hop a fast freight himself. A few days before his death, however, Brent had told a friend that he was clearing out immediately for eastern Canada. But he left it too late in the day to get to his safety deposit box. That night he had dined in Chinatown, leaving his car parked at the rear of the building, not far from the police station. He left the restaurant by the rear door with two men and an unidentified woman, probably hired to set him up, who unaccountably disappeared.

Brent slid behind the wheel of his car, lit a cigarette, and smoked it half-way down. Then he was shot in the back by one of his two companions. The cigarette fell from his lips inside his sports shirt. The hit men, one sitting on either side of him, supporting his body, drove west towards the University Golf Course, inside Leonhard's territory. When Brent started to bleed heavily, they stopped at a newspaper box and bought a late edition of the morning *News-Herald*, folded it double, and rammed it against his stomach under his shirt.

Brent died en route to the tenth green, where they shot him twice more. Then they abandoned his car some distance away, leaving in it Brent's life's blood and grass clippings that would match the strain found growing near the tenth hole, but nothing else that would ever identify them.

"Who killed him?" I enquired.

"Quebeckers," McGann responded.

"We're square," I thanked him.

"We'll never be square," he said.

When police located and opened Brent's safety deposit box on the fourth day, they found $75,000 in cash. On the fifth day, through the courtesy of another headline, the RCMP asked the public to help find the killers. On the sixth, an inquest confirmed my already written summary of Brent's passing. Seven days after I had received that early morning telephone call, the *Sun* offered a $1,000 reward for confidential information leading to the arrest of the killers.

Ten days passed with no mention of Brent's name. Then, quite suddenly, a major headline announced that a dual RCMP and Vancouver City Police Department investigation was being mounted, and that the local police commission had offered a $2,000 reward for information. No further reports were published, and the case appeared to die a natural death in police circles. But it did not die with me, because McGann had told me something I didn't write for the newspaper: that Jacob Leonhard and William Semenick, the city's two drug barons, would be executed in the immediate future, heralding an all-out drug war in Vancouver. Then a major crime family from the United States would take control of Vancouver's leaderless and lucrative market in illicit narcotics.

A ONE-DOLLAR
LOTTERY TICKET

ON OCTOBER 1, 1954, seventeen days after Danny Brent was hit, I bought a one-dollar lottery ticket that set in motion a chain of events triggering twenty-seven consecutive page-one headlines, and sowed the seed for one of the largest and longest news stories in Canadian history.

I had been having a beer in a Main Street beverage room, a scab among a festering collection of decrepit buildings, cheap cafés, three-dollar whores, and the bulk of Canada's drug-addict population. I was nursing a minor sulk over the *Province*'s refusal to reinstate the Hidden Witness Plan, a scheme that police reporter Jack Steppler and I had designed two years earlier. It was a great idea and had worked reasonably well. Any person could tell Steppler and me by mail whatever information they had concerning a crime. They didn't have to identify themselves in any manner; they simply printed on the message any five numbers in any sequence. They then copied the same sequence of numbers on the letter's corner, tore it off and retained it. If the information helped solve a crime, they could claim from the *Province* a cash reward and still remain unknown. I had wanted to use the plan again for the Brent murder, but management did not, so the *Sun* stepped in with a pale imitation and sold more papers.

While I was considering other angles for flushing out the killers, a waiter shoved a book of lottery tickets under my nose and asked me to pick one for a dollar. Intrigued, because selling lottery tickets was illegal even for Lions, Kinsmen, Kiwanians, Rotarians, Optimists, and other assorted chicken-à-la-king luncheoneers, I pulled the tenth ticket off, and with it, unintentionally, the back cover of the book. It was fortunate that I did, because the information printed on the inner side listed "The Official Results of the Fifteenth Drawing Held August 26, 1954, of the Western Canadian Employees' Sweep."

I had urged Forst many times to give consideration to creating a unique position for me on the paper, one that would permit me to operate as a reporter on my own initiative. We had agreed that if such a job could be designed, I would still act as the *Province*'s pilot. All he was waiting for, before turning me loose from my full-time police bureau duties, was the right situation. It came when I told him about the lottery ticket. An immediate $25 weekly raise brought my salary to $140, a lordly sum in the newspaper business. (It was a higher salary than that paid to the city editor and only $52 less than Chief Mulligan's lawful income.) As well, I was to have a car allowance and a reasonable expense account. My assignment was to operate alone and in any area in which I sensed a news story, using those gems of information left over from articles I had written, in my own bylined, thrice-weekly column, on the front page of the second section. My new desk hugged a private corner of the news-room and bore two telephones, one connected to the main switchboard and the other direct to outside. I worked whatever hours I wanted and reported only to Forst.

I began my lottery-ticket investigation by attempting to get the telephone numbers or addresses of the 120 winners listed on the prize sheet. All were identified by surname and, in some cases, first initials, or by *noms de plume*, and the names of their city, town, or village. Each was preceded by the number of the winning ticket. Listed were twenty winners of $50 each, fifty of $100, twenty of $200, twenty of $500, five of $1,000. At the very top of the list, there was one winner of $2,000, one of $3,000, one of $5,000, one of $10,000, and one of $35,000. In all, 120 winners shared $80,000 for an average pay-off of $666. The amounts stunned me, since the mean income of local workingmen at the time was less than $3,500 a year.

Since I had never heard of the Western Canadian Employees' Sweep, which I would learn had sold tickets on one draw every other month for ten years, and reportedly paid out staggering prizes compared to any other lottery known in Canada, I called the city editor of the Regina *Leader Post*.

"Have you heard of anyone in your city or surrounding area winning $35,000 in a lottery since the 26th of August this year?" I asked.

"Irish Sweep?" he questioned.

"No," I responded, "but the ticket number was 1726111, and the *nom de plume* and address used was Dog Goner, Regina, Saskatchewan."

"I'll call you collect when I check it out," he promised.

Next, I enlisted the co-operation of the city editors in Prince Albert, Saskatchewan, for Harry Burris, a $2,000 winner; in Lethbridge, Alberta, for P.M. Sixty-Six, who was listed as receiving $2,000; and in Edmonton, Alberta, for Black Horse, shown as having won $3,000. I kept only one of the five top names for myself, Calliope of Vancouver, the second-prize winner of $10,000.

By day's end, the editors' reports were in, and all were negative. The next day I made another round of long-distance calls, and again local checks revealed no identification. Among the twenty listed winners of $500 were only two proper surnames, P. Bosnik of Vancouver and S.T. Sampson, of Winnipeg, Manitoba. But exhaustive checks failed to locate either of them, or the three local *noms de plume*. It was time to alert Forst to the indisputable fact that the lottery was not only illegal, but probably phony as well.

He shook his head as I explained my findings, and agreed that time was of the essence in publishing the facts.

"How much help do you need to wrap the first story up for page one tomorrow?" he asked.

"Three people. One to correlate the information received from the other two. I'll need a couple of smooth talkers to call all the city editors in western Canada and get them working on it without tipping our hand, then to check out every local winner listed. It'll be an all-night job if you want it for the first edition," I explained.

Tom Hazlitt, Herc Munro, Ed Moyer, and I made a great team. Ed patched together the incoming information in sequence from the other two, and I wrote the main article. Then the old Tinkers-to-Evers-to-Chance routine started at dawn, with Forst grabbing each page out of my typewriter as I finished it, checking it for libel and possible errors in continuity, passing it to Stan Sutherland, the news editor, who totalled the length and blocked out the space he'd need on page one, and on to a deskman who corrected all errors and wrote the three headlines that would blow the syndicate and its front men right out of their socks. Forst went all the way, giving it a triple, eight-column headline and all but a corner of the front page:

Vancouver Province Exclusive!
REPORTER EXPOSES FAKE LOTTERY HERE

He slipped in a photo of me on top of a fourteen-point byline and inset a large "Exclusive" slug vertically into the lead.

The story practically wrote itself:

> A million-dollar sweepstake is operating in western Canada, with an advertised pay-off of $85,000.
>
> Identified only as the "Western Canadian Employees' Sweep," it is one of several for which tickets are sold in Vancouver. Sweepstakes are illegal in Canada.
>
> Unlike the Irish Hospitals Sweep or the Army and Navy, the operators of the sweep are not named on the tickets or on the prize list. Nor has the *Province* been able to contact a winner.

I went on to detail the enormous sums of money we learned could have been generated from the operation, which was headquartered in Vancouver. Pictures of the tickets and prize list were displayed prominently, with special attention drawn to the fact that a printer's union seal was displayed on them. The last paragraph, inserted right on deadline, explained that not one prize winner could be located.

As soon as the beverage room opened that day, I bought a beer and a whole book of tickets from a waiter. I asked him for a receipt and requested he mail the tickets to an address—my own—in Vancouver. The tickets arrived the next day. I kept the unopened envelope as proof of a federal offence: sending lottery tickets through the mail.

My next step was to drop in on Chief Mulligan for a chat. He was, I was told, out of town, so, as a substitute, I bearded the surly deputy chief, Gordon Ambrose. I asked him if he had any knowledge of the sweep. He replied that he did not, nor had he any information of any other lottery operating within his jurisdiction.

Detective Sergeant Ian McGregor, head of the police gambling detail, was next on my hit list. I knew he had never told me an untruth.

"No comment" was his reply to my questions.

Another detective said it all in a clipped sentence: "Stay the fuck away from it, or you'll get hurt. It's too big for any of us, even the man in the corner." That reference was to Chief Mulligan.

The first edition hit the streets to a complete sell-out. The *Sun*'s editorial room was reported to be a scene of panic, as management tried to design a catch-up story for the final edition. They did, by scrounging around to locate several other smaller lotteries, and introducing them in major headline form, not as an adjunct to the *Province*'s news break, but as their own startling exclusive. But that was the name of the game and the tenor of the times. If you weren't one up, you were one down.

I handled each call from the switchboard in order. The first was from the mayor's secretary asking me to see him, to which I replied that he could meet me at my desk instead. The second was more welcome.

"Munro? McGann." There he was again, surfaced from the slime with which fate had covered him. I gave him my private number, and he called me back on it to tell me that he'd left an envelope for me at the paper's front desk with enough in it to keep me going for awhile.

"I'll phone you in a few days," he said and hung up.

He'd left me two lottery tickets, one on the Army and Navy Sweepstakes, an illegal but acceptable Canadian institution, and the other on the Irish Sweepstakes. "Guess which is phony?" he had written on the envelope, and beneath it, "Both!"

I couldn't believe it; they looked so perfect. I hustled up to Vancouver General Hospital, after borrowing a pair of tickets known to be authentic, and made use of one of their microscopes. Under only 20-power magnification, I realized that a child could have picked out the counterfeit. This added a new and distasteful element to the investigation.

Forst felt that the phony ticket issue should be kept separate for a day or two from the Employees' Sweep, so as not to dilute the impact of our investigation of the WCES perpetrators. I stepped out of the anchorman position for Hazlitt, who was replaced in this spot by Clare Anderson, another dynamic and well-rounded investigative reporter. The second day's headline echoed the latest development: NEW LOTTERY FRAUD UNCOVERED IN CITY. This story dealt with a monthly sweep sold by the "Canadian Racing Ass'n," and the ticket we came up with was for a race at Bay Meadows, California, to be run on November 30, 1954. The brutal fact was that racing there had already been terminated until the spring of 1955.

While six senior reporters took care of the ongoing developments and checked out the hundreds of telephoned leads, I concentrated on the two phony sweepstake tickets. My first break came from a woman at Red Cross headquarters who would not identify herself.

"You did such a brave thing in taking our blood to Powell River in the storm to save that man's life that I must help you. Go to the men's locker room of our downtown building, and there you will find the tickets." She was almost in tears.

Ten minutes later I was alone with Detective Sergeant McGregor. I told him the facts as I knew them. His men struck so fast that all entrances and exits to the building were covered within minutes, as was the locker room itself. There, they found thousands of phony Irish tickets stuffed into lockers, all ready for sale on the next race.

Tom Hazlitt and I shared a major byline on the story, which made the front page of every daily newspaper in Canada, and some in Ireland. The story was taking on international proportions but we still didn't know who printed the tickets. To learn that we would have to find the two engravings used to print the front and back of the counterfeit Irish tickets.

On October 4, McGann telephoned to say that the engraving plates for the fake Irish Sweep tickets were hidden in a printing shop that was locked during the owner's absence on a fishing trip. I went to the address he gave to find the back door jimmied and the place ransacked. McGann phoned again to say there was a parcel at the front desk for me. It was the missing plates.

In the meantime, in major headlines across the nation, newspapermen pressed civic authorities to strip away the deceit and incompetence that permitted lotteries to operate. In the *Province* these headlines appeared in succession:

NEW LOTTERY FRAUD UNCOVERED IN CITY
POLICE KNEW ABOUT LOTTERIES
CHIEF DID NOT TELL PROSECUTOR OF SWEEP
ELEVEN FINED IN FAKE CITY LOTTERY
CHIEF MUST EXPLAIN FAILURE ON LOTTERIES

I was asked to appear in secret before the Police Commission and the chief constable. The night before my appearance, some very distinct threats were made by telephone to other newspapermen concerning my welfare. The paper printed them in detail, except for the vulgarities, and trumpeted their gravity through another massive headline: VIOLENCE THREAT IN FAKE LOTTERY. I felt no concern for the messages; experience had taught me that when a threat was sincere it was never stated for public consumption.

In the midst of all this, another person came to me with information. He was Parnell Johnson, the same man who had tipped me off to the marauders of Lover's Lane, and whose identity I had kept a secret until he himself revealed it. Several years after that episode, he had run into financial trouble with his automobile dealership and had crawled into bed with a man named William Couper, about whom I knew quite a bit. Couper was bagman for Ralph Campney, a local federal member of Parliament and Minister of Defence. Couper was the architect of Campney's power in his district. I had tied Couper to illegal gambling activities previously, but all complaints had been ignored by the police. As one beer-parlour waiter put it: "You work for the Campney/Couper ticket, or you don't work here at all." Couper clearly had Chief Mulligan's ear, or, as he liked to boast, his throat.

Couper had made Parnell Johnson a director of his Quadra Club, a downtown drinking establishment, then placed him under the authority of a retired West Vancouver businessman, who acted as operational head of the WCES. Johnson, by then, was a thoroughly frightened man, but he managed to generate enough courage to give me the names of the top distributors in Edmonton, and the name of the biggest Vancouver distributor.

I called the city editor of the Edmonton *Journal* immediately, and laid out the names and addresses Johnson had given me. Within hours, their places of business and residences had been raided, and all were arrested, and charged, and subsequently convicted. But, according to Edmonton police, they were all warned immediately after their arrest, from pay telephones in Vancouver, that they would be "dealt with immediately" if they named their suppliers. Nevertheless, two of them talked, and fingered two people as their superiors. These men were traced to a Vancouver address on Beatty Street, where the trail was lost. The next gem of information McGann gave me placed the headquarters of the Sweep at the same Beatty Street address, across from the old *Sun* and only a block away from the *Province*. It was the business location of the Army and Navy Club of Canada, who also ran a national lottery. But all traces of a double operation had vanished.

Johnson appeared twice before the Police Commission in secret session. He was so debilitated by fear at being in the room with Chief Mulligan, whom he knew was tied to Couper, that Clare Anderson and I took him to his secluded home and sat with him through most of the night. He slept for awhile, then woke up, claiming he heard a car outside. We investigated surreptitiously and found there was, indeed, a dark sedan stopped across the street. It was partly masked by the fog but it clearly contained moving figures. As Anderson dialled the police, I loaded a shotgun that Johnson had stored in a cupboard. My plan was to ease out the side door into the fog, cut around the back of the house, nestle up against the porch, and wait for the occupants to make a move.

I crouched there for almost half an hour, watching the black sedan and the figures moving inside it. Then from a block away I saw the halo-like effect of an approaching car's headlights. The driver of the sedan saw them too, because he fired up his engine and drove off immediately. Soundlessly the oncoming car edged to a stop in front of Johnson's home. I was startled to recognize it as Forst's blue convertible. I pulled open the passenger door and told Forst to wait there for Anderson. Back in the house, I learned that after calling the police Clare had phoned Forst to come as well. Knowing a patrol car could be there at any moment, we made Johnson lock the door and had Forst drive us to the *Province*, where we put together the balance of the day's events in story form.

The lottery scandal gradually eased off the front page to make room for more serious charges, made by the police themselves through their union, against Mulligan's administration. The hue and cry for a full-scale enquiry was joined by elected city representatives and even some government voices. The mood of the city was an angry one. The violent nature of overnight crimes increased enormously, and gang warfare erupted into the streets.

It wasn't long before I got another late-night phone call. I'd been receiving a number of calls from people who assured me that more than one person would feel relieved at my sudden passing, and I did not need another, especially one that would require me to leave the premises and transport my body to another location. But the thought fathered the act, and the telephone rang.

"Munro?" queried the flat, unemotional voice.

"Christ, what now?" I stretched the sleep from my body, as I noted the time — 11:55.

"The pavilion near Lumberman's Arch in Stanley Park. Soon as you can. Park and wait." A click signified our parting. I was never to learn his identity.

I dressed quickly in warm clothes, stuffed a mickey of rye in my coat pocket for any thirsty officer I might meet, and gave the car a good check for dynamite before starting it up and rolling towards the Lion's Gate Bridge.

The treacherous fog delayed me, and when I pulled onto the northern perimeter road leading to Lumberman's Arch, I had a sinking feeling that I was too late. Two detective cars, some uniformed police officers, and Park Constable Bill Lindsay, whom I knew well, were in conference near an ambulance just closing its door.

"Who is it?" I asked the driver, a former partner of mine on the old weekend shifts.

"Semenick's the only name I heard. He's been shot, but he's still alive and we gotta go." They roared off with siren wailing.

I called the night editor from my car and gave him the little information I had, then went to talk to Bill Lindsay. Confidentially, and off the record, Lindsay filled me in on what he knew. Near midnight, while patrolling the park in his Jeep, a nightly occurrence since 1949 after the great rape case broke, Lindsay had pulled in behind a car containing three men. While the car was still moving, a body hurled itself from the front seat onto the roadside. Shots were fired. The car stopped quickly, discharging one man. When Lindsay's presence on the scene stopped the action, the car sped off with no lights, and the man left behind ran past Lumberman's Arch and into a densely wooded area.

Lindsay identified the victim as William Semenick, a convicted narcotics dealer who was known to be the head of a major drug ring in Vancouver. He had apparently been driven to the park for execution, and had flung himself out, roiling along the shoulder of the road. The gunman, then on foot, fired at him in the dark, hitting him once.

McGann, it now seemed, had been correct in his prediction that the two senior operators in Vancouver's drug underworld were marked for death.

Before dawn I heard from McGann again. He called to name the two contract killers who he said had tried, but failed, to kill Semenick. They were Joe Marcoux and Eddie Sherban. Sherban had already been arrested by the police, who had trailed him from the park to the Vancouver Rowing Club docks, where he had hidden submerged in the water. Marcoux too would eventually be arrested and charged, as was Semenick. Semenick, however, refused to identify his would-be assassins. For his consistent refusal he received the nickname of "Silent Bill," and was committed to Stony Mountain Penitentiary.

The lottery story was still seething, and came to another quick boil with the discovery of the body of a city printer named Robert Hopkins in his tiny bachelor home. He had been shot and strangled on the evening of Semenick's trial by gunfire, and was believed to have been involved in the printing of sweepstake tickets.

While the public was besieging the mayor's office to stop the carnage, little concern was being paid to the insinuation into the city of certain persons from Chicago, who posed as businessmen seeking real-estate investments. In fact, they were the cleaner-cut, college-educated front men for that sinful city's own syndicate. Within days they had selected their target, recorded his moves, considered the pattern of his activities, and established the timing of his death. Dynamite was stolen from a construction project on the outskirts of Vancouver. At least six sticks were taped together and fitted with detonators and one common electrical connection. At dusk, on the evening of Monday, February 15, 1955, at approximately six o'clock, the explosive charge was taped to the steering wheel column beneath the dashboard of a late-model heavy Buick sedan, parked in the driveway of 5690 Heather Street in south Vancouver.

At about this time I received a telephone call at the *Province* from a most pleasant chap who suggested that he had some information for me concerning a crime, but that he could not give it to me for a couple of hours. I thanked him for his courtesy and waited downtown for the telephone call I knew would come. It did, at 7:40.

"Mr. Munro, you might have some interest in a situation that will reveal itself shortly. If so, you should leave now, and drive at normal speed south on Burrard to Heather, where you should turn west and park at eight o'clock in the 5600 block." And he hung up.

I was tempted to tell the news desk, or to advise someone on the police force I could trust, or even to speed to the area to look it over in advance, but I did none of these because they would have served no purpose. Subconsciously I knew that I had no control over whatever situation was waiting for me.

Heavy traffic delayed me by perhaps two minutes. I was moving easily along Heather, just as night had fallen, when I both heard and felt the shock of a tremendous explosion. The car windows were down, and the sound smacked my eardrums. As I drove the last half-block I could smell the dynamite.

Jacob Leonhard, the third man whom McGann had said would die, had stepped from his home into his car, turned the key in the ignition, and blown his car completely away from his body. One part hung from the thirty-foot TV mast atop his house. Windows for blocks around were smashed, and structural damage was done to nearby homes as well as his own. Inside his house, his wife and children lay stunned by the blast. Outside, Leonhard fell, a mass of ruptured flesh, from what was left of his car onto the cracked cement driveway.

I had the office on the line in a minute, as neighbours called for police and ambulances. I was on the lawn taking pictures of the still-smoking mess when at least eight detectives arrived. Leonhard was rushed to hospital still alive, and traffic police sealed off the area, while other uniformed officers took statements from neighbours and collected those car parts blown up to 100 feet away. One of Mulligan's henchmen grabbed my arm to ask how I got here so fast. I told him real hard that if he touched me again I would break whatever he touched me with.

It had been a bad day, a bad week, a bad month, and a tough year, so when the story was wrapped up and my pictures were printed, identified, and left on the news desk, I drove home, slept the clock around, and spent the next couple of days with the children, without even touching a telephone.

GOD HATES QUITTERS

THE POLICE GRAPE-VINE had it that Chief Walter Hugh Mulligan was extremely upset with my activities as a newspaperman. He had passed the word that I was to be watched carefully for any infraction of bylaws or traffic laws, and any encroachment into a police situation without his permission.

I reasoned that of the 728 officers on the force no more than 10 per cent would have held out a free hand to save the chief from drowning; and of the other 90 per cent at least half would have held his head underwater until he no longer made bubbles. His appointment as chief in 1947 had followed a contrived probe of the force, and it still rankled most of the personnel, who thought him unqualified and incompetent.

If it was to be war between us, I had two choices: I could stay clear of the department, or I could pick up the gauntlet. Mature thinking ruled out avoidance; to Mulligan, that would have signalled fear of his authority. Besides, I had been reared to believe that God Almighty hated quitters.

So I set about learning as much as I could about the situation. From certain officers within the department, who had their ears to the ground and respect for my integrity, I learned that my actions during the Stanley Park Caper had annoyed Mulligan, since the episode had placed him in a bad light. He was also irritated by what he referred to as my "omnipresence at the scenes of numerous accidents and sudden deaths." And my exposure of the fake lotteries had again publicly embarrassed him, painting him as incompetent. More than either of these reasons, I suspected that he wanted to rid himself of my involvement because he knew about the massive file I had built on him over a four-year period. I had, during private meetings, communicated some of the lesser information in it to the mayor, and he had probably passed it along to Mulligan.

In the spring of 1955 I made up a summary of the file—the file itself was kept in my safety deposit box—and gave it to Bill Forst. I had decided that the best course of action was to put the whole story before the public, and I wanted the *Province* to let me do so.

The file I gave to Forst read:

Chief Walter Hugh Mulligan is a thief, a liar, an ally of criminals, a suborner, a betrayer of public trust, an inept administrator, a nepotist, a purveyor of grace and favour, and a moral leper.

1 He conspired with known criminals to permit gambling and bootlegging operations that they controlled to operate with impunity, while closing down other illegal operations outside the syndicate's control.

2 He conspired with others both within and without the force to subvert justice.

3 He suborned senior officers under his command.

4 In concert with another police officer, and while a member of the force, he is alleged to have stolen a sum of money from the residence of a person whose premises had been broken into previously.

5 He arbitrarily demoted and promoted persons within the department to serve his own personal ends.

6 While lawfully married and living with his wife, he maintained a mistress with funds gained from permitting organized crime to operate with impunity.

7 He used police vehicles for improper purposes.

8 On two singular occasions he permitted the continuance, for extended periods of time, of specific criminal acts, which both placed the lives of citizens in peril and bilked them of money.

9 I am prepared to state the names of those persons involved in the above charges and enlarge upon the details to the management of the paper once it has accepted the allegations as being worthy of publication and agrees to publish them.

MULLIGAN'S CAREER SUMMARY:

Born in Liverpool to policeman father. Came to Canada with parents at age fifteen. First employment was as seagoing steward. Second was ashore, installing electrical batteries. Third was as a third-class policeman in 1927, patrolling Vancouver's skid-road district. Promoted to detective rank in 1945, and from there jumped ranks of sergeant and inspector to become superintendent of the Criminal Investigation Branch. Continued to befriend individually the mayor, members of police commission, and some judiciary.

In 1946 created a fictional scenario of corruption within the force for private presentation to police commission, which body accepted his charges without investigation, then named him as lone prober. His report to commission caused dismissal of numerous ranks, promotion of many more, and early retirement for Police Chief Alex McNeill. In 1947, only eighteen months from detective rank, he was named Chief of Police with enlarged powers of command. Has served as vice-president of Chief Constables' Association of Canada, a director of city Boy Scout association, and on YMCA executive.

The response was immediate. The day after I handed the statement to Forst I was summoned to Moscarella's office, with Forst and Ross Munro. Moscarella asked me to substantiate the allegations. I reminded him that, as I had stated in the file, I required assurance that the paper would begin an immediate, in-depth investigation of the charges I'd made before I would give the names of those involved to the paper.

Moscarella insisted that I detail for Forst all my information. The paper would then have a close look at the finished product before making a commitment. While I had full faith in Forst and Munro, I thought that the publisher was being unduly cautious. I refused, and was ordered by Moscarella to refrain from further investigation, since I was a highly visible employee of the *Province*, and he did not wish it to become known that a *Province* newspaperman had been investigating the police department.

Afterwards, Forst and I had a long talk about a newspaper's responsibility to the public versus its responsibility to its shareholders and advertisers. He was in favour of instituting an immediate investigation of all my allegations, he said, but he admitted that he could not move without Moscarella's sanction.

"I am in the unhappy position of requiring you to cease and desist as ordered, and of firing you if you proceed," Forst spelled out.

"I could resign and go it alone," I pointed out.

Forst quickly ran through the problems I was sure to face were I to embark upon a one-man crusade against Chief Mulligan and organized crime in Vancouver. His argument was very persuasive, and I began to think that perhaps Moscarella was right and that I should let the bad guys go and allow the rape of the city to continue.

Understanding the quandary I was in, Forst granted me a week's paid leave to consider my position. I gratefully accepted his offer. I needed a chance to remove myself from the cocoon in which I had so long laboured, and lean upon Nature for a few days of solitude in which to think the matter through.

I hugged the children extra hard, borrowed an open-cockpit biplane on floats, lashed into the empty seat my sleeping bag and rucksack, and flew north along the sabre-toothed coastline.

When I returned, I met with Forst over a bottle of wine.

"What do you think I should do?" I asked him.

"No other daily newspaper will print the story." Forst was adamant in his judgement. "If you quit because you disagree with the *Province*'s policy, it will be the paper's loss as well as your own." He went on to point out that I would be without income and faced with increased expenses, and that my life would be placed in jeopardy, threatened by the whole spectrum of organized crime in the city, and by any police officers and members of government who were involved.

"You will come under attack from every quarter, including the daily press. Your entire life will be exposed to public scrutiny, and all blemishes found will be publicized. These people have the power to reach into every file in this nation." He made no apology for his brutal summation.

"Your children will be subject to abuse at school, both physical and verbal. Many policemen will deny you to their own neighbours. Win or lose, the fact that you made the charges, whether they are proved or not, will deleteriously affect your chances of employment in the future, especially in British Columbia. What's more, your credit history will be screened, and perhaps altered to damage you. You will have great difficulty in acquiring insurance on your life. If you continue to drive a car you may be harassed and charged with traffic offenses you did not commit, and since you are unmarried you may well be set up, or pictured in such a way as to appear morally bankrupt. And your life would certainly be at risk."

All in all he painted a bleak picture. Even if I managed to have the charges published, my chances of surviving the war, let alone winning it, were slim.

"If I resigned, what support could I count on from you?" I put the question to him squarely.

"On the face of it, nothing," he spoke candidly, "because the paper has already ruled out my involvement. But privately I would assign a reporter to work with you covertly, and pay some reasonable amount towards hiring a professional bodyguard to try to keep you alive. But if it became known..." He left that outcome hanging.

I had another area to explore before making up my mind: the feelings of my parents and my children. I explained to them the basics of my venture, not the intricacies. My mother replied I should do whatever I felt had to be done. My father, however, tried to dissuade me, concerned no doubt with possible stains on the family escutcheon, whose arms he had merely inherited, not earned, and with his obligations to the children should I not survive the foray. The children understood the problems they might face at school, but assured me they could handle them. On the strength of their feelings, and the value I placed on my research and abilities, I elected to proceed.

To succeed in the venture, I needed to lay the groundwork carefully. First, I had to find someone to publish my stories; second, I had to establish a source of facts from within the police force itself; and third, I needed to ensure a stable source of income to care for my family over whatever period of time the operation took. Since I would be on my own, I would also have to keep a vigilant eye on my own motives. I cautioned my mind to be analytical in dissecting each requirement, assured myself that I had control over each point, then handed my resignation to Bill Forst.

I cleared out my desk that evening, picked up a five-year severance pay-cheque the next morning, sold my car in the afternoon, and banked enough money to support my family's needs for sixteen weeks. Then I took my gun and permit to Neil Fleishman, a lawyer with whom I had served as an officer in the Irish Fusiliers, and explained to him in confidence the nature and scope of my venture. He locked my gun and carrying permit in his safe, against a timed and dated receipt, and I gave him my power of attorney in all matters. I retained only the gun's empty shoulder holster, to give the impression that the bump under my arm was the weapon I was known to carry.

My first act as a free-lance newspaperman was to contact Stewart McMorran, the city prosecutor, and broaden his knowledge about Chief Mulligan. His office would be the prosecuting authority if charges were to be laid. Because of past dealings with him, I knew I could trust his integrity. Besides, he was healthily ambitious, his goal being to occupy the mayor's chair at city hall. He had the talent and the drive; all he needed was the support of the populace, which, he knew, he could get if he were seen to be the white knight who reformed the corrupt and mismanaged police department.

After I met with McMorran, he and I went on to an appointment in Victoria with Robert Bonner, the provincial attorney general. McMorran quietly set the stage for my submission with a preamble of Mulligan's regime. When I had finished my summation, Bonner thanked us both and said he would ruminate on the matter. He also asked McMorran to keep him apprised of any specific information concerning corruption that came to his attention.

Howard "Red" Somerville was the editor of *Flash Weekly*. Published in Toronto, it was Canada's equivalent to America's *National Enquirer*. He was erudite, hard-nosed, inquisitive, and dedicated to publishing every stripe of article dealing with injustice, criminal acts, con artists, and shady situations.

Owner and publisher of the paper was Louis Ruby, a self-made millionaire, who had parlayed his profits from mixing raisins and peanuts together in Cellophane bags and selling them for a nickel apiece, into cornering the Canadian market for coloured comic books, which he sold by the hundreds of thousands to overseas troops during World War II. He then founded a prestigious racing stable and a classy horseflesh magazine, which Joe Morgan, a well-known radio luminary, edited in the *Flash* offices. It was doubtful that *Flash* made more than enough to pay its bills, but it gave Ruby an outlet for his pet peeves, and it was a telling weapon in his hands. Ruby numbered among his closest associates Willes Chitty, the most highly regarded libel lawyer in Canada; Smirle Lawson, chief coroner of Ontario; and John Chisholm, the chief of police of Toronto. But no person at any level who abused the public was safe from Ruby's columns.

After two weeks spent updating myself on current events within the force, I called Somerville and gave him a thumb-nail sketch of the story and its awesome possibilities. He explained the situation to Ruby, who flew to a meeting with me the following week. During two days of discussion, we explored every avenue down which the publication of my charges might lead.

"Munro," he said, in the airport departure lounge, "here's the deal. I'll print everything you send to Somerville, subject only to his editing the copy for libel. You will be referred to as the paper's Vancouver editor whenever it becomes necessary to use your name. I will pay a reasonable wage to whomever you choose to hire to watch your back, because you'll be a ripe target for a hit man. Lastly, you must have the first two chapters of this major exposé on my desk ten days from now, and thereafter whenever Somerville requires them." We shook hands on the bargain.

I kept my word and delivered the first two instalments on time, and he kept his word. But oh, how he kept his word! Unknown to me he had earmarked half of each of two succeeding editions for the stories, printed 10,000 extra copies of the first issue and 30,000 of the second, and shipped them hot off the press by air to Vancouver's airport, where they were picked up by special trucks. Within hours they were delivered to most news-stands and store outlets in the city. I pushed my way through a crowd of people surrounding a kiosk at Granville and Georgia streets to find the mobbed vendor selling them to eager buyers. I tore one out of his hands and felt faint as I read the front page: RAPE OF VANCOUVER! MUNRO TEARS MASK FROM CROOKED LAW IN GANGLAND EDEN. And beside this startling headline was a large picture of me at a typewriter, pointing a finger at the camera.

Boxed in the upper-right-hand corner of the page was another announcement: NEXT WEEK! REVOLT OF THE MORALITY BRASS.

It was splashier inside; across the two centre pages, emblazoned in two-inch-high type was the order: CLEAN UP THIS MESS! Set into the major story carried over from page one were pictures of Chief Walter Mulligan, Detective Sergeant Leonard Cuthbert, and others. Page three was devoted entirely to coming events:

THE LID IS OFF VANCOUVER VICE AND ITS ALLIES

Starting this week, Ray Munro, veteran reporter and head of *Flash*'s West Coast bureau, will bring you the true story of how police corruption, City Hall conniving, and Gangland money turned Vancouver into Canada's crime centre, the story it took months of patient checking to uncover, the story which Munro hammered out on his typewriter as paid bodyguards shielded his every move, the blazing story of the rape of a city!

- Read about the police chief and the vanishing piggy bank.
- Read of the society playboy's sinister double life.
- Read why Vancouver today is Hophead Heaven.
- Read of the scarlet women and their highly placed lovers.
- Read of the senior detective who spilled his guts to Victoria.
- Read how the politicians sold out you, the public.
- Read how the Syndicate captured City Hall.
- Read the price tags on Vancouver officialdom.
- Read why press photographers are banned at police courts.

READ THE WHOLE SHOCKING STORY IN FLASH!

I called Forst immediately.

"Jesus, but when you go, you *really* go," he said.

I explained about Somerville, Ruby, and the deal, and asked him what action the *Province* was taking. He told me that the paper, and probably the *Sun* and *News-Herald* as well, would remain silent until some legal action was taken against either the *Flash* or me by one of the persons named.

"Jack Whelan's waiting for you at the Irish-Canadian Club. He's going to cover your back. Just don't connect me with him in any manner," Forst closed off the conversation.

I knew then that he was really worried for my safety. Jack Whelan, brother to Superintendent Harry Whelan, was my bodyguard. The force had already begun to polarize, with Harry as undercover leader of the white shirts. Harry wanted me alive to tell the whole story, and he'd arranged to have his brother named as my bodyguard. Forst and Ruby were sharing his salary and expenses, and Superintendent Whelan was secretly deploying a second screen of loyal patrolmen around the two of us.

Jack Whelan was big, and he was tough. When he left the force a few years earlier after a dispute with the brass, he turned wrestler. I knew him only because a few months earlier I had prevailed upon him to tell me all he knew about Mulligan. I now had in my vault an affidavit signed by him, detailing the circumstances of how he and Mulligan, when they were detective partners, stole a loaded piggy bank from an apartment where they were investigating a theft. That story was in the current issue of *Flash*.

The only hard items Jack carried on his person were two ball-point pens with the caps removed, which he clipped to an inside pocket. I saw him use them—or almost use them—just once, when a man came at me like a thunderbolt from a car. Jack suddenly had one pen in each closed fist, points downwards, and was moving between my attacker and me like an express train, slashing the wicked devices at obscene speed. Had they landed, they would have inflicted horrible lacerations. The would-be assailant leaped away between two moving trucks and escaped. A check of the car he vaulted from revealed that it had been rented at the airport by a man arriving from Portland, Oregon, and showing identification found later to be stolen.

Some months earlier I had met secretly with a senior detective of unblemished record, from whom I had received information in the past. He had at one time been assigned to the gambling detail, then headed by Detective Sergeant Leonard Cuthbert, but had requested a transfer because he knew that some members of the squad were receiving cash from Cuthbert. Cuthbert, in turn, was receiving a pay-off for permitting specific games to operate while raiding others and charging those running them.

"There is no way consistent pay-offs can be made by any squad leader to his men, unless the chief of police is in on the deal," my informant stated bluntly. "Mulligan was taking a big envelope on a regular basis, giving back a smaller envelope to Cuthbert, who in turn was paying off his key men."

I had known it was going on, but, lacking any substantive proof, I had not been able to state it publicly. I now decided, however, that this angle might be the one that would force Mulligan into the open to defend himself, thereby opening the door for the Vancouver press to report. I chose to act out a daring scenario.

I slipped on my empty shoulder holster and hailed a taxi to take Jack Whelan and me to Cuthbert's house, a small cottage in Vancouver's east end. I rapped smartly on the front door. Cuthbert answered it almost immediately, staring at me from a face swollen by lack of sleep. Lethargically, almost as though he had been expecting my visit, he stepped aside and motioned me in.

"Len," I cautioned him, "you're in trouble. And unless you get up off your knees and tell either McMorran or the attorney general the whole goddamn truth, you're going to wind up the fall guy and in jail."

"Why are you telling me this?" he questioned through clenched teeth.

"Because I think you've been made a pawn. By telling your story now, you can come through the carnage in good shape," I explained. "You have only three choices. You can come with me now and tell your story to the prosecutor and to the attorney general in Victoria, or you can wait to be arrested, or"—I opened my coat to reveal a bit of the leather holster—"you can shove yours in your mouth and pull the trigger." With that suggestion I walked to the door, turned, and said, "I'll wait five minutes in the cab for you, then I'm leaving to write the rest of your story, and the names that go along with it."

His door remained closed, and we drove off, hoping against hope that my visit would trigger some immediate response.

The main headlines of all three Vancouver newspapers that day of June 23 trumpeted the fact that Chief Mulligan had commenced action for libel against *Flash*, Ruby, Somerville, the local *Flash* distributors, and me. Furthermore, the Senate committee investigating narcotic drugs had laid the blame for Vancouver's notorious drug problem squarely on the city police. The door had been opened for the press to investigate my charges, and the onus had been put squarely on the Police Commission to take some form of action. And they did, within the hour. The commissioners, comprising the new mayor of Vancouver, Fred Hume and two judges, placed Mulligan on temporary suspension and requested Bonner to institute a commission to enquire into the allegations I had made.

At 8:15 the following morning, Detective Sergeant Len Cuthbert sat behind his desk in the police station, placed the muzzle of his service revolver to the left side of his chest, and pulled the trigger. He was rushed to the hospital, where surgeons worked successfully to keep him alive. The bullet had missed his heart by an eighth of an inch.

A COMMISSION OF ENQUIRY

THE FOLLOWING DAY both the *Sun* and *Province* devoted a full page to the report of Senator Tom Reid, chairman of the Senate committee investigating narcotic drugs, which stated: "Where law enforcement is lax, that's where you find the big traffic in dope. In narcotics, Vancouver is Canada's capital." The committee had pointed a finger directly at Chief Mulligan and his men.

Unknown to me, while I was in Cuthbert's home, Attorney General Bonner had been closeted with Prosecutor McMorran and the three members of the Vancouver Police Commission to discuss the charges I had made against Mulligan, in the affidavits I'd given to McMorran. That meeting followed immediately on the heels of my second major *Flash* exposé, in which I named the major gambling dens in the city and their operators, and in which I exposed links between organized crime and the local athletic commission. I explained how the crime syndicate divided up Vancouver, and concluded with a short article on how it felt to take on the cops and the robbers at the same time.

The next day Mayor Fred Hume announced that Chief Mulligan had been placed on indefinite leave of absence, that Traffic Superintendent Alan Rossiter had been named temporary acting chief, and that R.H. Tupper, Q.C., a Vancouver lawyer, had been chosen by the attorney general to conduct a Royal Commission. He was given "the widest possible reference, with full power to summon witnesses and to punish for contempt."

Two days later Tupper began taking voluntary statements from a small number of police officers. On July 5, the commissioner opened the hearings to standing-room-only crowds. Those who gained entry were told that his enquiry into the police force would be three-pronged: it would look at suggestions of corruption involving police officers and men, at allegations that the Criminal Code of Canada was not being properly enforced, and at suggestions that the force was badly administered. He then declared it was not within the commission's jurisdiction to subpoena any person outside British Columbia. When that news broke, those members of the criminal fraternity not already vacationing outside the province, or lying low on the fringes of Vancouver, departed immediately.

The first person served with a call to appear was Detective Sergeant Leonard Cuthbert, who was still in hospital recovering from his suicide attempt. The second white paper bore my name. I called Ruby, and he asked me to fly to Toronto for a day to meet with his legal counsel. (Tupper had written Ruby and Somerville, asking them to attend. Both of them accepted the invitation, with a proviso that all their expenses be paid. Tupper refused, and neither appeared at any time before the commission.)

On my return to Vancouver Ruby hired Neil Fleishman, the lawyer I recommended, to represent me, him, Somerville and John Blunt Publications, the company that published *Flash*.

On July 13, 1955, the probe called its first witness, Detective Sergeant Robert Leatherdale, a highly respected career officer, who testified that, after Mulligan promoted him to sergeant in 1949, the chief gave him command of the liquor detail, on the condition that he would allow a number of bootleggers to operate without interference. "The offer was that I would receive money for the freedoms to operate, and split it with the chief constable," he stated to a stunned audience. He refused to honour the chief's request, and gave details of the conversation to City Prosecutor Gordon Scott, Magistrate Oscar Orr, and Mayor Charles Thompson, but heard nothing further of the matter from any source.

Leatherdale also testified that he shared an office with Detective Sergeant Cuthbert, then head of the gambling squad, who told him he was expected to pick up the pay-off money and take it to Chief Mulligan, who would give him back half, a portion of which he should divide among his men. Cuthbert was later replaced by Detective Sergeant Archie Plummer, another highly respected officer.

Plummer was next on the stand. He explained that he had made a typewritten copy of Leatherdale's notes. When he had faced Cuthbert with them in his own home, Cuthbert assured him that they were correct, and that he, Cuthbert, had indeed taken money to let bootleggers operate. He had given the money to Chief Mulligan, he said, and received half back.

I had expected a feeling of euphoria to sweep over me when these damning statements were made, because, no matter what other evidence was given, the charges made by those two respected detectives, and backed up by the original notes made at the time, removed Mulligan from the Vancouver Police Department for all time. But only a hollowness came, enhanced by the knowledge that I had started a juggernaut rolling, and that it would not stop until it ran its course. I knew, too, that every man on the force would feel ashamed of his badge, and that only with the fullness of time, and a massive dose of purgative, could the force once more walk in honour.

CHIEF MULLIGAN ALLY OF CRIMINALS, screamed the headline in the next morning's *News-Herald*. And from that moment on, it became a guessing game among members of the press as to when and under what circumstances the chief would flee the country. There were still many witnesses to be heard from, however. The commission had requested subpoenas for Mayor Fred Hume, ex-Mayor Charles Thompson, Prosecutor Stewart McMorran, ex-Alderman R.K. Gervin, Detective Inspector Peter Lamont, and ex-Detective Sergeant Percy Hoare, as well as many persons known to have been the subject of internal police investigations, including former convicted crime tsar Joe Celona, and the shadowy club owner and known companion of Chief Mulligan, William Couper.

Couper's name on a subpoena was welcome news; only weeks before I had written a story for *Flash* revealing that Couper and Minister of Defence Ralph Campney were associated in real-estate dealings. I stated that certain major Vancouver buildings registered in Couper's name had been leased to the Department of National Defence at exorbitant rentals. In most cases, the annual rents paid were one-third the value of the property. On the day the police probe opened, a member of Parliament from the Vancouver area repeated my charges in the House of Commons. That prompted a government investigation that eventually substantiated the charges. The Royal Commission subpoena bearing Couper's name was never served; he had fled the province.

I assumed then that with a parade of witnesses yet to be heard it would be some weeks before I would be called to testify. Both Jack and Harry Whelan felt that the most crucial time for my safety lay immediately ahead. Once I had testified, the only motive for removing me would be revenge.

They were immediately proven correct.

While I had answered the telephone to numerous cranks, messengers of filth, and promisers of death and dismemberment, no one had threatened harm to my young children. Then it happened.

"Munro?" the soft male voice enquired. "Your son Rob and daughter Joanne will leave school one day soon, and you'll never see them again."

I stifled my rage and the urge to bang down the receiver.

"Joanne has worn a different dress to school each day this week," he went on. "Today it's blue. And Rob is wearing grey shorts and a blue shirt, with a bandage on his left knee. I already have his Wolf Cub cap, which he thinks he lost, and yesterday I watched him fly a kite from his back porch." The silken, unemotional voice raised the hairs on my neck. "It's too late to stop what you've started, but I'll—" and the caller disconnected.

I told my parents to stay inside with the children, and was at Staff Sergeant "Red" McBrain's RCMP detachment office within fifteen minutes. When I told him about the telephone call, he assured me that within minutes a screen would be placed around the children for as long as needed. No further threats were made against the children, no one was seen watching them with an ulterior motive, and no harm was to come to them.

But I did make a foolish mistake during that period, which could have cost me my life. I was lunching in a downtown café without Jack Whelan nearby, when a young chap tapped me on the shoulder, asked if I was Munro, and passed me a handwritten note. It told me to leave immediately and proceed to a door at the top of a flight of stairs, next to a drugstore across the street. Mr. Whelan was waiting for me, the note said. I assumed the sender was Jack or Harry.

It was high noon with streams of people passing in front of the shop. I crossed the street, pulled open the door, and trotted up the stairs two at a time. I rapped once on the door at the top of the stairs, and it was pulled violently inwards. I heard a man shout, "Grab him!" I wheeled around instinctively but caught a massive blow on my forehead, which lifted me clear off the top step and arced me backwards into a prolonged fall that ended when I landed on my shoulders at the bottom of the stairs. My feet swung around and smashed through the large glass panel, leaving me half in and half out of the building. I saw people bending over me as I sat up amid shards of glass, then lifted my arms for someone to help me to my feet. There were voices asking why someone didn't call the police—on that word I staggered around the corner into a taxi-cab.

Ed Moyer, the *Province* reporter whom Forst had secretly seconded to me for a month as a casual legman, and who had excelled himself as a rumour-confirmer, had a ground-floor room a few blocks away. I was there within minutes. The door was locked, so I slipped inside through a window, stuck my face into a sinkful of cold water, and washed the blood away. Then I phoned Harry Whelan at the police station with the facts. I learned later that two uniformed policemen went into the apartment like gangbusters, one in the front and one in the rear, but my attackers had fled.

I wore dark glasses for the better part of a week because of the purple pouches under both eyes, and was accused of "playing Hollywood."

Somerville was breathing down my neck for more copy, but I told him he'd have to wait. I had already written six stories, and the threats and attacks had frayed my nerves somewhat. I needed a few days' rest to revitalize myself, gather my thoughts, and implement another course of action to capitalize on the momentum that my original stories had established.

The next issue of *Flash* contained a full-page story below a two-inch headline: GET WITH IT! MULLIGAN SHOULD BE BEHIND BARS NOW! On another page was a story titled: CHICKEN PRESS HELPED CROOKS WIN VANCOUVER. The first was a direct slur on Tupper's commission and worthy of a contempt of court charge; the second was merely contemptible. I had written neither.

In shock, I sent a telegram to Ruby, resigning from our agreement. While it disconnected me from the medium I was using to get information to the public, I reasoned that enough charges had been made in *Flash* to cause the daily press to start investigating on their own and to publish their findings.

Jack Whelan was next on the witness stand. His description of stealing the piggy bank with Mulligan and their splitting the $11 in coins in the police car was hilarious, and brought a stern reprimand from Tupper. Then he told the commission that he and Mulligan were partners, and that he had set up a deal for gambler Pete

Wallace to pay Cuthbert $5,000 a month. The audience was soon stunned into silence. He went on to explain that former Alderman Gervin and Mulligan's friend William Couper operated the largest gambling game in the city with complete immunity from police interference.

The press corps came to full attention when Superintendent Harry Whelan took the stand. He was considered to be as straight as a die, and with no price on his integrity. It was his refusal to bow to Mulligan's improper requests that saw him reduced from deputy chief to head of the uniformed division. He confirmed that Mulligan had made an illegal proposition to Cuthbert.

"Cuthbert was terrified of being arrested and going to jail for his crimes," stated Whelan, "and as late as June 14 he was considering suicide. The day before he shot himself, he told me he was going to McMorran, to tell it all."

Suddenly, and without prior warning, Attorney General Bonner ordered the RCMP to probe "all criminal aspects" of the testimony coming out of the enquiry, and just as suddenly the hearings were set down for fourteen days, until Cuthbert was deemed well enough to take the stand.

ON
THE STAND

INSIDE THE COURT-HOUSE on the day Detective Cuthbert was slated to testify, the scene was tense. Surging crowds muscled each other for seats or standing space, awaiting the arrival of the star police witness.

In a dramatic move, T.G. Norris, Q.C., counsel for Chief Mulligan, requested that Ruby, Somerville, and I be cited for contempt of court, because of the content of the most recently published articles in *Flash*. I had not written the articles or even known about them until I bought a news-stand copy. Norris damned the articles as libellous and scurrilous attacks on the integrity of the commission and his client.

"It might be thought the person responsible for writing this material is insane." Norris waved a *Flash* at the commissioner. He held it between two fingers, like a leper's bandage. Then he asked that all the charges made in the paper be "blown away by the fresh winds of justice." He was good, all right, an intelligent and erudite actor, and one of the most expensive lawyers in Canada. But knowing the size of Mulligan's staggering pay-off kitty, I didn't concern myself with whether or not he could afford Norris's legal fees.

The commissioner, after a morning of discussion, ruled that if Ruby, through his esteemed counsel Willes Chitty, would undertake to refrain from publishing further articles of a like nature, he would not inflict punishment. That judgement, unacceptable to Norris but approved by Chitty, made me breathe a little easier; I had sufficient on my plate without another and very serious charge being placed on it.

Cuthbert's long-awaited appearance was highlighted by his faltering walk to the witness box on the arm of a nurse. Before a mob of scuffling spectators he took the oath, placed a hand over his heart where the near-fatal bullet had entered, and tried to make peace with his troubled conscience. Rocking back and forth in agitation, he stunned the court with his admission that he and Mulligan had split large sums of money over a six-week period in 1949 when he was head of the gambling squad. In a thin voice and with visible emotion, he transfixed all present with his tortured testimony. He counted off on his fingers the amounts and dates he accepted the bribes and named the gamblers who gave him the money, then related how he would take the cash in a paper bag into the chief's office. There Mulligan would count it out, giving half back to him, a portion of which he gave to the officers on his squad.

At this point, some members of the press, in a scene like something out of a movie, rushed for the telephones to ensure that headlines would be readied for the next edition.

Then, in a second dramatic revelation, which sent another bevy of newspapermen running to the telephones to suggest different headlines, Cuthbert told of my visit to his home and the three options I had spelled out for him.

"Ray Munro was known to me as a reporter who stayed with a story until he got it, and when he came to my home and spoke with me inside, I knew I was in trouble. He had a taxi out front, and I could see Jack Whelan inside it. Ray wanted me to get into the car and have a talk with both of them, but I refused, as I was only partly dressed and without shoes."

Cuthbert then said that I had asked him to come with me to McMorran and then to the attorney general, and tell his story about the Mulligan pay-offs.

"I asked him if there was anything else I could do, and he replied that I had three choices." He repeated what I had told him.

CUTHBERT TESTIFIES: "I SPLIT GAMBLING GRAFT WITH CHIEF MULLIGAN"

MUNRO SAID: "BLOW YOUR BRAINS OUT, CUTHBERT. YOU'RE STUCK"

The two massive headlines faced me on every corner, and punished my conscience for having placed such a thought in Cuthbert's disturbed mind, even though my intent had been only to scare him, to make him understand how serious I was about bringing Mulligan to justice.

None of the numerous routines Norris used on witnesses succeeded in shaking Cuthbert's testimony. The trembling man even refused to name any of the members of his squad who shared in the dirty money. Soon afterwards the Police Commission met and fired him, permitting him to take only a portion of his pension. At a later date, when he had recovered, he accepted a position as a security expert with a local manufacturing plant, and faded into obscurity.

For some time immediately after accepting Ruby's writing offer, I had mailed dozens of one-liners to *Flash* about persons associated with the enquiry. I had written them only as a source of background information for Ruby, but I suddenly had a queasy feeling that I had erred in transmitting them. My uneasiness proved justified when, in the next issue of *Flash*, some of these quips appeared in a column headed with my name, although I had resigned my position weeks earlier. One of them dealt with a bullish lawyer who was known to drink to excess in a private club, then regale his listeners with so-called "inside" information on known personalities. He had made the error of taking my name in vain, so I responded by telling Ruby in a note that the lawyer's adult daughter had been committed to an institution, for reasons best known to her overbearing father.

Well, when I read it, I knew I was in trouble. The very next day Norris exploded. He read the item to the packed assembly and to the commission, mentioned that I had written it, and said that it referred to him and his daughter. He demanded that I be charged immediately with contempt of court. It was a serious situation, and a summons was issued, calling upon me to show cause why I should not be committed for trial. Fleishman advised me to retain Harry Bray, Q.C., an outstanding libel lawyer. The battle lines were drawn.

More screaming headlines blazed my name across the full width of the dailies: RAY MUNRO FREED IN CONTEMPT CASE and MULLIGAN'S LAWYER QUITS POLICE PROBE.

The following day the lawyer and the client were pictured on page one leaving the court-house, Norris for the last time as a probe counsel, and Mulligan, unbeknownst to the press, en route to the American Consulate to apply for a visa to enter the United States. Headlines in the *Sun* stated that Norris was leaving for personal reasons. But no one could fool the reporters who had watched Mulligan's defences crumble into believing that statement.

The afternoon before Superintendent Harry Whelan was due to take the stand for the second time, he and I walked on the court-house lawn and talked easily about life in general and the fishing trips we had taken in his little outboard, trolling for salmon in the Strait of Georgia. He seemed deeply concerned about the image of the force. He realized that the cancer had to be cut out, but he hated having to take the stand and tell all he knew about fellow officers who were involved in corrupt practices. He also knew he would have to undergo a most personal cross-examination.

That night I disconnected my telephone to get some extra sleep and was stunned mid-morning when I heard on the radio that Whelan had been found shot in his home several hours earlier and had died en route to the hospital. Most of page one of all newspapers was given over to the story, headed in circus-size type: TOP COP KILLS SELF.

Some witnesses claimed they saw an unidentified man running away from the house moments after they heard the shot, but several teams of detectives working around the clock for days could not prove their statements to be correct. The inquest, which I attended with his brother Jack, ruled Harry's death to be a suicide. And I knew in my heart of hearts that one reason he had been concerned with taking the stand was that he feared being labelled as unstable. His father, some years before, had killed himself with Harry's own police revolver. Later, Harry's daughter had taken her life while visiting in the United States. Both of these facts would have come out in the cross-examination.

I needed a night out, so I invited Roy Bradner, a schoolteacher friend, to have a few drinks with me in West Vancouver, where my face was not known, followed by an after-midnight dinner at a quiet suburban restaurant. As the last two remaining diners, we were about to leave when two husky men dressed in workmen's clothes entered, took a table, and began a loud discussion of current happenings at the police enquiry. They made liberal use of my name in company with the most vulgar adjectives. When I saw the proprietor slip quickly into the kitchen, I told Bradner to go straight out the back door, run to the front, and start the car. I would be out in a moment.

I stepped smartly to the front door and pulled it open. Without a word, one of the men threw his full weight onto my shoulders, sending me crashing to the concrete, scraping my face and chest. I knew I was hurt and would have to fight for my life, but what I feared most was a knife thrust. We rolled under a small truck, where I managed to smash his face into the drive shaft, as his partner grabbed a leg and pulled us both out from underneath.

I heard the engine of Bradner's car racing as he drove in my direction, just as the wail of a police siren cut through my pain. Without a word the assailants scrambled into a late-model sedan and roared down the highway, away from the oncoming red light.

My face was a mess. Strings of skin had peeled away and the bone of my nose was showing through. I knew my chest was bleeding from the erasure of skin, and one fist was already swelling (I had inadvertently smashed it into the truck's under-side).

We agreed that I should go to Vancouver General Hospital and get patched up. To leave a blind trail, I used Bradner's name and his cottage address. He paid the repair bill for me, and after midnight offered to drive me home. We were almost to the centre of the Lion's Gate Bridge when the same late-model car in which my attackers had escaped raced alongside, pulled sharply in front, slammed on the brakes, and made a complete reverse turn, coming to a sudden stop facing us, a few yards away. There were three men in the car. The driver and another man, the same ones who had attacked me earlier, leaped from the car and ran towards us. I picked up a huge wrench Bradner used to secure his trailer hitch and, with an overpowering urge to bring it down on someone's head, leapt from the car and ran right at the nearest man, who turned and hurried back to his own car.

Suddenly Bradner slammed his accelerator down and drove straight into the attacker approaching his side, glancing him off the hood and onto the roadway. The man staggered to his feet, bent double, and crabbed his way hurriedly into the car. His partner had climbed behind the wheel, and they roared away towards Vancouver as Bradner tried to smash his car into theirs and missed.

I was on the narrow sidewalk, and suddenly sensed a figure behind me. Bradner shouted out the car window for me to look out. I swung around in time to see a man on the railing behind me. He was holding tight to a vertical beam. As I grabbed for him, he lost his footing and fell backwards off the bridge and towards the water, 200 feet below. Another car pulled in behind ours, disgorging an off-duty Vancouver policeman, who made a run for the rail.

Through the light rain we could see the man's body, face up to us, his arms flailing, spinning slowly. He grew smaller, as did the sound of his scream.

We raced across the bridge to the north end, where Bradner told the toll collector that a man had jumped off the centre section. At the Indian Reserve's small dock was a simple skiff with oars, which I used to row out into the ebb tide for the body. I knew roughly where he had hit, and after about five minutes I saw him, floating face down. When I pulled him into the boat, I knew he was dead.

The flashing red lights on the shore led me back against the tidal flow, and when I couldn't row any farther, two ambulance men waded out and towed the boat in. While the police were searching the body, Bradner and I left quickly. Later, he telephoned the RCMP in North Vancouver with his name and address, in case they wanted to ask him some questions.

My face and chest were glued with dried blood to the pillowcase and bedsheets when I awoke late in the morning. After donning dark glasses, I made my way downtown and bought a *Sun*. A short article described the recovery of the body of a middle-aged logger by two unnamed citizens. In the early morning hours, the paper said, the man had jumped from the Lion's Gate Bridge. He had been pronounced dead on arrival at hospital.

The occasional concerns I had had for my own safety diminished somewhat with the bridge episode. Since the chief and the rotten cops had been named and publicized, along with their gambling and liquor-trafficking counterparts, and since my evidence would merely confirm their actions, revenge would be the only motive remaining for an assault on me. I was further reassured by the old adage: "Never kill a cop or a reporter." Police never close any file on the unexplained death of one of their own, and the press never sleeps until a newspaperman's slayer is apprehended and brought to trial.

I kept a close check on Joanne and Rob during those perilous months. But although my name was frequently in the papers, often in headline form, and always connected with wrongdoing or violence, they had fortunately been only mildly teased as a result. Thankfully, our relationship did not suffer. I told them truthfully what was happening, and kept reminding them that soon it would be over, and we would return to a normal life.

But as the summer went on, the parade of witnesses continued. The head of the policemen's union, Detective Fred Daugherty, castigated Mulligan for the innumerable times that men had been improperly demoted, promoted, suspended, and dismissed, suggesting that Mulligan had surrounded himself with a screen of personal lackeys. Daugherty implied by innuendo that members of the Police Commission, past and present, were equally to blame. His forceful testimony brought the ordinary policeman's life under Mulligan's rule into sharp and distasteful focus.

Those facts and statements were supported most tellingly by Patrol Sergeant Milt Walker, as fine a man as ever donned a uniform, with a splendid career behind him as a combat major in the Canadian Army overseas. He stated that as a leader Mulligan did not have the qualities of an ordinary non-commissioned officer. Coincident with his testimony, a member of the provincial legislature in Victoria rose in the House to charge openly that the probe into my charges had been deliberately delayed to permit the gravest offenders to flee the country.

Throughout it all, Mulligan sat beside his freshman counsel, Jay Gould, grim-faced and making copious notes.

Another close observer of the proceedings was Jack Webster, a Scotsman who had been hired as a reporter at the *Sun* shortly after I was. He turned out to be one of Hal Straight's better investments, although Straight rarely made full use of his talents. Webster was talkative and histrionic, but he could also be canny and resourceful, and he had a masterful interviewing style. His other forte was that he could take shorthand as fast as a person could speak, for long periods and without error. He put this skill to good use at the commission hearings. By then he was working for radio station CJOR. No day was complete for most households on the lower mainland until they had heard Jack Webster narrate, in the most fascinatingly accurate manner, not only every word spoken by every person before the commission, but the actual feel of the events. I've never known of any newspaperman to equal him. Every word was taken down in shorthand, then repeated on the telephone every half-hour or so to be heard live on radio. Then, in the evening, he repeated the entire day's events to the largest listening audience in Vancouver's radio history, to that time.

SECRET WITNESS

ELECTRIFYING is the only word to describe the shock that rippled through the jammed courtroom when my secret witness entered. In the strange silence, only the dainty footsteps of a diminutive female echoed. Down the narrow aisle she walked, between spectators, past the rows of lawyers, commission officials, and the press. Then she entered the witness box, and took the oath. Layers of black veil covered her head and neck completely, to remove all possibility of her face being photographed en route to the courtroom.

Mulligan leaned forward anxiously, staring at the witness in an attempt to establish her identity. Suddenly it came from her own lips. She was asked by the clerk to state her name.

"Helen Elizabeth Douglas," she answered, removing her veil.

Mulligan paled visibly. He licked his lips, then slowly, ever so slowly, eased his large body back in his chair and shoved his ever-present pen and notebook resignedly away from him. One hand came up to form a mask over the lower half of his face.

Helen Douglas was my surprise witness, my trump card. It was a strange road I had followed to place her in that chair, starting with only the feeblest intuitive reasoning six years before, and leading down numerous culs-de-sac and through nearly impenetrable mazes.

It began when I saw her profile, at dusk, as she entered the rear door of an unmarked detective car with a bag of groceries from a market. She was not a policewoman, and yet the driver must have been familiar with her, as he remained behind the wheel and permitted her to enter and close the door by herself. I was intrigued enough that I noted the officer's name and the licence number of the car. My sixth sense had come into play again. With patience I finally located and identified her, then placed her name, address, and circumstances before Chief Prosecutor McMorran.

Even before she spoke, the newspapers were setting the incident in bold headlines: 'MYSTERY WOMAN' ON STAND. But the story was better than any reporter could have hoped. Helen Douglas testified that she had been Mulligan's mistress from 1945 through 1949. She had known he was married, and had met him in company with Detective Laurie McCulloch in a drinking club owned by William Couper, who had introduced them to her.

WOMAN WITNESS CHARGES FRIENDSHIP WITH CHIEF, the *Province* headline shouted. The word *friendship* was used in the same sense that *Time* magazine used "very good friends" to describe a more than platonic relationship.

Calm and composed behind her blonde wig, heavy-rimmed glasses, and large-brimmed hat, Helen Douglas explained that she was now married and had altered her appearance to prevent public involvement of her husband in the distasteful affair. In her testimony she described a trip she and Mulligan had taken across Canada for a two-week holiday to a police convention in Montreal, and other trips to the United States and Vancouver Island. She had travelled with him, she said, in a police car on many occasions, and had often been chauffeured by a plain-clothes officer. Mulligan had spent mornings, afternoons, and sometimes all day or night with her, and had given her various gifts of jewellery and small amounts of money.

The second shock wave hit when she told of receiving $2,200 in cash from Mulligan to buy a small property for him in her name in the Fraser Valley. Later, when they were separated, she sold it for $500. The press perked up even more when she recounted some prominent people mentioned to her in connection with money and favours during what she intimated was pillow talk. Despite frequent clashes between Jay Gould, the chief's lawyer, and Victor Dryer, a commission counsel, she was permitted to continue her testimony. Immediately she named two known gamblers the chief had spoken of as being behind some money he was getting.

Neighbours of her Georgia Street home were questioned as witnesses, and several recalled the occasions of Mulligan's visits. One man told the exact time of night Mulligan arrived and the breakfast hour at which he left, after having been kissed goodbye at the door by Helen Douglas in a robe.

Then the big rocket went off, the one for which I had waited. Clearly and distinctly, Helen Douglas told the commission the chief explained to her that he had $38,000 in cash, received from gamblers, hidden in a safe place for their future needs.

Newspapermen erupted from the hearing to grab the few available telephones. CHIEF GOT $38,000, WITNESS TESTIFIES, the headlines said, in type at least as large as that which noted the sinking of the *Titanic*.

Despite intense cross-examination by Gould, who faced her with a lengthy list of male callers to her home, and charged that as revenge for Mulligan not wanting to marry her, Helen Douglas had gone for his client's jugular vein, she refused to be swayed from any of her statements. Immediately after she left the box, Gould startled the commission by announcing that both he and his client would leave the hearings and not return, that they were ready to face trial on whatever charges would be laid.

With the hearings adjourned again, Mulligan, then fifty-two, asked the Police Commission to fire him, instead of presenting his resignation, so that he would qualify for an additional pension of $50 a month. To be sure that no one would miss the import of the event, the *Province* headlined the story in large type again and labelled the edition an "Extra." MULLIGAN ASKS TO BE LET OUT. His request was accepted, with a rider that his pension not commence for three years, at age fifty-five. One week later, RCMP Superintendent George J. Archer was permitted to leave that force and accept the position of chief of police of Vancouver.

A new hand was on the tiller, but the probe was not yet over. A few more, including Mulligan and me, were still to be called as witnesses. Mulligan didn't wait to be called, however. His flight from Canada was announced in another black headline: MULLIGAN GOES TO U.S.; WON'T RETURN TO PROBE.

With him went the libel suit he had laid against me, the one that brought the Police Commission, the press, and the attorney general into the act, and had resulted in the Royal Commission.

A number of other officers testified to the control known criminals seemed to have in the police department and then, in late October, on the Royal Commission's thirty-third day of actual sitting, I was summoned to testify.

It has been said, and I am sure it is true, that a man who acts as his own lawyer has a fool for a client. I disregarded that proverb because I had nothing to fear. All the statements I had made in print about Mulligan, Cuthbert, the morally bankrupt senior police officers, and the gambling syndicate, as that illegal fraternity was called, were true. Also, I had something else to reveal, something I had kept quiet about until then.

I had known the year before when, after my marathon seventeen-day reporting ordeal I had exposed the phony lotteries and the fake Irish sweepstake tickets, that all the phony and illegal lotteries operated courtesy of Chief Mulligan. But owing to the *Province*'s dictum against naming persons who had not been charged with or convicted of a crime, I could not present the whole story.

The commission had no such restrictions, however. So just as soon as I had been sworn in, I told the packed courtroom that ex-Chief Walter Mulligan had paved the way for all lotteries to operate in the city. Away went the press again. The *Province* finally printed the enormous headline they should have published a year earlier. In type the religious editor had privately reserved for the Second Coming the paper announced: CHIEF RAN LOTTERY—MUNRO CHARGES. But it would have made me prouder if I had been standing in the witness box as a *Province* reporter, instead of as a gypsy airplane pilot.

After Tupper had wrested control of the hearing back from the unruly spectators by hammering his gavel and threatening to clear the court if the audience interrupted again, commission counsel asked me bluntly if I had written a number of specific stories in *Flash* both before and during the enquiry. I had written some of the articles; others had been enlarged or amended by editors in Toronto. I therefore declined to answer, on the ground that I would leave a record for any civil suit that might follow. That answer was accepted gracefully, but I sensed there was something else they were going to hit me with, and they did.

Gordon Towne, manager of Couper's Quadra Club, had told probe investigators that some weeks prior I had entered his club, asked for him, and then suggested that for $3,000 I would refrain from using Couper's name when called to testify. Three witnesses, he said, would swear they heard me make the offer.

What really happened, as I explained to the commission, was that Towne asked me in for a chat. In a roundabout way he had advised me that my future in Vancouver would be more tenable if I didn't refer to Couper again in any forum. I thanked him for his opinion, told him to stick his thinly veiled threat in his ear, and departed.

I was then directed back to the lottery exposé and to the twenty-seven consecutive page-one *Province* headlines they had fostered. I explained to the commission in detail the times, dates, and circumstances surrounding valid information I had received and taken to the appropriate officials. And that after I had given the same information to Detective Sergeant Ian McGregor, the raids were immediately carried out, arrests were made, and convictions were obtained.

I explained that I had spoken individually to each of the three members of the Police Commission about Mulligan's involvement in the WCES, and that they had done nothing. I had nailed down Mayor Hume again and gone through some of my information and evidence in two private meetings with him in city hall. I had shown him affidavits from my secret witness, Parnell Johnson, who was involved in the phony WCES operation at a high level. I even produced Johnson at a later date, as well as the locally made engraving plates for printing phony Irish Sweepstake tickets. I then testified that when the mayor declined to act, I took the whole issue to Stewart McMorran, who eventually brought it to Commissioner Tupper's attention, and he called me as a witness concerning it.

Suddenly the enquiry ended, after six months, 1,280,000 words of testimony covering forty hearings, 126 witnesses, and 144 exhibits. Commissioner Tupper departed to assess his findings and write a concluding report. The RCMP and Vancouver City Police Department investigating teams met to draw their own conclusions.

The shadowy figures from the city's sewers, who had fled in fear of exposure and criminal charges, began buying tickets back to Vancouver from foreign climes. The minions of the law took deep breaths and embarked on the tortuous road back to their proper place of authority. Many reputations were deservedly destroyed, and others tarnished. Only the handful of officers who dared to take the stand in defence of truth came away with their reputations enhanced. It had been a catharsis, a cutting away of the cancerous rot that had eroded whole sections of the Criminal Code and had begun when Mulligan stole the police department from the people and sold it to organized crime.

Some weeks later a headline appeared: MULLIGAN CORRUPT — TUPPER. As the story beneath reported, Tupper had released his summation. Among other things, he concluded that former Chief Walter Mulligan bolted the probe and fled to the United States because he knew he couldn't clear his name; that he accepted bribes for the purpose of dissuading him from his duty as a police constable; that former Detective Sergeant Leonard Cuthbert accepted bribes from gamblers and shared the monies with former Chief Mulligan and certain members of the gambling and liquor details; that ex-Detective Jack Whelan's testimony of the stolen piggy bank was untrue, and that the allegations against Couper, who was conspicuous by his absence, must be accepted.

The final headline on the matter read: MULLIGAN WON'T FACE CORRUPTION CHARGES, which came as a surprise to no one. And with that headline ended the longest-running news story in Canada since the end of World War II. In the final analysis the bad guys had been recognized for what they were, and I had accomplished what I had set out to do, with some regrets.

A cold rain was falling in lower town on the last-minute drugstore shoppers, the hollow-eyed drug addicts seeking a fix, and the ever-present lurching winos during my last Christmas Eve in Vancouver. There were still a few Santas on the glistening sidewalks, and my sixth sense told me to follow one whose red suit didn't seem quite right. He stumbled his way into an alley near the police station, where he tossed the traditional metal tripod into the darkness, along with the noisy bell. He then ripped the protective screen from the metal pot's contents and, by the fistful, stuffed his uniformed pockets with money. It was all so reminiscent of Chief Walter Hugh Mulligan.

TO THE EAST...
AND THE
MIDDLE EAST

I HAD ALWAYS, it seemed, used my flying skills to add a bit of excitement to my life and a bit of money to my bank account. Since quitting the *Province*, I had leaned more and more heavily on this means of income. In the spring of 1955, I had bought on credit a well-maintained Republic Seabee airplane, removed the heavy retractable undercarriage, and used it as a flying boat. For months I flew outdoorsmen into secret and forbidding places in northern British Columbia, the Yukon, and Alaska. Many of the pristine waters I kissed with the keel of my airplane had never before been touched by man. I was also involved in a number of rescue flights, but finally, in the winter of 1955–56, I had to admit that my dream of surviving in the cutthroat world of independent charter flying was not going to be. It was a hard reality to accept, but I knew it was time to move on to new endeavours in less restricting climes. With the wholehearted approval of my parents and the children, I sold the Seabee, bankrolled the family, and planned my return to Ontario.

As soon as I arrived in Toronto, I called Louis Ruby, publisher of *Flash Weekly*. We met for lunch at Winston's, and I refused an offer of $150 a week plus expenses to set up and run a duplicate of *Flash* in Montreal. It had gone against the grain for me to write for a non-newspaper such as *Flash*, but during the Vancouver police exposé I had done so anyway, for reasons of expediency. Howard Somerville, the hard-hitting editor who handled the Vancouver police probe stories, had left that job for the CBC news department, and Ruby was dickering with Joe Morgan of radio fame to take over the editor's chair. I suggested that he change *Flash* into a hard-hitting investigative weekly, and he promised to give it some thought.

Next, I met my old friend Ray Timson, with whom I had worked at the *Star* and the *Sun*, who was making another name for himself with the London *Free Press*. Timson explained that the *Free Press* was not my kind of newspaper; it was too wary of publishing contentious issues. He suggested I visit Thomson Newspapers in Toronto. I left him with the promise that when I had my own newspaper I'd offer him the job of running the news-room as managing editor.

My meeting with the two Thomson heavyweights, Brian Slaight and St. Clair McCabe, went well, although Roy Thomson's penurious streak was evident in their manners: not even a cup of coffee was offered during the almost two-hour meeting, which edged into lunch-hour. After we discussed my newspaper credentials and the Vancouver police affair, they asked if I would consider joining one of their daily newspapers in a southwestern Ontario community.

"It's a city of 35,000 people in a farming area, a few hours' drive from Toronto. There's no pressure, as there is on a big city daily," explained McCabe.

As soon as he mentioned that section of Ontario I mentally ran through the papers Thomson owned in the area: the Guelph *Mercury*, the Galt *Reporter*, and the Chatham *News*. Since the only city fitting all descriptions was Chatham, I asked two point-blank questions.

"Is it the Chatham *News*? And what would the position be?"

They were taken aback momentarily, then Slaight laughed and told me I had guessed correctly.

"We have a problem there we must resolve," Slaight explained. "When we bought the paper, we inherited the general manager as well as the editor, managing editor, and city editor. The editorial heads are all advanced in years and are holding back the progress of the paper, but for reasons beyond our control we can't remove them from the payroll."

They offered me the position of managing editor, but explained that for morale's sake I would have to start as a reporter and receive rapid promotions. They expected me to take over the editorial department almost immediately, and I could work at my own speed with the general manager's full consent.

I asked about salary, but was told it was up to the *News'* management. I admitted that, while their proposition gave me cause for consideration, income was my main concern. They promised me a starting salary of $125 a week, with raises for each position I advanced above that.

I caught the afternoon train to Chatham, where I was met by the paper's manager, J. Keith Stewart, who had been filled in by Slaight. Stewart had started with the paper as a youth under the previous owner, who had sold out to Thomson. I spent the night at Stewart's home, and listened to him describe the make-up of the paper and the litany of its problems until near dawn.

The next day I stepped into my new position as a reporter. After I looked over the antiquated composing-room equipment, an editorial office that would make a boiler room look decent, and a staff of seven reporters, one photographer, and three dispirited, elderly editors, I realized the enormity of the task lying ahead.

My first call in the city was on Clare Bagnall, chief of police. He already knew that I was the Ray Munro who tackled the Vancouver police force, and that I was starting at the *News* so I didn't waste any time setting him straight on my views.

"I'm here as a newspaperman. I do not like crooked cops, and I will do anything I can to see them go to jail. I trust I will have no reason at any time in the future to have another conversation with you, and would hope that I never have cause to investigate and report on any facet of your department for conduct detrimental to the public good." I left him on that note. (I must have done something right, because during my time with the paper no information came to my attention to discredit the force.)

That supposedly private meeting was the subject of immediate gossip among the reporters, who guessed my mission at the *News* was to revitalize the newspaper. Two of them made the mistake of inviting me to participate in a sexual orgy in the engraving department with three local belles that very night, which I declined with a laugh.

Within a week I had pin-pointed the problem areas that caused the *News* to be what it had always been, a small-town newspaper and never a responsible daily, and within a month I assumed the position of managing editor. The *News* had an aging and uncaring editorial management, amateur reporters, disgruntled composing-room personnel, and a crew of fast-buck advertising salesmen led by a huckster who was allowing advertisers into the composing room before press time to check over their ads. When I learned he was also telling would-be advertisers that he could get articles about them into the news columns, I wrote him a memo telling him that the practice would stop. That afternoon he charged into my office without knocking and demanded to know what my memo meant.

"First things first." I closed the door. "You will never enter my office without my inviting you, and you will never raise your voice to me. In answer to your question, I meant simply that you will never attempt by any means to place a story in the news columns of this paper."

"Who in the hell do you think you are, coming in here and turning this place upside-down?" He was apoplectic.

"I'm the fellow who is going to see that things are run properly around here from now on. If you want to give me an argument and think you're tough enough to take me, let's step out in the alley." I opened the door for him. He passed through it without accepting my offer.

The life-blood of any newspaper is its advertising revenue. The money made from the sale of the papers themselves only partly offsets the cost of the news gathering department. By publishing free stories about local business ventures, the *News* was losing money it should have been making from the sale of advertising space. The advertising manager was not the only one to complain, however, when I brought the practice to a halt.

My next complainant was the owner of the largest undertaking firm in town. He started out by being most friendly, then he asked me to continue placing stories of deaths and interments in the paper, using the name of his company and referring to him as a "funeral director." I pointed out that I was a simple man, who used simple words. The word *undertaker* was, I felt, the best one to describe his occupation. For his edification I opened the dictionary and read its meaning as "one whose business it is to prepare the dead for burial and to conduct funerals." He was very upset with my response and stormed down to see Stewart, whom he had known most of his life. Stewart, however, agreed with me, and from then on, save in advertisements, the term *funeral director* never appeared in the *News* again, during my time.

The following week, I was visited by a man who introduced himself as the new minister of a local church, just arrived in Chatham. He wanted the paper to write a feature article about his career so that his new parishioners would know of his background. From the moment he introduced himself I knew I had seen him before. By the time he had finished his pitch I had him identified.

"You were in the RCAF during the war in England," I stated.

"Why, yes, I was." He seemed startled.

I smiled. "You were the padre at the hospital, where I was treated for burns."

"Certainly. I remember. You too were in the air force."

"Well now," I stood up, "I knew I had a good look at you when you were lying on your back in the grove behind the hospital with that WAAF officer writhing about on top of you, but I wasn't sure you had seen me well enough as I passed to remember my face."

"Now see here," he bristled.

"No, you see here. What you did there is your business, but if you want your life's story in the *News*, that'll be part of it." I opened the door for him to leave.

My next move was to call Jim Kingsbury at the Toronto *Star*, and ask him for names of a few reporters with experience whom he would employ if he wasn't fully staffed. By nightfall, I had hired two of them over the telephone to start work the next day. I then fired on the spot the two staff members who had invited me to the midnight orgy. In turn, I called in each member of the editorial staff and learned something of his or her previous employment and present qualifications. To each I offered two weeks in which to perform like a professional or clear out.

The brightest reporter on staff was Ralph Hicklin, an alcoholic who honestly admitted he couldn't handle the problem, and had given up trying. Since he had a superlative command of the English language, having been schooled privately in England, it was to him that I entrusted the largest story the *News* had ever undertaken: a six-part history of Canada's Air Defence Command. Final permission for Hicklin to live with and be privy to all facets of the operation I gained from RCAF headquarters in Ottawa, and he gave himself to the task for a month, flying in all types of aircraft to the fringes of space and the top of the world. The result was a superb series, which all twenty-eight Thomson papers in Canada published, and which won, for Hicklin and the *News*, the National Newspaper Award of Canada. It was the first of twelve awards for writing and photography the paper would win in a two-year period. It was also the first award the paper won; in their previous history, they had never been awarded anything.

On my appointment to the position of editor-in-chief, which gave me the responsibility for the content of the editorial page as well as the news and feature columns of the paper, I offered Ray Timson the job of managing editor. I knew the possibility of gaining his expertise was slim, because he was considered the brightest news mind on the London *Free Press*, and I could not pay him the money to which his skills entitled him. He refused the offer with thanks, then made his way back to the Toronto *Star* (where he had started his career) as managing editor of that newspaper, the largest in Canada. In need of a city editor as well, I called Slaight for suggestions, and he offered me the services of a senior reporter with experience, from a Calgary newspaper. I listened to his resumé, then requested Slaight to hire him for me, sight unseen. His name was Peter Gzowski and he proved to be a sterling choice.

During this formative period, I was in close contact by telephone with my parents and children in North Vancouver, and I lived in a comfortable parlour room in a fine old home owned by an elderly widow, a family friend of the publisher. When I sensed that Stewart was satisfied with my handling of the newspaper, I approached him with a request that he confirm me as editor-in-chief. He agreed readily, and we shook hands on the deal, which included a three-year verbal contract.

I located a fine home in Blenheim, a smaller community a few miles away, with decent schools, clean air, and fields in which to roam. My parents sold our house and a month later arrived with the children, who settled in well to their new surroundings.

The only woman I had seen regularly while I lived in Vancouver was Thora Bock, who worked as secretary to Neil Fleishman, my lawyer during the first stages of the police probe. We had dated occasionally, and she had visited my home frequently enough to become somewhat of a big sister to the children. I had not expected to see her again after I left, but suddenly she surfaced in London, only a short drive from Chatham, where she was employed as private secretary to the publisher of the London *Free Press*. I drove to see her, and we had a pleasant reunion. Later she spent a day with me and the children at Blenheim. We continued to meet but the distances between our homes and the demands on my time limited the amount we saw of each other.

Finally, my new life seemed to be falling into place and settling down. I had a secure job and recognition for the work I was doing, a comfortable home for my family, and companionship. Assuming I could leave others in charge for a while, I jumped at the opportunity to cover the Arab-Israeli war in 1957, which had started the previous October and was still smouldering. My assignment was to act as military correspondent. I would visit the Middle East, Italy, England, and Iceland, and report on the problems currently besetting them for the *News* and Thomson's twenty-seven other Canadian newspapers.

Getting over the effect of the required innoculations gave me a day in Montreal with Larry Robillard. During this time we discussed entering into business together, he having quit his job as a Canadair test pilot. Then I boarded an RCAF North Star aircraft and flew to the Azores, thence to Gibraltar, where I tested the defence perimeter surrounding the RAF's bomber station, climbed without challenge into the belly of an unguarded and uncrewed Canberra jet bomber, and then wired a story to Canada about the lack of security on that front-line base. It was picked up by an international wire service and caused angry questions to be asked on the floor of the British House of Commons.

The hastily formed United Nations force charged with keeping the uneasy truce between Israel and Egypt was commanded by Canadian Major General E.L.M. Burns. His RCAF air armada was based at Naples' Capodichino Airport, and its personnel were housed in a third-rate downtown hotel. Their duties were to ferry any and all items required by UN forces throughout the demilitarized zone, and to transport personnel and observers to and from the troubled lines of demarcation.

The officers' mess bar in the hotel was the focal point of all non-flying activities. There, alcohol was consumed in great quantity, aviators' lies were added to, distorted, and distended, and all seventy-two verses of the RAF's infamous song were drunkenly rendered, commencing with "In ancient days there lived a root, of ill repute, a prostitute..." and ending with "... the Harlot of Jerusalem." And through that portal passed perhaps the finest transport aircrews in the world. Their flight diet consisted of meeting and defeating the worst vagaries of weather offered over the Mediterranean Sea, including deadly thunderstorms, hail-stones the size of baseballs, devilish sand clouds rising to stratospheric heights, desert brown-outs that erased all view of landing strips, and the ever-present possibility of attack from fighter aircraft of both antagonists, or a third intrusive power.

My schedule called for immediate departure from Naples to Abu Suweir in Egypt as a passenger with General Burns aboard his DC-3 aircraft. However, an oversight by the duty officer, who failed to advise me that the flight had been rescheduled for departure three hours earlier, meant I had to board a C-119 Flying Boxcar, which was transporting a huge generator to my initial destination. I had just squeezed between two crates and readied myself for take-off when it was determined that the plane was overloaded, so I was bounced until room could be found aboard another aircraft, later in the week.

Already behind schedule, I boarded a civilian cargo plane headed for Athens on a flight that took us through a hail-storm that put fist-sized dents in the nose and wings. I saw the Acropolis and Parthenon by moonlight, then talked my way aboard an El Al flight to Tel Aviv. It was crammed with Jews from Europe going to their homeland.

Upon arrival in Israel, I learned that the general's plane had been forced back by weather, and that my C-119 had crashed on the island of Crete. My next story described the UN's overtaxed airplanes, resurrected from graveyards and reconditioned with cannibalized parts, that were forced to fly in dangerous skies where sudden death awaited any craft and crew found off their approved course or in the air after nightfall.

Over the next few weeks, I travelled by army vehicle, military aircraft, donkey cart, and on foot across the length and breadth of that fabled land, from Nahariya in the north to Elath on the Gulf of Aqaba. I passed unnamed battlegrounds marked only by twisted steel shapes and border kibbutzim by the dozen, infiltrated by marauders at night and assaulted by rockets during daylight hours. Small children carried machine-guns as they watched over their flocks of sheep. I cradled one doll-like form of brutalized flesh until she fell silent forever; a mine had exploded beneath her baby feet.

Each facet of war and the incessant training to kill were recorded in my photographs, and in the simple paragraphs I wrote to describe the torment in the land God gave to Cain, where lives were measured not by calendar years, but by the rising and setting of the sun on a time gone mad.

The border police and I established a rapport, and they permitted me to join their night patrols. On one sortie they killed four intruding saboteurs, an action I wrote about at length.

My first request to the commandant of the Israeli army's parachute school to jump with the soldiers on a night exercise was refused, as were my second and my third. Finally, Major Daniel Man permitted me to exit an aircraft at low level above the invisible sand, which I smashed into with stunning force. I fired the prototype of the world-famous Uzi sub-machine-gun, drove a tank, eased myself into the cockpit of a battle-weary Spitfire at the Tel Aviv airport, and was captured by camel Bedouins in the Negev Desert.

In Beersheba I met two escapees from the French Foreign Legion, whom I hired to lead me though the minefield surrounding the Gaza Strip. I wanted to go to Egypt, but I could not enter the country legally. The Israel admittance stamp in my passport ruled out any chance of gaining a visa, and the heavily patrolled UN line stood between me and my target. We began in the bitterly cold hours shortly after midnight on the rim of the Negev Desert near the village of Abasan. I followed one step behind one of the ex-legionnaires. He had joined the Foreign Legion to forget a lost love, then fled the military life after three years of torturous training, drunkenness, and lack of contact with an enemy he had hoped would kill him. On our bellies we passed close enough to a UN tent to hear the sounds of the soldiers' snores, then crossed back again past the frost-covered bushes and icy rocks to the wadi, where the second man waited.

But he was not alone. He sat on the sand surrounded by eight darkly garbed Bedouins, each carrying a bolt-action rifle and all heavily bandoleered. They searched me and my guide and took all our possessions, finding even the thin plastic envelope containing several photos and my writing papers that I had carried inside my undershirt. For two hours, we walked silently in single file beneath white stars and a thin moon to a gathering of black tents outlined against the lighter sky. A fire sent our shadows dancing on the sand and hot fingers of pleasure onto my shivering skin. For a moment I feared the shaking of my freezing body was the beginning of malaria, but when the palsy subsided as my marrow warmed, I eased into a dreamless sleep.

He was standing over me when I awoke, just as false dawn broke. He looked like the awesome genie that filled the sky above Aladdin's head in the picture-books, except he carried a large silver-sheathed dagger and Mauser machine pistol hanging from a wide leather belt. He turned to my legionnaire guide and asked a question in Arabic. I rose quickly.

"Of what nation is this man?"

"Of Canada, next to the United States," my guide answered.

"I well know its place, and must know why he is here."

After receiving a translation of the exchange, I explained very slowly my assignment in Israel and the reason for my venture through the minefield with the deserters, whom I did not describe as such. While he spoke no English in my presence, I felt the Bedouin understood a few words.

"He wants to know who is in the pictures." My guide pointed to the papers our captor held. They were my papers, the ones I had carried in the plastic envelope.

"I don't want to upset him, but I would like to know to whom I am speaking," I replied.

"To Sheikh Suleiman al Huzeil, lord and master of some thousand Bedouins camped hereabouts, and whose territory you passed through without his authority," he explained.

"The children in the pictures are mine, and the wom—" Before I could finish, the sheikh shoved the 8 × 10-inch glossy in front of my face.

"Marryleen?" he asked.

I had almost forgotten it was there. I had taken it to Montreal to show Robillard. It was a picture of Marilyn Monroe and me together as we entered the dining room of the Hotel Vancouver.

"Sure is," I explained to my guide. "That's Marilyn and me."

"He wants to know if you fucked her." The ex-legionnaire moistened his lips, awaiting the answer.

I was so startled by the crudeness of the question that I spoke without thinking. "That is a question only she should answer," I responded icily.

As soon as my comment had been translated for him, the sheikh put his huge hands on his hips, bent his torso backwards, and awakened sleeping camels with a violent and prolonged laugh that ended in a deep and gurgling cough.

"But he can have that picture if he wants it," I said quickly, hoping to improve his good humour even more.

We got along famously after that. I told him about the movie stars I had flown, and promised I'd take some pictures of him. He wanted me to send him copies and also to send one each to Marilyn and Eleanor Roosevelt. I told him the kidnapping story, after he had explained he wanted Marilyn for her body and Eleanor for her mind. Several years later I saw his face filling the cover of *Time* magazine. Inside, I read of his nomadic life, his predilection for naked blondes, and his offer of marriage to Mrs. Roosevelt.

By nightfall the legionnaires and I were back in Beersheba. I found a bootlegging joint near the camel market, where I propped a chair against a wall and drank myself into a state of mild intoxication. With my body relaxed and my mind set upon savouring the sights and sounds of the lost hell-hole, the like of which I had seen before only in movies, I shouted to the bartender, a friendly, bearded Jew who had cared well for my thirst, "Harry, you're a jewel, a goddamn jewel."

I guessed later that my slurred speech had come across as "Harry, you're a Jew, a goddamn Jew," to the squat man leaning against the makeshift bar who could have doubled for the movie actor Akim Tamiroff. He swung in my direction and at the same time hurled a bottle from a ham-like fist. It caught the forehead of a most unpleasant person sitting at the table next to me. "Goddamn Jew, eh?" Akim snarled as he ploughed into his bleeding target.

A stop-watch would have counted off less than sixty seconds before everyone except me was whaling away at each other with fists, feet, and hard objects. When I saw a knife held blade upwards in Akim's right hand, and watched him stalk, in a crouch, another man who was holding a broken bottle, I knew it was time to make an exit. In seven giant strides I was out the back door and over an eight-foot wall, through a morass of camel dung, and onto a side-street. From there I hired a car to drive me to Jerusalem, where I reclaimed my suitcase in the King David Hotel and bedded down for an around-the-clock sleep.

CLOSE CALLS

MY MONTH in the Middle East had ended. I caught a flight back to
Naples and spent a weekend on the island of Ischia lying in the sun.
I planned to fly back to Canada by way of Rome, and RCAF bases in
France and Germany, but at the UN headquarters in Naples a cable
from the *News* awaited me, saying that Keith Stewart, the general
manager, had suffered a heart attack. He was in bad shape in hospital, and my presence was required immediately. Two days later I
was back in Chatham.

It took me only one meeting to form an intense dislike for Stewart's replacement. A preening, vapid man, he had been assigned to
act as general manager until more was known about the long-term
effects of Stewart's stroke. His career in the newspaper business had
been confined to junior management of departments other than a
news-room. His idea of collecting and disseminating news seemed
to be to print anything that came over the Teletype, gather recipes
by the hundreds, and present it all in an advertising-laden special
section, for the prime purpose of increasing revenue at the expense
of reduced news coverage.

Stewart soon began recovering from his stroke, but his doctors
doubted that he would ever return to his desk. The prospect of
being saddled with the new and incompetent general manager
loomed like a black cloud over my staff, who were cheered only by
the militant stand I took against his numerous and continual efforts
to impose his will upon me.

No attempt had ever been made by the powerful International
Typographical Union to bind together the compositors and press-
men at the *News*, nor had any foray been made into the news-room
by the American Newspaper Guild. That was the greatest fear of the
Thomson group, that their employees would unionize and they

would lose control of their payroll to an alien presence. It was to forestall those eventualities that the now-confirmed general manager addressed himself.

He summoned me by telephone while I was in conference. He told me to report to him immediately, but I ignored his request. When I finally entered his office he upbraided me for not appearing when ordered.

"I'm too goddamn busy to listen to your usual nonsense," I said. "If you want to talk to me in future, come to my office when I'm not busy."

"You'll wait right here until I'm finished with you, because what I have to say concerns the handling of your department. There's a move afoot to unionize the reporters. I've learned that material is being mailed to them at this newspaper." The veins were standing out on his temples.

"I have no idea what you're talking about," I told him truthfully.

"Well, I am ordering you to open all mail addressed to newsroom employees at this address. Bring me anything related to union matters."

I shoved a forefinger under his nose. "Wait right there," I said, then returned to my office, where I grabbed my copy of Canada's Criminal Code and thumbed through it to the section covering the laws against tampering with the mail. I slammed back into his domain and shoved the opened book in front of his face, pointing to the significant paragraph.

"What you have just ordered me to do contravenes a federal law. You are an idiot, an incompetent fool, and a disgrace to newspapering." I tore the volume from his grasp.

"You're fired," he shouted.

I forced myself to leave before I rammed my fist past his yellow-stained teeth.

"Put it in writing," I shouted over my shoulder.

I had some more arguments with other people in the organization. Then without explanation to anyone I cleared out my desk, and drove to see my lawyer. I told him the facts and asked him to take immediate action to recover all monies owing to me from my contractual salary, profit sharing, and whatever else was honourably mine, and not to call me until Thomson, McCabe, and Slaight had either paid, or been sued. Eventually I sued, went to court, and won.

Lou Ruby of *Flash Weekly* learned I had left the *News*, and invited me to Toronto, where he explained his plan to reshape his paper into a hard-hitting investigative journal of quality within a six-month period. He offered me the editorship and twice the salary I made at the *News*, for a four-day week. I would have a six-man staff and Joe Morgan as a feature writer.

It was an offer I could not refuse. So for six months I spent each three-day weekend in Blenheim with my family, then returned to Toronto, where I bedded down in a hotel on week nights. But our best efforts to transform the paper were unsuccessful, and I eventually parted company with *Flash* on an amicable basis, and the paper went back to being the *National Enquirer* of its day.

I dropped a note to Robillard, letting him know I was a free agent again, and he responded with a prepaid airline ticket to Montreal and a request that I join him for a serious discussion about our business futures.

He met me at Dorval airport and drove us, in a limousine borrowed from one of his wealthy friends just for the occasion, to the Queen Elizabeth Hotel, where he ushered me into a fine room. We relaxed over drinks while he updated me on his adventures since last we met in his Westmount penthouse, where I had stopped over en route to the Middle East.

How, I asked him, did he pay for this luxurious life-style.

"I'm running on nerve, in a sense," he replied. "I had a falling out with my dear wife some months ago, and moved to this inn. I am employed by Morgan and Company, stockbrokers, as a securities salesman, and service a lengthy list of stock-buying clients. I have just learned today, from a private source, that tomorrow Diefenbaker is going to announce the continuation of the Avro Arrow programme. All evening I've been busy making arrangements to purchase, at the market's opening, a large block of shares in that company. And speaking of gambling situations, what do you know about Cuba?" he asked.

"It is mountainous and exports raw sugar. Until Castro ran out Corporal Batista it had a zillion whore-houses and gambling joints. And it is teetering on the rim of bankruptcy," I responded.

"Correct. But did you know that Batista, who is now a paying guest of dictator Trujillo in the Dominican Republic, is planning to mount a major offensive to wrest control from Castro?"

"I assumed as much, but what I suspect Batista has not got—and which he must have to mount a responsible assault—is a number of fast, weaponed aircraft."

"That's where we come in, you and I." He winked. "Because we are going to involve ourselves in that little venture."

"Count me out," I responded. "I have a good relationship with the Mounties, and a slim file that says nothing but great things about me. I have no intention of messing around in another country's war, not even from a distance."

"Neither have I. But I'm meeting a friend for lunch who has been involved with Castro since before the revolution."

Lunch was served in the room, so Larry's friend would not be seen with us. He was Andy McNaughton, son of the late General A.G.L. McNaughton, who led the First Canadian Army division overseas in World War II, and who, had he been alive, would have died of shame. McNaughton had made a deal with Castro during the planning stages of the revolution in the Sierra Maestra. In return for a commission on each delivery, McNaughton had become the sole purchaser of arms for Castro. The drawback was that McNaughton did not have the huge sums of money required, nor had Castro. A plan was therefore worked out, whereby McNaughton, who had code-named himself Esquimalt, would travel the world seeking out arms merchants. The deal he had offered them was that for the delivery of weapons and ammunition to Castro they would be paid double as soon as he took power. In this manner, McNaughton had got Castro his arms, and Cuba had been liberated. Then the arms dealers came after Esquimalt for their money.

All had been going well. Final negotiated payments, out of which McNaughton would receive his commission, were readied for transmission from Cuba to assorted Swiss bank accounts. Then a sudden hold was placed on the pay-off.

"Some son of a bitch in Wisconsin bought a whole squadron of Vampire jet fighter aircraft from the War Assets Corporation in Ottawa. They had lifted them from squadrons that Richard Rohmer formerly commanded. The U.S. buyer has been given an export permit, which takes effect in three days' time." He drummed his fingers nervously.

"So what?" Larry asked.

"They're going to be trans-shipped to Batista in the Dominican Republic. He will use them to attack Cuba, that's what! And I have been advised, in plain English, that if they leave Canada I will not receive the money owing to me." He hammered the table.

"What," I enquired, "do you want of us?"

"I can't be identified in any manner with this operation. But if you can somehow block that permit, and stop those planes from leaving Canada, it would be worth money to me."

I explained to him that, while it could probably be done in time, speaking for myself, I would want some up-front money. He made us an offer. He would escrow $3,500 immediately with the Merchant's Bank around the corner. If the government rescinded the export permit, he said, Larry and I could pick up and share the money as we chose.

"Ten thousand," said Larry.

"No," responded McNaughton, "that's all I've got. And most of the money I'll get from Cuba is already spent on a deal in Lebanon, a sure cure for cancer I've been working on at the University of Beirut for several years. But I'll give you some cash money today to cover your possible expenses to and from Ottawa."

"Ten thousand," repeated Larry.

"No, $3,500 escrowed and $500 cash now," concluded McNaughton, as he arose to leave.

"Okay with you?" Larry asked me.

I nodded.

"If that's all you can come up with, then add to it a telephone call," I said. "I want you to call whomever it is you report to in the Cuban government and tell them that Larry and I are the ones who are caring for the matter," I added.

He accepted the proposition, and within minutes was speaking to a Teresa Casuso at the Cuban Embassy in New York City. Larry listened in on the extension telephone, and heard McNaughton identify himself as Esquimalt and mention that the Ottawa matter was in the hands of two trusted friends, whose names he spelled out as J.G.L. Robillard and R.A. Munro, giving our hotel address.

"I'll be in touch frequently by radiophone from my car. I have to leave now for a skiing date in Vermont." He walked with us to the bank, where the proper arrangements were made: the money held in escrow would be ours if, within two days, any major Canadian daily newspaper reported that the export permit had been killed.

Logically, the best way to have the permit cancelled was to get a member of Parliament to question the Conservatives about the matter. Prime Minister John Diefenbaker was four-square against any death-dealing machinery of any description being delivered to any destination that did not fly the Union Jack. To have an M.P. question the P.M. on the floor of the House might do the trick, but we needed immediate action. I suggested that we utilize the services of a radio reporter with whom I had worked in Vancouver. I called him, explained the situation, and asked him to return a favour he owed me. He agreed to help and passed the word on to a Liberal M.P., who somehow arranged to raise the issue in the House the following day.

The morning edition of the *Globe and Mail* carried a page-one story about the summary cancellation of the Vampire shipment permit in their late-night edition. Larry and I were elated, although he was less pleased when he read that Diefenbaker had summarily cancelled the Arrow programme.

We got the money from the bank, squared away the massive hotel bill, and telegraphed $500 each to our respective homes. Then Larry borrowed an aircraft from a friend, and we took off late that night for a dawn rendezvous with an executive of Republic Aircraft at a private airport named Deer Park, on Long Island, New York.

After we cleared customs at Burlington, Vermont, the weather soured and forced us to seek a low-level approach to the area, with me chart-reading and Larry flying. I had my finger on Deer Park's identity symbol and kept shoving it in front of Larry's eyes, until finally he pushed it aside.

"There it is, just ahead to the left." He pointed into the enveloping black mists, through which I could see only the occasional dim light. "I'm going to cut around and dump this beast in. Our only other choice is to fly to Newark and get a radar approach, and this plane is not equipped for an instrument landing."

"Go for it," I agreed.

He did, pulling a tight spiral to within 100 feet of the black earth, then kicking the nose high in a vicious side-slip that allowed me to see, out his window, two short rows of lights set very close together. Suddenly we were down, with one hard bounce followed by another. Larry reined the projectile to a halt underneath the last two lights, which from the air we had assumed were set at ground level alongside a runway. They were not. Through the striations of mist we could see they were streetlights. We had landed not at Deer Park Airport, which proved to be seven miles to our east, nor at any other airport, but on a narrow, partially developed street in a new housing subdivision.

We tried three homes before we located one with a telephone, and called our Republic man, who sent a company car to drive us to New York City for the night. He also promised to explain our landing to the local police and the FAA.

At dawn the next day, with most of the embryo community's residents watching from the grass verge of the street, Larry hauled the plane into the air. Six minutes later we landed again, at Deer Park Airport, where we left the plane while we spent three days in New York trying unsuccessfully to conclude a deal between Republic and Canadair for a batch of jet aircraft drag parachutes.

Back in Montreal we moved into the Queen Elizabeth Hotel again and, owing to our dwindling finances, charged everything possible to the room. From a fine haberdasher in the lobby we fleshed out our wardrobes, through the florist we telegraphed bouquets to our families, and at the Beaver Club we took our meals, putting all purchases on our tab. That week our old squadron leader Stan Turner, now a group captain, arrived to take command of the RCAF station at Lachine, and we celebrated his arrival by wining and dining him and his wife.

By the time the account reached $2,000, the fussy assistant manager began pestering us for payment. Therefore, when Castro's New York-based lieutenant, Teresa Casuso, called to thank us for staving off Batista's attack on Cuba and to offer me a job, I accepted with alacrity. The position was as public-relations and press representative for Castro's visit to Montreal in four days' time. I would receive an advance of $500 to set the wheels in motion, plus another $500 from Cuban Consul Flores Solis in Ottawa when I signed my accreditation papers.

That day I drove to Ottawa, and by nightfall I was back in Montreal with the accreditation documents and the funds. We paid $500 towards our hotel bill and telegraphed $200 to our homes, then began planning the operation.

The next morning, I was reading a *Globe and Mail* story about my appointment when a telephone call came that signalled the second most important event in Cuba's history.

"Ray Munro?"

"Yes."

"What was the name of the owner of the hardware store in White Rock, British Columbia?"

"Earl Barge," I answered, startled by the question, but guessing that someone wanted confirmation that I was who I said I was. He was obviously satisfied with my answer.

"This is the Mountie you swam with," he went on, "and we'll mention no names. I am now at a more senior level in Ottawa, and know that the wisest course you could follow—and I suggest you do it today—would be to return the accreditation you received yesterday and resign publicly from the position. Trust me, and good luck." He terminated the call.

I immediately awakened Larry. He agreed that I should heed the strange advice, and we drove to Ottawa. I first had my documents photographed, then returned them to the Cuban consul with the explanation that I had to leave the country immediately and could not handle the assignment. Solis asked for the $1,000 back. I replied that I didn't have the money and explained that it would be accounted for in due course.

I then telephoned several reporters of my acquaintance in the Press Gallery and informed them of my resignation. The story was published, coincident with a release from Cuba that Castro's visit had been called off.

At noon two days later, the world learned of Cuba's military alliance with Russia. No demand was ever made on me for return of the funds, which Larry and I felt we had earned for the Vampire operation. McNaughton could not be located, even by Ottawa's security section. By chance, I later learned he was in Lebanon, setting the wheels in motion to distribute to the world what would become the most argued about, damned, and thoroughly disproven so-called cure for cancer ever known—Laetrile.

STOCK MARKETS
AND PARACHUTES

IT WAS three weeks since I had seen my family. Because Larry Robillard had not seen them for ten years, we borrowed an airplane and flew the 500 miles to Blenheim and stayed several days, then returned to Montreal.

Larry tried his key in the lock of our hotel-room door without success, before taking it to the front desk with a request for a replacement. We were ushered into the assistant manager's presence.

"I've secured your room until you pay your account, which now stands at $1,728.64, including today's rental. We will reopen it for you only on payment for the account," he intoned icily.

"Here is a cheque for the entire amount," Larry offered in a superior tone.

"The only cheque I will accept must be certified, unless, of course, you agree that the room may remain locked until the cheque clears our bank." His rejection was firm.

"I have some items inside that I need immediately," I explained.

But he was insistent. All our possessions were to be boxed and stored until the account was settled.

Over coffee, we agreed to share between us the hundred-odd dollars of our bankroll. I would lodge myself in the local YMCA, while Larry went to his home town of Ottawa to settle some personal matters.

Next morning I awakened in an ancient room that smelled of stale clothes and chlorine from the swimming pools only a floor below. A spring snowstorm had just begun, and pedestrians leaned into the cold wind that drove my spirits even lower.

My finances totalled $48 when I slipped into my only suit for a coffee downstairs. I then enjoyed a hot shower, and returned to my room to find the door had been forced open and my trench coat stolen. In a determined effort to slough off the trapped feeling that started crowding me, I walked briskly to the park near the Sun Life building, where I brushed the wet snow from a bench and sat down to ponder my next move.

I knew from experience that it was in adversity that I became best acquainted with myself. First, I knew, I needed to care for my creature needs: food, warmth, and shelter. To do that, I required immediate and gainful employment. The first step, therefore, was to acquire a proper physical presence.

The Mount Royal Hotel answered all my needs. I purchased underclothes, a shirt, socks, and a hand-rolled silk breast-pocket kerchief, into which I changed in the wash-room. While I was shaved and trimmed in the barber's chair, I enjoyed a manicure and counted the cadence of the bootblack's canvas as he brought a mirror-like finish to my shoes. Over lunch in the Hunt Room, I finalized my plan for immediate employment. My target was Edouard DesRosiers, owner of a small stockbroking company bearing his name, who was about to promote, among other more secure ventures, stock in a company called Copperstream Mines, whose mining engineer, Gordon Forbes, I had met with Robillard several days earlier. Forbes had told us about a major copper discovery in the Mattagami area of Quebec. The claims were owned by DesRosiers, who was going to start selling shares to finance a major drilling programme to ascertain the extent and value of the find.

My plan was simple. I drew up a list of persons I knew of financial substance and committed them to memory. I then assured myself by telephone of my target's presence in his office and hailed a taxi to the financial district. His building adjoined a fashionable men's apparel store, whose single window displayed a male mannequin wearing a striped tie that fairly screamed sincerity. I bought it, leaving the small change from my last $11 on the counter, along with my discarded tie. Penniless, I strode purposefully past Des-Rosiers's greying secretary, pausing only to mention that her beauty made my heart beat faster, rapped lightly on his oaken door, and stepped into his presence. I introduced myself, shook hands, seated myself, and explained my reason for calling.

"It has come to my attention that fortune has smiled upon you in the form of a most salubrious mineral discovery now owned by Copperstream Mines. I understand that you are now seeking funds for immediate exploration work."

"I'm surprised at your knowledge of my affairs." He smiled. "I would appreciate knowing your source."

"It would be improper for me to admit my informant's name at this moment, except to tell you that he is a respected name in the industry," I responded. "But my purpose in mentioning the copper find to you is, first, to get an absolutely correct reading on the price of Copperstream stock at this moment, to ensure myself that the bid is solid and that control of the stock is wholly in your hands."

He assured me of his command position of the company, then dialled a number and passed the receiver to me. When I heard a male voice say, "McCuaig and Company," I knew I was connected to a major brokerage house. I asked for a market on Copperstream. "Wait one minute, please," came the response, followed almost immediately by the statement that it was offered at thirty cents with twenty-five bid.

"Twenty-five, thirty," I reported. "Now, here's my proposition. I must, due to circumstances I will not discuss, recoup immediately a modest sum. To do this, I am prepared to cause to be purchased from your holdings of Copperstream, within the hour, at twenty-eight cents, an amount of stock equal in commission to the funds I require. In return, I ask a commission of 20 per cent, paid to me as soon as you receive confirmation."

"To your friends, over this telephone, through their own brokers?" He stood up.

"Certainly," I responded, rising from my chair.

"I will give you three cents a share." He pointed to the telephone and walked around the desk to look closer at my tie. "University or military?"

"Cambridge." I used the name of the store from which I purchased it, and over the intercom I asked the secretary to get me Dr. Smirle Lawson at the coroner's office in Toronto. Then he passed me the receiver.

I could hear the operator asking the Lombard Street building's switchboard for Dr. Lawson, and suddenly he was on the line.

"Smirle, it's Ray Munro. I'm calling from Montreal." We chatted for a moment, then I told him my reason for calling.

"I am well acquainted with a senior mining engineer, who has just now returned from examining a property near Mattagami that he claims is pregnant with high-grade copper ore. I have already purchased a few shares. Because I know you are interested in the penny market, I thought you'd like to know," I said.

"What's the name and the price," he asked excitedly.

"Copperstream Mines, and I paid twenty-eight cents," I answered, adding hastily that he could check with his own broker and buy it from him through the over-the-counter section of the Canadian Stock Exchange.

"Thanks, Ray, and come in to see me when you get back." He rang off.

"Mr. DesRosiers." I turned to him. "Within a few minutes, you will be able to find out what size of a buy order Dr. Lawson has placed. Please understand that I would not like to find a discrepancy in the figures."

He smiled, and pointed to a framed photograph of himself and Quebec Premier Jean Lesage on the wall.

"Mr. Munro, that is the circle in which I travel."

"I saw the picture, and that's why I asked the question," I responded easily. After that we talked about the slumping newspaper business in Montreal, and his recollection of the Vancouver police probe. Then he took a phone call, during which he raised his eyebrows at me while jotting down some figures. After giving instructions to the caller he looked at me strangely.

"I have just sold, to A.E. Ames and Company of Toronto, 10,000 shares at twenty-eight cents," he marvelled.

"That's $300, Mr. DesRosiers, if you will be so kind. And I would prefer the money now, as I have another appointment." I stood up to leave.

"Would you consider employment with me?" he asked, writing the cheque.

"We'll speak of that tomorrow." I shook hands with him, folded the cheque, and walked out into a gentle snowfall. I hailed a taxi to take me first to his bank and wait while I cashed the cheque, then to the train station, where I wired $100 to Blenheim, and lastly to the Ritz-Carlton Hotel, where I took a room. At the Marine Bar I revelled in my good fortune.

"Nice tie," the bartender smiled.

"Yes," I agreed, "it sure is."

I started work the next day for DesRosiers as a salesman after giving the Quebec Securities Commission five dollars, along with a simple personal-history form co-signed by my new employer. Without even a telephoned background check I received a licence to sell stock. Out of the seventeen persons of my acquaintance I telephoned urging them to buy Copperstream, fourteen acted on the suggestion, and over a period of two weeks collectively purchased 115,000 shares at prices ranging from twenty-eight to thirty-four cents, earning me $5,347. (I had agreed to work for DesRosiers only if I received a 15 per cent commission.) I eventually learned he'd bought the stock from Copperstream's treasury at ten cents, while I had sold it at an average of thirty-one. After paying my commission he had quite legally put the difference in his pocket, although he had originally told me that all the monies raised were going into development work on the property.

I moved out of the YMCA and rented a furnished bachelor apartment by the week. When Robillard came back from Ottawa with some capital, we paid off the delinquent hotel bill, only to find that much of our clothing was missing from the storage room. When I learned that I couldn't sue the hotel for negligence, I embarked on a three-year degree course in law, which I eventually completed successfully.

In September 1959, after five months in Montreal, during which time I had made repeated trips to Blenheim, I arranged to meet Thora in Montreal, where I proposed marriage and she accepted. In October, we were wed. She and the children moved to Montreal, where I had rented a spacious apartment, and we started a new life.

The price of Copperstream was going up and down like a yo-yo. Then a vice-president of McCuaig and Company broke the unwritten rule against hiring an employee away from another brokerage firm. He offered me a job with a $500 monthly draw and a ready-made clientele, comprised of new accounts and some diverted from other salesmen. I accepted the offer, and my first act was to catch Copperstream on a rise and sell out all my clients' shares. Smirle Lawson's original investment of $2,800 returned him a profit of $1,100 in five weeks. All my other customers acted as wisely, and with their near-unanimous agreement I plunged their profits into a sleeper called Bunker Hill Mines. A bush pilot of my acquaintance had tipped me off to the fact that some extremely high-grade mineralization had been found on that company's northern property. I bought them in at ten cents a share, and within days the stock leaped into the eighty-cent range, at which point I sold them out. It continued trading to one dollar before it fell back to the twenty-cent level. My clients had made enormous profits, and many took my suggestion of converting their windfalls into CPR common stock.

To ease the tension of my stress-filled life, I decided to take up parachuting. I bought a complete set of equipment, and hired an airplane with a pilot to take me up seventeen times one weekend. Each time I jumped. Within a year I earned the highest-world-class professional licence. I subsequently operated my own parachuting firm, assisted in the design of a military operation, captained a United States Air Force parachute team, and received undeserved credit for saving the lives of three persons when our aircraft's engine exploded only 300 feet above a forest.

I also once lost control during a jump, and slammed through a canvas-covered garden swing on which were seated two octogenarians. I bounced off the swing onto a table set with their afternoon tea, and caromed from there through a greenhouse. When I struggled free of the entangling parachute lines and noticed great gobs of red oozing from my neck, I ran into the house for help, until I learned with relief it was plum jam.

In 1962, I also began to teach parachuting. My first student was Ivan Christopher, a mining engineer. He had completed his ground and theoretical practice during the filming of my school for CTV. But at 2,800 feet, after climbing out of the plane and holding onto the wing strut, he refused to let go, causing the aircraft to list to the right and the pilot to consider an emergency landing. I solved the problem by jumping out the open doorway and grabbing him around the waist as I passed. I pulled him away from the strut, when his parachute opened automatically, before kicking myself away and activating my own parachute just before I slammed into a forest. He thought it was great sport and wanted to go up again, along with the cameraman, who was also awaiting his first jump.

I enjoyed having company during the long preparation for my jumps, and once asked Alphonse House, the new manager at my bank, to join me. He was fresh from Newfoundland, where he and his friends used to play poker in the vault on Friday evenings. Until his family arrived to join him, House lived in the Mount Royal Hotel. He accepted my invitation to drive with me on a Sunday morning to Swanton, where I was to make a free fall from 15,000 feet, to a rip-cord pull at 1,000, allowing the parachute to fully inflate at about 500 feet. It was part of the experiments Major André Coté of the Canadian Army and I were completing for our High Altitude Low Opening project. I had the plane's right seat removed, and told House to sit on the floor facing the rear, alongside the opening. I sat on the back seat and at jump altitude merely fell past him and out of the plane, activating a white smoke bomb that would track my descent to the ground.

House admitted afterwards that it had been the most exciting moment of his life. Some time later, I had reason to hope that he remembered that excitement when I asked him—or rather his bank—to loan me $40,000 to buy a new airplane for my next endeavour—northern bush flying.

RESCUE

FROM 40,000 FEET the pilot of the B-52 bomber could see the lazy curvature of the whitened earth, bold against the slate blue sky. As he flew northward, he saw Great Slave Lake to his left, then the Peacock Hills, the jagged rim of the North Polar Sea, and the western shore of northern Hudson Bay, where it marries the striated shoreline of Chesterfield Inlet.

Yet all the pulsing, intricately miniatured devices surrounding him could not detect the terrible need of three fellow humans directly beneath him. He might have seen a brief and tiny wink of light on his parabolic approach over the downed plane, but this faint flicker was indistinguishable from the myriad points of cold polar sunlight reflecting back from ice-covered rocks and giant crystals of fractured ice.

Eight miles below him, give or take the distance a shout could carry in still air, a portly man stumbled and fell forwards into the deep snow, his arms tracing angel wings in uncontrolled rage.

Past where his tracks ended on the shoreline of the pot-hole-sized lake, the pilot of the broken plane shook his head back and forth. His discouragement bordered on hatred for all mankind as he slipped the metal signalling mirror back into his shirt pocket and kicked the metal belly of the canted aircraft. The woman, swathed in a stained canvas engine cover and slumped over against the biting cold behind a screen of chopped undergrowth, stared ahead dully through ornately shaped sun-glasses.

The southern senator pushed himself to his knees from where he'd expended his rage. He stared angrily at the woman, and wondered what he'd seen in her that had brought on such a terrible sweetness whenever he touched her. He had never before known such desire. They'd met three nights before in his hotel bar in Yellowknife. He'd been scheduled to leave for home in a few hours, and she'd been planning to fly to Baker Lake in the morning, then directly on to a nursing job in Uranium City. They had spent the night together, and awoke to find that her scheduled flight had already left. He'd chartered a bush airplane to fly them both to Baker Lake, then on to Uranium City. That would give them two more nights together before he caught the twice-weekly flight to Edmonton, the first leg of his journey back to Tennessee.

The pilot was paying too much attention to the goings-on in the back seat and not enough to his task of monitoring the flight when the ice-plugged oil breather tube on the engine over-pressurized the system and blew the dip-stick out of its sheath. Within seconds, the slip-stream had blown hot oil along the underside of the engine cowling and back to the windscreen, where it flowed upwards with the wind to obscure the view.

He could have landed without damage, located and repaired the problem, and been on his way within the hour if the plane's left ski hadn't caught a snow-covered shoreline rock and bent double, then sideways.

They were down on what a northerner would call a frozen pond. The pilot had not filed a flight plan, because his airplane's licence had expired, and this bootleg trip was to pay for the needed inspection. No one knew they were missing. No one knew of their plight.

On the morning of the third day of their ordeal, I was 150 miles north of their position, awaiting a Beaver bush plane from Yellowknife that was already two hours late. The cook was fussing over the icing on two dozen cup-cakes, while chaffing silently at the rude suggestions hollered at him by the four-man drilling crew and the college-kid engineer. He finally stamped a foot on the plywood floor, shouted a now-familiar "You *men* you," and huffed off to his own tent to freshen up his talcumed face and regain his composure.

I shifted the kerosene lamp to read again the agreement that had brought me into this forsaken land, double-checking the typewritten facts against a terrible craving to leave for civilization and Christmas among crowds. It was tightly written:

During November and December 1968, a preliminary exploration programme will be carried on in the Ellice River area of the North-west Territories. The approximate location of the claims group is 65 degrees North Latitude and 104 degrees West Longitude in the Mackenzie Mining District.

The property consists of 40 claims which are contiguous and comprise approximately 2,000 acres, said property to be traversed by a Cessna 180 aircraft carrying a spectrometer to detect and measure uranium plus thorium radioactivity. Traverse lines will be in an east-west direction at quarter-mile intervals, to be flown at a height above ground of 150 feet, plus or minus 25 feet, and following the contours of the terrain.

Control will be maintained by checking against aerial photographs and ground markings. The results will be recorded by instrument, and fiducials will be marked manually. Results of the survey will provide exploration targets to be investigated on the ground with packsack diamond drilling by field personnel.

The agreement went on to describe the location (380 miles northeast of Yellowknife and 300 miles northwest of Baker Lake), the general geology of the area, the fact that all supplies would be flown in by chartered bush aircraft from Yellowknife, that sleds would comprise the local transport, and that my contract would end with the last line-mile flown. That had happened. I would leave for home when the load of fuel arrived.

What the contract didn't spell out was that the camp would be three canvas tents on a frozen, treeless wasteland overburdened with glacial till and boulder fields; temperatures would plunge to forty-five degrees below zero Fahrenheit, and mean-fisted winds would whip out of the long nights to pound the few hours of daylight with white-outs and canvas-tearing uppercuts. I'd known from bitter experience what flying dangers and physical hardships the contract would embody, but the financial reward had been too great to pass up. One week's travel time and no more than three weeks on site, with all fuel, food, and lodging provided, would return me almost $15,000, one-third the cost of a new float-equipped bush plane. While this fee was near double the average contract price for a similar job, the mining engineer for whom I worked knew from experience that the flying survey would be done properly and that all records of earth's hidden treasures, inscribed on the flow-sheets from the airborne instruments, would be treated by me as state documents.

Three weeks together with the same crew in confined quarters had bred foul thoughts and short tempers. Twice, men of the drilling crew had beaten each other until one could not return to the scratch line. The battery-operated high-frequency radio connected to the Yellowknife flight office worked only in the fairest weather, and the locker-room lies had turned tasteless in their retelling.

I had been told a story about the early days of the previous survey that seemed to capture the mood of the place. Two prospectors and a cook, with his pet raven and a load of food, had been flown in six months earlier, to set up a camp and map the local outcroppings of rock. After four weeks of eating preserved ham and tinned pineapple, the cook's favourite meal, and being wakened each dawn by the raucous rasp of the big bird, the prospectors agreed on the killing. They tied a stick of dynamite with a short fuse to the bird's legs and tossed it into a clump of bushes. Then they ran like hell.

The bird struggled free of the imprisoning branches and into the air, with the fuse sputtering beneath it. It had chased the screaming men at head-height into the cook tent when the dynamite exploded. The canvas shelter was blown apart, and the lighted stove with its burning embers was turned into flying shrapnel, which started a fire and burned most of their supplies and the radio transceiver, their only link to civilization.

One man lost a yard or so of skin and his hearing for several weeks; the other lost his hair, hearing, and a portion of one arm. The cook wasn't hurt at all; he'd finally tired of his daily diet, and had gone trapping for fresh game birds to stuff with fresh wild berries and roast for dinner.

Fat with the late-arriving Beaver aircraft's discharged load of fuel, I powered off the frozen lake for the last time. The B-52 entered my field of view some 100 miles south, like a sharp white line etched on smoked glass. The eight contrails, individually undetectable to the naked eye, merged into one tubular form behind the silvered arrow tip, as the rapidly cooling vapour from the jet's engines metamorphosed into ice crystals.

I levelled out atop scattered cloud, put the plane on course, and let my mind review the changes my life had undergone during the five years since I walked away from my seventeen-year career as newspaperman. My family was enlarged. Thora and I now had a son Donald and a daughter Janet. My career in the stock market had been financially remunerative. I had attained the highest international parachuting licence without lasting damage to my body. Robillard was employed by Canadair as sales director for their new passenger bus. Stan Turner was serving his second tour in Russia as Canada's military attaché, having lost his bid to head up the Air Defence Command, of which he had been a key organizer. My parents had moved to Long Sault, Ontario, to be nearer the children, my fledgling one-plane airline had just got off the ground, with help from a loan arranged by Alphonse House, my bank manager, and we lived in a country setting, in Lancaster, Ontario.

One hour and twenty minutes outbound on the five-hour flight to Lynn Lake, a dancing brightness on the silver underside of my port wing led my eyes downwards to the tortured landscape, unrolling like a map 2,000 feet below. A pin-point reached me again and again from the rim of the taiga forest.

Slowly I was able to distinguish the outline of a small, oval lake, lying awkwardly in a crease of the ruptured land. As I curved in flight to examine the blinding whiteness, I saw an airplane 100 yards or so off the shoreline, sideways to its landing path. Then two running, waving figures emerged from the edge of the scrub towards the plane, and a third figure jumped up and down near a huge X trampled in the snow near the lake's centre.

Lessons learned from mistakes forgiven are the sum total of a pilot's skill, and while occasions that call for immediate action do present themselves, success is usually determined by cold calculation. This was such a moment. I rocked the wings in the time-honoured signal of recognition and, knowing well their agony at my next manoeuvre, climbed away in a flat spiral to gain the height I needed to accurately plot their position.

The lake was not marked on my chart, but I knew its approximate location and that it drained into the Thelon River. I noted the co-ordinates as 64 degrees north latitude and 103 degrees 27 minutes west longitude. I guessed they were 200 miles east of Fort Reliance, 250 miles west of Baker Lake, and 350 miles north of Uranium City. Except for the bush camp 200 miles behind me, the only trace of human life in that wretched wilderness was a long-dead native campsite 100 miles east on the Dubawnt River. The flight I had begun as a joyous trip to civilization had suddenly become a life-or-death affair.

Experience had taught me that improper freeze-up of northern lakes could result in a crust of wind-packed snow masking a layer of slush that could swallow an airplane up to its propeller hub. The parallel tracks of the downed plane were still faintly visible as grey-shrouded indentations. But despite the awkward angle of its wings there was no indication it was mired in slush or had broken through the surface ice.

I flew the plane slowly past the waving trio, close enough for them to see the earphones I waved out the opened window. On my next pass, one figure, whom I assumed to be the pilot, pointed to both his ears and then crossed his arms negatively in front of him. I knew then their radio was inoperable. When I came low past him a second time, he had already stamped out a large T in the snow as my landing direction. I scouted the shoreline again from near-zero height looking for clues to the lake's surface, then made a slow approach over the short trees to hit the snow a deliberate *thwack* with both skis. Then I powered ahead from the bounce and turned back to double-check the surface for tell-tale signs. There was no sign of water in my ski tracks, so I gentled the plane to a mid-lake landing and taxied to the survivors: two grinning men and a crying woman. They had both doors open before the plane had stopped sliding.

"Jesus Christ Almighty, am I glad to see you!" The pilot almost leaped into the cabin to hug me.

When their jubilation had subsided, I had the pilot leave a note on his plane's instrument panel explaining he'd been picked up and taken to Uranium City. The odds that another transient pilot would spot the downed plane were impossible to calculate, but I didn't want that pilot to assume the occupant had wandered off and died. Because of the shortness of my take-off space, I packed my tent and spare oil into their plane, then drained 100 pounds of gas into the snow. With the pilot and nurse bundled in sleeping bags in the cargo space and the senator up front with me, I broke free of the cloying snow and climbed to cruise altitude.

During the long flight to my landing site on the lake under the town's bluff, the whole story unfolded. The senator was so glad to be alive that he offered to pay the entire cost of recovering and repairing his pilot's airplane and the air transport of the nurse to Baker Lake. Then he offered payment for my services, which I refused. In the spirit of Christmas, I agreed to omit filing a report to the authorities, and the pilot guaranteed return of the items I had left at the crash site. Eighteen hundred miles later, still in my bush clothes, I shopped for Christmas presents for my family.

Some months afterwards, I learned from the rescued pilot that the senator had received a traumatic shock shortly after his arrival home, when police advised him of the death of his wife in the company of another senior government official. Both of them had been found half-naked in an automobile that had collided with a transport truck. The scandal caused the senator's immediate retirement, after which he refused to pay the $6,000 recovery and repair costs of the downed airplane.

TOP
OF THE WORLD

STAN TURNER HAD LEFT the RCAF and retired to Fort Chambly, Quebec, a quiet backwater where there was little excitement. One Saturday morning, to add a little bit of the unexpected to his life, I set a helicopter down in his tiny backyard, alongside his deck chair. He gave me a quick smile and said, "Fuck off, I'm reading." After that, I got him aloft occasionally in my bush plane. I'd land at his dock and coax him into the pilot's seat. There, surrounded by familiar instruments and engulfed in the pleasurable aromas of high-octane gas and hot engine oil, he would come alive, lifting the floats smoothly from the water and revelling in the purity of flight.

His management capabilities then landed him a senior position with Expo 67. The celebration of Canada's 100th birthday since Confederation had the whole population in a party mood, and the 1967 World's Fair, held in Montreal, was the country's birthday cake. Turner placed my name before the Expo board of directors as his choice for polar ambassador. The appointment was a significant honour, requiring the piloting of a single-engined aircraft on a 10,000-mile midwinter flight through the high Arctic, to pay homage to Canada's first-generation bush pilots, and to take Expo 67 in film to thirty-eight northern communities and twenty RCMP outposts whose inhabitants would never visit the fair.

For the flight, I chose my 1966 Cessna 180 on wheel-skis. I had christened the plane the Arctic Sun Express, because I flew it so often in the northern polar regions.

The first leg of the journey was from Montreal to Winnipeg. I took Ivan Christopher with me as a passenger. In Winnipeg, where the city laid on a civic reception, I acquired a replacement passenger, the legendary Murray Watts, the most successful mining engineer in Canada's history. Better known as Mr. Ungava, he was the man who outlined the great Mary River iron range. From there the flight touched The Pas, Lynn Lake, and Uranium City, where a wild storm grounded us overnight after the townsfolk had assembled to see the movie and accept the souvenirs we had brought from Expo. During an all-night drinking and story-telling session, which I avoided, Murray bought a Turbo-Beaver aircraft for $150,000 from a local bush pilot. He planned to use it in opening up a mineral discovery he had made at Coppermine, on the rim of the Arctic Ocean, and he radioed for his pilot, Ron Sheardown, to pick it up.

At Fort Smith, RCMP Superintendent Harry Nixon, an old friend who later took command of the western arctic division out of Whitehorse, met us with an honour guard and sat us down to a civic banquet hosted by the townsfolk.

Each mile we flew thereafter was across uninhabited wasteland into the deepening darkness of the polar days. At times we were forced to tree-top height by snowstorms, ice fog, perilous white-outs, and ice accretion, all of which added to our respect for those first-generation pilots whose exploits had guided me for thirty years: Russ Baker, Bernt Balchen, Matt Berry, Leigh Brintnell, "Punch" Dickins, Walter Gilbert, Harry Hayter, Herb Hollick-Kenyon, "Lewie" Leigh, "Wop" May, Grant McConachie, Stan McMillan, Archie McMullen, Jack Moar, H.A. "Doc" Oaks, Bob Randall, Pat Reid, Romeo Vachon, Tommy Williams, and others unnamed but ever-remembered.

Across the deep-frozen northern tundra and enveloped in night, we sought our way by the stars and eternal landmarks to the rim of the Arctic Ocean, then west towards Tuktoyaktuk on the delta of the Mackenzie River where it empties into the Beaufort Sea. A South Carolinian sailor saw the Arctic Sun Express as a blip on his radar screen, in the bowels of his United States Navy weather-ship frozen into the ice of the bay. Only his skill and my belief in those skills brought us safely to earth through the otherwise impregnable fog that suffocated us. The next day he guided us again on radar through weather that blocked our view of earth, to 70 degrees north latitude over the sea, satisfying a long-slumbering desire of mine and gaining me admittance to the Cold-Nosed Order of Arctic Pilots, a confraternity founded by the legendary Matt Berry.

The reception by the people who crushed into the communities' meeting places was second only to that on Christmas Eves, when the RCAF played Santa and para-dropped gifts and supplies to a people starved for a sense of belonging.

We tackled the awesome might of the Richardson Mountains at first light from Fort McPherson on a 400-mile leg to Dawson, in the Yukon, and stayed almost level with the peaks until weather forced us into a rat race through the valley bottoms to a risky landing during a white-out on a tiny lake, where we spent fourteen hours battered by tearing winds, while the temperature sank to fifty-two below zero Fahrenheit, creating a wind-chill factor of some eighty below.

I broke the rules of flight again between Mayo and Whitehorse, when heavy snow forced me upwards through the overcast, relying solely on instruments and the map heights of surrounding mountains, until the engine quit without warning. I raised the RCAF's radar, which fixed me dead centre over the valley at the top end of Lac Labarge. Just as we broke through the cloud to the sight of Robert Service's memorable locale, where the legendary Sam McGee was cremated, the engine caught to my urgings, and we sputtered our way to the town's airfield. During my radio conversation with the Whitehorse tower, I learned that a CPA flight was readying for take-off to Vancouver with M.P. Erik Neilsen aboard. Since Watts had expressed a desire to leave for warmer climes, I successfully urged Neilsen to delay take-off for thirty minutes so they could fly south together. Then I tackled the muscle of the Stikine Mountains alone, hopscotching 1,200 miles to Telegraph Creek and Fort St. John, over the Swan Hills to Edmonton and the cradle of bush flying.

No welcome touched me more than that given me by my childhood heroes. They crowded into my suite for a whole night of drink and discourse. When they left, they presented me with a copy of *Airborne From Edmonton*, the book by Eugenie Myles on northern Canada's flying history. It was signed by thirty-eight living aviation legends, and the presentation page was inscribed by "Punch" Dickins. Riveted to the front cover was an oblong piece of aluminium, salvaged from some long-dead airplane, on which was engraved: "To commemorate the flight of CF-UGK [the call sign of the Arctic Sun Express] through the Canadian Arctic during the centennial winter of 1967 in tribute to Canada's pioneer bush pilots, this volume has been autographed and presented to bush pilot Ray Munro, by those he remembered."

Not long after that, in the fall of 1968, I met two other important figures in aeronautical history: General Dick Lassiter of the U.S. Air Force, and the aeronautical wizard Bill Lear. I spent an evening with them and my old friend Allan Jones in New York. After a hilarious trip down memory lane, Lear and Jones admitted to having started the infamous Mile-High Club in a DC-3 a mile above Lake Michigan. They had been flying in Lear's first autopilot airplane, and had left the controls to the new invention while they disported themselves horizontally with two young women in the passenger compartment.

The subject of conversation then turned to the perils facing aircrews of the USAF Strategic Air Command. Their missions included overflights in B-52 bombers of Canada's pie-shaped area of polar sovereignty, whose apex was the North Pole. Each crew member was checked regularly in ground-based pressure chambers for physiological and psychological aberrations, but no amount of training could prepare them mentally for a forced ejection into the troposphere above the most alien and inhospitable place on earth, the Arctic Ocean. This body of water, the mostly-frozen roof of the world, was 5 million square miles in area and 13,000 feet deep in places.

Later, that conversation sparked in me a desire to learn more about survival under arctic conditions. Before long, I had started thinking about accepting the challenge and parachuting onto the north polar ice cap, as close to the North Pole as conditions would permit. My goals were many: I wanted to be the first person to parachute onto the area of the North Pole; I wanted to write a paper on the physical effects encountered both during and after the jump; and I wanted to use the adventure as a basis for a novel. Since I was determined to treat the attempt as a sporting event and not stain it with commercialism, I had to absorb the whole cost, which I estimated at $10,000.

I began by seeking permission for the jump from those governmental bodies having control over that geographic location, the departments of Indian and Northern Affairs, of Transport, and of Defence, the Surgeon General, the government of the Northwest Territories, and the Arctic Institute of North America. Using the shotgun approach, I advised each of my intention and purpose, setting the target date at the last week in March 1969, because by then the sun would have risen from the long polar night to touch the horizon.

I also had to arrange air transport from Montreal to the North Pole, a back-up jumper, and the most professional equipment available. I divided the journey into four flights: Montreal to Frobisher on Hudson Strait by Nordair's inaugural northern jet flight, due for a late March take-off; thence by cargo aircraft across the Arctic Circle to Resolute, on Cornwallis Island; and from there by Twin Otter on skis to Alert, on the northern tip of Ellesmere Island. From there I would emplane in the Otter for the pole, 540 miles over the ocean. I first chose Max Ward's airline, which operated from Yellowknife and points north with Bristol Freighters and Twin Otter aircraft. But after three months of trying unsuccessfully to make arrangements with his operations manager, I wrote his company off and sought a deal from Weldy Phipps, owner of Atlas Aviation based at Resolute and a veteran arctic pilot. He responded immediately in the affirmative, and within three weeks we had hammered out a prepaid contract and set the date.

The back-up jumper would be needed if I was injured in the descent. In that event, he would parachute from low level to my position on the ice and render immediate first aid. For the job, I chose Norman Jones of Montreal, a hardy individual who was dedicated to completing any task he undertook, and who was able to control his fears. While he completed a professional course in cold-weather first aid, I took him aloft thirteen times and parachuted with him from low level to ensure he could get to my side in the shortest possible time.

The final requirement was the clothing and parachute gear. I acquired goose-down garments from Sir Edmund Hillary, with whom I had been associated as Canadian representative for the Arthur Ellis Company of New Zealand, a firm of which he was a director. The parka I would wear had been used by a doctor who climbed in it with Hillary to the second camp from the top of Mount Everest.

I had narrowed down my choice of parachutes to a Security with a large T-U configuration for fast turns, or a Pioneer with a dangerous turning problem but greater target accuracy. Since I was familiar with the Pioneer, which I envisioned Jones using, I planned to make several jumps with the Security rig before making a final decision. In any event, I had decided to wear a small reserve parachute in a chest pack, in the unlikely event my main chute malfunctioned.

On the day I planned to test the Security parachute, my regular jump pilot failed to arrive at the small country airport on time. I therefore prevailed upon an off-duty fireman and amateur pilot to let me sit sideways in the back seat of his little Taylor Cub airplane with my feet hanging over the side, while he flew me to 3,500 feet. There I would fall out, activate the main chute, and test the steering capabilities. All went well until I realized at 2,000 feet that both my legs had gone to sleep. I therefore merely tapped him on the back and fell into the slip-stream. Once I had stabilized my free-falling body, I turned towards the airstrip and pulled the rip-cord. When no sudden jolt shook me, I peered over my shoulder to see an amazing tangle of canopy and shroud lines flopping across my back. There was no hope of transforming them into a life-saving device.

To pull the rip-cord on the reserve parachute, which I had packed with a small pilot chute for fast opening, would have meant certain death, because it would have entangled itself in the streaming and useless main canopy. Counting off the ten seconds I knew I had left before slamming into the ground at 120 miles an hour, I pulled each of the emergency capewell releases on my shoulder harness to free me from the main parachute, which was torn away from me by the rushing air, then yanked the rip-cord on my reserve. The small chute appeared instantly as an explosion of white in front of my face, followed by a severe jolt. It blossomed just as I passed through the top branches of a large oak tree. I then fell feet first at a low angle into a rockpile, and bounced from there across a fence into a field of cows. One massive pain suddenly flooded my body and I thought I had died, because I knew my eyes were open yet I could see nothing but a dark red haze. I pushed away my goggles, then sat up to wipe the blood that had collected behind the lenses. A tree branch had slipped under my helmet and reopened the old Mexico wound. After rising slowly and testing each joint, I knew that a few stitches and a hot bath would put me right.

I gathered the parachutes into a field pack, and trudged through the forest to a side-road, where I thumbed a ride in a truck back to the airfield. Ahead I could see the flashing red lights of a provincial police car. The officer was joining a knot of people who had started to run towards the grove of trees, into which someone had seen me fall without a parachute. I prevailed upon the truck driver to accept five dollars for his trouble and to catch up with the officer and tell him I had gone to the hospital for some needlework.

I learned later that the malfunction had been caused by a loose screw in a U-bolt holding the suspension lines. I finally chose the Security parachutes anyway, for what would be my 528th and last descent, this one onto the polar ice cap.

All the governmental departments responded favourably to my requests. I suspect their enthusiasm might have been prodded by a formal request from General Lassiter, and by a serious communication to them from Dr. Wernher Von Braun, director of the U.S. National Aeronautics and Space Administration, with whom I was acquainted. His prime interest in the descent concerned its application to the well-being of the astronauts under his command.

Before the government agencies would give their approval, they demanded a number of protective measures be taken, among them proof of proper knowledge of polar survival techniques, approved transportation and equipment, understanding of the laws governing human conduct in that strange and lonely land, and a very stiff medical with X-rays and psychological examinations, all under federal supervision. Then Brigadier H.W. Love, head of the Arctic Institute of North America, confirmed the institute's sanction of the experiment, and Stuart Hodgson, commissioner of the Northwest Territories, personally issued me an Explorer's Licence, permitting the operation to proceed.

With everything in place we met the press at Montreal airport, then boarded Nordair's inaugural jet flight to Frobisher, 1,300 miles north. We were promptly stranded in Frobisher for four days by a raging blizzard. From that lonely outpost we flew in an aging Constellation to Resolute, a small Canada/U.S. weather station 1,000 miles farther north and 100 miles east of the magnetic north pole. It is to this pole that all compass needles are irresistibly drawn, and it is confused by some with the true North Pole, another 1,300 miles away. I later learned that the Constellation and its crew continued on to Biafra, where it was shot down and destroyed by an enemy night fighter.

Our schedule called for an immediate take-off to Alert, the world's most northerly community, 800 miles away at 82 degrees 30 minutes north latitude. We were delayed though, first by 100-mile-an-hour winds that grounded all aircraft and then by a mechanical problem. To keep our bodies fit during this trying period, Jones and I slept outside in arctic gear in wind-chill temperatures reaching 117 degrees Fahrenheit below freezing.

On the morning of the third day, we packed the cabin with gasoline drums, and Weldy Phipps and his co-pilot, Jasper LaFrance, took off for a point on the frozen ocean half-way to our goal, where a cache would be established. With our long-range fuel supply in place, marked only by coloured weather balloons floating on foil-covered lines above the drums, we took off, grossly overloaded, in an outside wind-chill temperature of 135 degrees Fahrenheit below zero. In that environment, oils solidify to taffy-like consistency, steel can be snapped with a child's blow, and rubber smashes like glass. And in those barren and friendless wastes, a person must spend most of his time just trying to stay alive. Human flesh exposed to that degree of cold freezes in less than a minute and mistakes are measured in silent death. The physical drain on a person is far in excess of his normal daily expenditure, and 5,000 calories are required just to replace the heat lost by the body.

For navigation we used sextant, gyro-syn compass, drift meter, and two astrocompasses, and on the first flight to set out the gas drums, Phipps drew a strip map of the route showing the shapes of the largest leads, or areas of open water, they'd flown over. These cracks in the polar ice pack open suddenly and widen from a few feet to a few miles within hours. Meanwhile, the smell of the raw gas in the cabin was overpowering as we watched our map come to life, showing us less than a mile off course and half-way to our target.

The cache, however, was gone. The ice had opened beneath the drums. Where they had been was now nothing but open water. The plane used seventy gallons of fuel an hour at a ground speed of 130 miles per hour. To go the full distance to the Pole and back, a distance of 1,100 miles, we'd need 595 gallons. We'd taken aboard all we could carry, 630 gallons, which gave us a margin of only thirty minutes. If the fuel consumption remained constant, if we had no engine problems, if we didn't hit bad weather, and if we did not stray off course, we could make it.

On the horizon appeared the target, but under us and around us as far ahead as we could see was fractured ice laced with enormous areas of black water. Quick figuring showed we had just enough fuel to reach the now-visible North Pole, but not enough to climb above our present height. I had planned to land first on an ice-floe and mark it with flares for me to aim at, then take off again for the jump. Now I'd be forced to dive out the doorway into the unknown and risk hitting the water and dying almost instantly, or landing on a floe too small for Phipps to retrieve me from.

It was impossibly dangerous, and I knew then I'd lost, that I'd never touch that storied place.

Slowly we turned away. Our hope was to find a floe large enough and smooth enough for the plane to land on. Shortly we spotted it. It wasn't the best, but it was passable. Phipps got the plane down, but not without trouble. The nose ski had been damaged.

The small, rough ice pan was rimmed on one side by towering boxcars of sea ice and circled the rest of the way around by open water and rubber-thin ice that wouldn't support a footstep. Norman Jones, who confessed to having lived a full life, offered to stay alone on the floe and mark it with flares for me to aim at. We had enough fuel for one take-off, a climb to 10,000 feet for the jump, and then a last take-off for the return low-level flight to Alert, four hours away.

In what I suppose could now be described as a dramatic moment, four grown men on a small ice pan on the roof of the world quietly agreed that if I missed the target and entered the water, there would be no attempt at recovery, and that if I missed the floe and hit an area of distant ice and couldn't be saved without risking the airplane, they'd return to Alert without me. It was also agreed that after take-off, if fog or blowing snow hid the target and we couldn't spot Jones from the air within fifteen minutes, we'd return to Alert without him, refuel there from the last of our gas supply, and return to search until no hope remained.

The temperature over the polar ice cap is permanently so low that it seldom snows. Indeed, what snow blankets the area might well have lain there for decades. But the great arctic dread was ice fog, which forms when water vapour turns directly into ice. The wild polar winds whipping the powdered snow into dense clouds can obscure vision within seconds.

Jones checked his flares and emergency gear, accepted our lone bottle of brandy, and stood alone on the drifting ice. I climbed into my jump gear as we lifted safely off. It was fifty-four degrees Fahrenheit below zero.

We lost sight of Jones immediately in an ice fog. As we circled upwards into the twilight, I kept my head out the open doorway in the terrible cold of the slip-stream. I learned later we were at 8,700 feet when I saw one tiny wink of red beneath me and threw my body into the opening—and was jammed tight. My parachute pack had caught on the door-frame behind me, and the square aluminium panel that was mounted on my reserve chute, and which held the instruments that would monitor my height, time of descent, speed, and temperature, locked my chest to the frame.

I remember hunching over and hurling myself out and down into the awesome temperature that seared my lungs. The goggles iced up, and when I pushed them back, my eyelids froze together. I was blind. But even then I had to form my body into an arrow shape, hoping to hit terminal velocity of 180 miles an hour in free fall and record the wind-chill factor on my body instruments. Even that would be far short of what anyone falling from a sub-stratospheric overflying military aircraft could expect.

The disciplines I'd learned in my five years of parachuting paid off then, because, even blind, I was able to count off the seconds— in that case twenty of the longest in my life—when I spread-eagled to reduce my falling speed to 120 miles an hour, felt for the rip-cord, and pulled it. I heard, rather than felt, the canopy open. Then I tore off my gloves, and before my fingers could freeze I broke the seal of ice locking my eyelids together, to see with elation that my touchdown would be half-way between Jones and the thin ice.

I don't remember landing. I learned later my body had passed through a computed wind-chill temperature of 177 degrees Fahrenheit below zero. I also worked out later that if I hadn't jammed in the doorway, I would have left the plane too early and most likely hit the water.

Once more Phipps landed on that tiny floe, despite the damaged nose ski. It was a great moment for all of us. We opened the bottle of brandy, but instead of drinking it, poured it for luck into the gas tank. With the nose ski lashed tight to prevent further damage, all extra weight left behind, and a last-minute check of our position, which appeared to be 88 degrees 09 minutes north latitude, I froze a staff into the ice, on the spot where I had landed. From it streamed the flag of Canada.

It turned out that we could have drunk the brandy after all, because when we arrived back at Alert, Phipps ran the engines for six minutes before they quit.

Later, I completed my research responsibilities to the appropriate Canadian and American government agencies who were involved.

DOWN—
BUT NOT OUT

FAR OUT over the North Pacific Ocean, the constant western wind drank itself full of swollen winter clouds that the sun had formed by sucking water upwards. Pregnant with wetness, the sluggish mass trundled eastward to dampen Canada's ragged coastline, then struggled to lift its sodden bulk across the cold sprawl of the Rocky Mountains.

The roll of moisture washed the hills and, clinging greedily to timbered slopes, flowed upwards against the mountains' sides. Bleeding with wetness, it heaved its 1,000-mile width ever higher into cooler air, which chilled it into densely falling snow. Still pumping moisture from its ruptured belly, it swept up the range's muscled flanks into yet colder air, which froze the snow into needling crystals of ice. Then it rolled eastward past the highest peaks, and carried by faster, stratospheric winds it sped to the mountains' end and then arched down across Alberta's flatlands, slowly sinking back to hug the frozen earth as cold, clear air, sucked dry of exudation.

The chisel edge of the now-transparent mass scoured every hollow, mating with the warmer air rising from the larger lakes, and giving birth to snow-filled clouds that seeded all beneath as they themselves passed on.

Across the earth, where the Tropic of Cancer straddles the mid-Atlantic Range, a blanket of fetid air arose from the weed-choked staleness of the Sargasso Sea. Captured by a vagrant breath of wind, the lightly rising mass swam slowly northward into the waiting wall of cold. Then, pushed inland by the Polar Westerlies, it was sucked into those circling winds to blanket eastern Canada in an almost impenetrable fog.

Planing eastward from Lake Superior, the sovereign wedge of

cold, dry air trowelled beneath the warm front's curving snout and forced it upwards. And along this ever-climbing wall the coldness turned the wet, rising warmth into snow as dense as man had ever seen. Wind devilling out of the east, drawn off the Greenland ice-cap, was pushed along the Gulf Stream air, which in turn was spun even higher by the faster-moving prairie wind. The battle was joined above the Mistassini Highlands of Quebec, at 19:23 Greenwich Mean Time.

I would be one of the few airborne victims of this deadly weather phenomenon to survive.

It was the seventh day of my enforced exile at the isolated trading post of Great Whale River, on the eastern shore of Hudson Bay, where I had paused for what I thought would be the simple act of refuelling my single-engined, ski-equipped bush airplane for the final leg of a re-supply flight from Cape Wolstenholme on Hudson Strait to Montreal, a journey of some 1,200 miles. The afternoon weather had soured from snow showers to freezing rain, and the local weatherman, a federal civil servant with a low tolerance for urgency, handed me a printed forecast from Montreal's master weather office stating that the climate would be salubrious to my flying southward within the hour.

I was numb from boredom, solitaire, Salisbury steak under greasy gravy, and bread pudding, and fed up to the teeth with the ice fog, hanging roof-high over the lowlands and the seascape of the bay. So, when the tops of the tallest trees suddenly stood starkly separated from the grey blanket that had masked them from my view for a week of desperate wishing, I lifted my plane from the hard-packed snow and set course for Chibougamau, 300 miles southeast.

Within the hour the weather turned, until the space between the reaching trees and the underbelly of the cloying fog was less than fifty feet. Still, I was only an hour away from Abatagush Bay, where I knew I could warm my toes at a friendly fire if any Indians were camped within view.

When the ravine ahead filled with cloud, I deviated abruptly from my pre-planned course between two sidehills into a longer, deeper valley that beckoned me past its greedy walls. I felt sure that momentarily the light snowfall would stop and let me lift the plane to cloud-base height above the rolling hills and straighten out my track. But the trees faded into whitish green, as fists of snow swirled about me. I pierced them with the plane in futile anger on another deviant course, concerned that soon I'd have to turn back once more to seek another route.

The valley's width shrank even more as I felt the first faint premonition of impending danger. I banked sharply right then left in a tight blood-draining turn that reversed my direction almost instantly and saved me from a trap. For one human moment I longed for the loneliness I had just fled. There was no place to land within my view, only V-bottomed valleys and steep sidehills bearded with evergreen trees and pimpled with rocky protrusions. A frozen river would have done in a pinch, although I'd have preferred a frozen lake. But none appeared.

I twisted the plane through a series of small valleys, each narrower than the last, then dropped full flap to slow the forward speed and give me one more second of time if the end were near. The snow squall reached around me, and tugging winds fought my aching hands for control of the plane. For a brief moment, when I saw the water drops on the windscreen stay motionless as they turned into ice, I remembered the key point of a quiet lecture I'd had many years before, about flying in rain. A lifetime ago, Fred Gillies, my first flying instructor at Barker Field on the northern outskirts of Toronto, had said it slowly but with great conviction: "When you're looking through rain-spattered glass you'll be a hell of a lot closer to the ground than you think. And if those drops turn to ice, you'll be dead damn quick unless you land smartly or climb above the freezing level before you're a minute older."

I recalled another, even more basic lesson: "Lift overcomes gravity." But even as I thought it, the windscreen turned into a mirrored blind, and the sudden heavy feel of the yoke in my hands told me that ice had formed on the wings and the tail surfaces. I had reached the point of no return. I unlocked the reel of the high-frequency radio aerial, letting it stream out behind the plane, and flicked on the high-frequency radio set to try to give some human soul my last position, if I had the time.

Climb or land? How high was this storm that shouldn't even have occurred? Higher than the metal guts of my labouring machine could carry me? Would I encounter heavier ice, and fall to earth? And even if I clawed the plane above the storm, there was no airfield within my range that owned a system geared to let me land on instruments alone. And what danger would I pose to other pilots flying sightless like myself, and to those alive beneath me? No. I knew then I must land, even upslope into waiting trees.

Suddenly a lighter-coloured streak appeared ahead! I chopped the throttle off and kicked the airplane sideways into a sudden height-losing skid, then just as quickly kicked it back upon my chosen course and yanked the yoke back hard. The plane smashed through a massive snow-drift covering a ridge of broken ice and, smothered in a clinging shroud, turned sideways and came to a sudden stop.

I cursed aloud at my shaking hands for showing me the fears I had inside. I cursed the stupid fool I was for believing a weather forecast told to me by others. The panel switches all felt safely off to my probing fingers, reassuring me that at least my mental check-list had not failed me during that desperate life-saving gamble. Then I fumbled through my knapsack for the metal flask of brandy. I then opened the pilot's door to a smothering cloud of snow, which poured into the cabin. I quickly pulled the door shut. I was entombed until the great storm spent itself.

At 19:40 Greenwich Mean Time, I activated the oil dilution system that would permit me to start the engine without draining the oil to heat it, wrapped myself in a sleeping bag, and waited for the howling blizzard to drop the night upon me. I was alive, but I did not dwell upon how long that state might last.

A fitful sleep was broken by a sense that the wind had stopped. In the half-light of false dawn I shoved open the door against a drift of yielding snow. The plane was up to its belly in it. By the grey light I could see my landing place, a tiny lake, or more likely a frozen, stagnant pool, set in a pocket among the hills. It looked so short, too short, I feared, for me to get the plane aloft again, unless some head wind favoured me. What breeze there was only trifled with the evergreen needles. But even then, I was trapped like a dinosaur in a tar pit by the waist-high fall of snow.

The radio aerial was gone, entangled in the trees through which I had so lately passed, torn completely off the spool. My voice was stilled to the outside world. I was there until I freed myself.

I never laid out my aerial charts to plot a course to a destination north of Canada's tree-line without considering the possibility of my own death. There was always the chance that I would crash, terminating my life instantly, or leaving me to die of injuries, exposure, or starvation. To gain the edge against such an eventuality I stayed current on survival techniques and carried a proper emergency kit. And just in case I was unfortunate enough to be the only guest at my last supper, I carried a single place setting of Wedgwood china, Edward IV silver cutlery, and a Beleek napkin. The china had been given to me by John Arena of Winston's restaurant in Toronto, after which we had shared a bottle of Taittinger Comptes de Champagne, Blanc de Blancs, against that eventuality.

Although things looked bleak, as bleak as they had ever been, I hoped that it was not yet time for that final meal. Instead, I set up my Primus stove inside the cabin. Its hissing heat soon warmed the cramped space and boiled the water for a cup of tea—my breakfast.

There was only one way I was going to get my stupid person off that pond, and that was to get the body working. The body, I told myself silently, was nothing more than a means of transportation for the mind. My physical being was in damned good shape, considering the years of abuse to which I had subjected it, so I determined that it would perform any and all acts that my brain said it would perform, whether it rebelled or not.

I burrowed first beneath the plane's belly to examine the metal skis, which appeared to have somehow survived intact. Next, I strapped on my snow-shoes, and stomped to the end of the solidly frozen pond, counting each step and calculating the measurements in my mind. Six hundred feet, I concluded. Then I promised myself to track down the idiot bastard who had concocted that insane weather report that had so insolently been passed along to me. Occasional flurries!

Snow-shoes and a sharp bush axe were my only weapons against this hostile land. My snow-shoes weren't the silly little bear-paw type that some pilots shoved into their cockpits just to satisfy the rules. No, sirree. Mine were great, wide Indian-made beasts that hammered down three square feet of snow at every stride.

You will do it alone. Your great flat feet will pack down a runway four webbed yards in width and 300 flopping strides long.

The weakness of my body showed first in my lungs, which began to bleed from the frozen air. I had to rest, to revitalize myself. I drank hot tea again in the closeness of the plane's cabin, and ate special biscuits rich in vitamins. Then I took a mouthful of malted milk powder and went back out again and trudged to and fro until I could no longer drag one leg past the other.

The pain was only in my mind, I told myself, and I did not dwell on the broken, frozen skin on my feet, or on the blood that glued my woollen socks to the stiffened leather of my boots.

Finally, the 12,000 steps were behind me, and the snow was packed as hard as I could tamp it down. Then, hanging my weight from a wing-tip, I summoned every agonizing muscle into rocking the skis loose from the snow they had rested on all night. It was no use. They were frozen solid to the ice.

You will take your axe back over the ice ridge and you will chop down two small trees and clear the branches from them, then drag them back here one by one, never letting go the axe. This is an order.

My body obeyed. It protested the mind's unalterable decision, but it obeyed. It knew the eternal penalty for disobedience. Then I chopped both skis free of the ice and levered them up in turn on six-inch logs, so I could force my ungloved hands beneath to knife away the lumps of ice adhering to their undersides.

There was no time to stop or rest, only to work as I had never worked before. At last the metal runners were cleaned and resting on their little trestles so they would not stick again. The freezing rain had knobbled all the wing and tail surfaces, and the full length of the fuselage top, but using the old bush pilot's trick of whip-sawing a rough braided rope along their length, I cleaned them off. I packed the axe and snow-shoes back into place, fired up the engine after heating up its innards with a blowtorch under a canvas tarp, and waited impatiently for the oil gauge to show the slightest sign of life. Then, full power on, I started to move into the freshening breeze. Too slowly!

You must wait for the wind to course just so across the wing to form the perfect vacuum.

Abort! My senses screamed to stop the take-off run I'd started. Even as I cut the power I wasn't sure I'd acted quickly enough. As a last gamble to avoid an almost certain crash, I rammed full power again to the idling propeller and kicked the right rudder almost through the firewall. I swung around in a sickening half-circle, and stopped, safe again, for the moment at least, then I started the skis moving again slowly, back along the pounded path so they would not glue their friction-heated undersides to the snow as they had the day before.

Back and forth I taxied the plane, packing the runway harder and harder under the ton of weight on either ski, blasting around at each end of the strip in a cloud of snow and sound that for a fleeting moment teased the storm to strike again. It did.

Wind-whipped whiteness sped past the tiny cabin, where I huddled with the Primus stove and swilled hot tea and brandy and bound my broken skin.

A young fighter pilot, new to his trade and to the Tangmere Wing, once watched in disbelief as our squadron's leader, the battle-hardened Stan Turner, lighted his pipe in the cockpit of his Spitfire while a petrol tanker loaded high-octane gasoline into the tanks, just a reach away from the open flame.

"Doesn't he know that plane can explode?" the fledgling warrior asked a grizzled sergeant.

"It wouldn't dare!" was the reply.

That was the attitude I needed to develop as a shield from the forces of nature now visited upon me. I dared it to snow all night. I dared the raging blizzard to pack me in solid. It did, and with a venomous ferocity. At least eight inches of snow filled my trodden path, as though I'd never made it.

You will strap on those silly-looking webbed feet and you will stumble up and down that take-off strip all day long if need be. But you will beat a path for this plane to use.

My body honoured the command.

My feet were so swollen with broken blisters and abraded skin that I had to slice open the leather tongues down to their very tips before I could squeeze my boots on. When my legs first took the weight of my body outside the pilot's door, the pain was so great that I needed another long pull at the brandy. Then I pulled myself back into the cabin from the cold that hurt even my eyeballs, brewed another cup of tea on the faithful Primus, and forced down a whole enriched chocolate bar from the emergency kit.

Time to start the march again. Hup, two, three, four, hup, two, three, four.

It took me seven hours to finish the task of packing the night's snowfall. After the first two, there was no more pain from my feet. They were oblivious to hurt. Then I emptied the cabin of all unessential items: the rolled-up tent, two five-gallon containers of fuel, some cans of oil, a packsack filled with rock samples I'd gathered some weeks back from a promising outcrop, and even the heavy canvas engine cover. They were all I could safely leave to lighten the load. They would be lost to me forever, but that was a small price to pay if I made it aloft.

With the airplane cleaned of the new-fallen snow and the engine warmed to green-line heat, I powered it twelve times up and twelve times back. The only obstacle I faced that could physically deter me from my chosen course was that same man-high ridge of frosted granite that I had caromed off during my blind landing. A trap, set and waiting.

As ready as I would ever be, I snaked the trembling plane to the end of the narrow runway and then powered around fast into wind with the throttle locked fully on. The hand on the airspeed dial stood still. The 100-foot marker I had hammered into the frozen snow passed by. Then, as if by magic, the air-speed dial showed forty knots as I breasted the second measuring stake.

The rockpile loomed threateningly ahead as I tried in vain to coax an aileron to lift a wing and free one ski to cut some drag and speed me ever faster, but it would not rise. I was committed. There was no way out but straight ahead, for if I slowed the engine I could not help but smash into the waiting wall. Sixty knots on the dial. I unlocked the flap lever in desperation and yanked it up half-travel as I pulled the yoke back into my lap. The extended flaps met an invisible wall of air and vaulted the airplane sickeningly slowly above the last blockade.

Do not turn this plane one inch off its course or you will crash. Do not raise the flaps or you will sink into the trees.

My hands obeyed the orders. Gently then, when the second danger passed, I eased off the flaps, and just above the evergreens I left the challenge I had dared and won. The hills lay stark against the darkening sky, as south by east I flew towards Lac Mistassini, a landmark I knew I could not miss, even wrapped in winter's night.

UP, UP,
AND AWAY

AFTER my broken flesh healed, I accepted an invitation to address an aeronautical gathering in Austin, Texas, where I was fêted by the governor at a cocktail party. There I overheard a chance remark made by a man I later learned had been in charge of security in Dallas during President Kennedy's ill-fated visit. He commented on a national ballooning title that Texas had recently won and referred to the balloon as an aerostat and the pilot as an aeronaut. His remarks started me thinking, and eventually set me upon a new course of adventure.

En route home I detoured to Sioux Falls, South Dakota, where I visited the Raven Balloon Works. When I left I had made a $22,000 commitment to purchase three custom-made aerostats to be named Canada 1, 2, and 3. I also had a contract to act as sole Canadian distributor for their product. The fact that I had never been aloft in such an aerial device, which required a specific Ministry of Transport licence to operate, did not concern me. Within a week I was in Minneapolis with my family, and taking a one-day course in flying a Raven balloon from Matt Weiderker, a fine aeronaut who would eventually gain recognition for establishing a world distance record. Hurting from numerous sprains and bruises from horrendously hard landings, I returned to Canada and immersed myself in the science of aeronautics. When Canada 1 arrived, I had it in the air the same day, surviving five landings.

The ministry had never designed in-air or written examinations for the issuance of an aeronaut's licence, so after making certain declarations I received in the mail, in September 1969, a simple Department of Transport letterhead on which was typed a licence number, ULB-1, and the authorization for me to act as pilot in command of any size or type of balloon known to man. Two months later, I was named by them as an instructor and then as check pilot, giving in-air examinations to would-be licence holders.

I was then ready to start my own company, Balloon Systems of Canada, and to devote myself exclusively to training future aeronauts. I sold the Arctic Sun Express to a pilot-engineer, to whom I gave a dozen hours of concentrated instruction in bush flying, instrument landing onto water, and other life-extending techniques. He flew to Toronto, picked up Ivan Christopher, and took a southwards course. They ran out of gas over Lake Ontario, and had to be ignominiously retrieved. On a subsequent flight, the new owner, again with Christopher aboard, inadvertently landed my old airplane downwind on the main runway at Montreal International Airport, and caused great consternation.

Commander Jack Sloan was the first student to complete my aeronaut's training course. A Royal Canadian Navy senior pilot, just retired, he was working with Larry Robillard and Stan Turner in Ottawa. He suggested that, since Canada had never held a world record in aviation, I should consider rectifying the situation. When he agreed to join me in the project, I employed him to work through the International Aeronautical Federation (FAI) of France, the world body governing aviation endeavours, to gain permission for my attempts.

He learned that twenty-eight records existed in the hands of other countries for altitude, distance, and duration by hot-air balloons ranging in size from mine at 56,500 cubic feet to giants twice as large with a thermal energy of 3,000 horsepower and generating an amount of heat equivalent to eighty home furnaces.

The challenge I then accepted was to capture for Canada all those records. Again, I intended to maintain the true spirit of adventure and not stain the effort with commercial endorsement. I applied immediately for FAI sanction. After completing the paperwork and prepaying the cost of the licences, inspectors, and official flight observers, both on the ground and in a transponder-equipped twin-engined aircraft, I set out to break the altitude record, held by a ten-storey-high monster balloon in Britain.

At dawn on the morning of November 24, 1969, I lifted Canada I from the frozen ground at Russell, Ontario, and powered it to an altimeter reading of some 17,000 feet over Calumet, Quebec, when disaster struck. A copper line carrying superheated propane under pressure burst and spewed liquid flame in all directions, setting fire to my flight suit and melting great holes in the lower section of the balloon and skirt. In order to reach the trouble spot and correct it, I had to stand on the rim of the gondola and work my way up the superstructure. For this flight I had worn a simple back parachute. Its rip-cord caught on a projection as I levered myself upwards, the canopy falling into the gondola, where it caught fire from the spitting, fiery fuel. I ripped off the harness, gathered the whole nylon mess in my arms, and tossed it overboard. Then, in desperation, I climbed above the burners with a spanner.

The air in the balloon, meanwhile, had cooled to the subzero temperature surrounding it, the chase plane developed a mechanical problem that caused it to disappear, and Canada 1 began a frighteningly fast descent, slowed only by the natural ramming of outside air into the bag, which acted as a sort of undulating, rapidly descending parachute. Near 1,000 feet, and almost to the shore of the St. Lawrence River where the high winds had drifted me, I laid myself across the burners, turned on the fuel, and exploded them into life, wrapping myself for a moment in a ball of fire. With the throttle on full I was unable to slow the descent to a safe landing speed, and anticipated the pain that would soon commence when I smashed into the frozen earth.

A farmer's children watched me crash into a field adjoining their house, and within minutes had my battered body on a couch, while their mother poured hot brandy past my swollen lips. The father fired up his truck, and bundled in blankets I was driven to hospital, where I spent the night after being assured that although my body was deeply purpled, I had no serious injuries.

While the swellings subsided I learned I had broken the previous world record, reaching a height of 17,941 feet. But knowing Canada 1 was capable of greater glory, on December 17 before dawn I took off again from the same point, and reached an indicated 25,000 feet before my oxygen equipment froze. I was forced again to abort the flight, but this time I reached the aerostat's near-vertical limit and, still in control, was able to land gently in a level field. My unbroken barograph gave Canada an official world altitude record of 25,407 feet.

Within two weeks I had established eleven more world records for distance and duration, using all three of the Canada balloons, whose red and white vertical stripes became internationally known through pictures in newspapers and on television news programmes. One newsworthy landing was at a prison farm at Burritts Rapids.

During a telephone conversation with Wing Commander Gerry Turnbull, chairman of the century-old British Balloon and Airship Club, I learned that two great gas balloons were in place in Ireland, waiting for decent weather to attempt the first successful crossing of the Irish Sea. Both were capable of staying aloft for days at a time while covering vast distances. I decided immediately to fly the next day to Dublin. Despite its puniness and the shortness of its possible duration aloft, I planned to launch Canada 1 with the two giants. I employed a professional photographer to capture the attempt for posterity, and sent for Norman Jones and Jack Sloan, one of whom would accompany me on the flight.

The international press was awaiting our arrival. When one newspaper reporter joked that Canada 1 looked like a flea in comparison to the gas balloons, I signed and passed to the reporter for the *Daily Telegraph*, Britain's largest newspaper, $1,000 worth of traveller's cheques.

"Hold this money as my wager against the same sum from each of the others that Canada 1 will beat them to England," I said. "Whoever wins gets his money back, and the rest will be distributed by the *Telegraph* to charity."

The fact that neither of the other competitors would cover the bet was recorded on page one of British newspapers the following day.

We selected the coastal community of Wicklow, an hour's drive south of Dublin, for our launch site, and the old Grand Hotel as our headquarters. We had just settled in when a reporter called with the news that both our competitors had withdrawn from the race for obscure reasons.

So, mid-morning on January 26, 1979, with a 70 per cent chance of success, I lifted Canada 1 with Jones aboard into the grey coldness. Sloan was at Dublin airport, and over the radio he directed us to a brisk wind we picked up at 5,000 feet. At altitudes to 13,000 feet we chased favourable winds, caught some and missed others, drifted into voids, and finally lost the gamble twenty miles from the Welsh coast. With fifteen minutes of fuel remaining before an uncontrolled plunge would submerge us in the icy waters, I advised the RAF station at Valley of our problem and requested assistance. They were on the scene in a rescue helicopter just as we struck. The canopy of Canada 1 sank slowly beneath the surface, and the gondola turned upside-down, supported just under the surface by the buoyancy of the small fuel tanks. Jones and I remained afloat in our life-jackets.

Survival time in that sea was established at twenty-five minutes. After that, hypothermia would reduce our body temperatures until we reached unconsciousness, followed by the cessation of all vital signs, then death. The helicopter hovered overhead and lowered a thermally suited rescue specialist. He motioned me to take the sling he offered, and lock it under my arms. I passed it to Jones, who refused to enter it until I ordered him to do so. He was hoisted upwards and disappeared inside the helicopter. Again the airman was lowered. When he offered the sling to me I refused it, repelling his attempts to place it around me. I waved him off and then shoved him away bodily until he quit and was hauled back into the helicopter, which swung away and disappeared in the direction of Wales.

My reasoning was simple. The world had read of two Canadians challenging the Irish Sea in a balloon named Canada I. That we had failed in our attempt, as had every balloonist before us, was no shame, but to abandon that symbol of Canada's courage to the savagery of the sea was an unacceptable act. So I tied one wrist to the gondola by a nylon rope, then turned my mind to gentler times when the sight and feel of a baby's hand was reason enough to conquer the world.

Tim Phillips, captain of the chase plane carrying my cameraman, had followed the drama on his radio. When he learned that I was still in the water, he searched for and found an aged coastal freighter, made several wave-top passes across its bow, and then headed in my direction. The captain of the boat recognized the distress signal, which requested a boat to follow an airplane to the scene of an emergency. I have no recollection of the old ship wallowing around in ever-decreasing circles to come alongside the wreckage, or of the seaman in a rubber suit climbing down a rope ladder into the water and swimming to Canada I to tie a rope to us, or of being lifted by winch to the deck after an hour and twenty-five minutes in the icy sea. Once on board, I was swathed in blankets, and a cloth-wrapped wooden spoon was jammed in my mouth to prevent my teeth from breaking as the inner cold attacked my nervous system. Later, another RAF helicopter poised above the ship's masts and lowered a metal basket into which I was laid. I was then winched upwards and flown to the RAF hospital at Valley air base, where that evening I awoke to see strange patterns, which I learned were designs on the ceiling of the hospital room.

When the RAF station received the request for help, the marine section ordered one of its two great crash boats to the scene. Despite engine problems, it limped to intercept the freighter. But when it radioed that it could not make proper speed, a helicopter was sent. It was near nightfall when the crash boat intercepted the ship, whose captain had advised the helicopter pilot he was claiming Canada 1 as salvage. Since I was roped to it and alive, I was considered by the RAF to still be in possession. Accordingly, the officer commanding the crash boat ordered the vessel to stop, boarded it with an armed party, and seized Canada 1 in the name of the Queen.

With the balloon and gondola secured to the afterdeck, they headed home in then-stormy weather only to have the engine quit. They radioed for another craft to locate and tow them back to base. Early the next morning they were towed into harbour, dumping Canada 1 at dockside. This cavalier treatment so disturbed me that, when I could steady myself, I located Jones, who claimed to be in good shape, and together we acquired two sets of fisherman's clothing and boots, left the hospital, and surreptitiously hired a fishing boat to take us all back to Dublin.

Another problem arose with Irish customs. They claimed that we had removed the balloon from Britain without clearance and had brought it back to Ireland without papers. After a few minutes of that nonsense I called the *Express* reporter and told him the facts. Within the hour, a cabinet minister had ordered the release of the balloon. By nightfall we were reunited with Sloan in the Grand Hotel, where we slept the clock around.

I was ill enough to require medical attention for a week, but Sloan brought news that put me back on my feet. A major storm of near-hurricane velocity was spinning north from the South Atlantic Ocean and would pass west of Ireland, creating great winds headed for northern England. I telephoned Gordon McGregor, president of Air Canada, and asked him to have Canada 2 picked up from Lancaster and flown immediately to Dublin. When the balloon arrived, the same cabinet minister cleared away the importation problems.

With Sloan monitoring the great storm in the airport's radar room, I readied Canada 2 at the same launch site, surrounded by crowds of people, including the Wicklow schoolchildren, who had been given the day off to watch the second historic event. Since I could not exceed the all-up weight of the aerostat without voiding my FAI licence, I decided to go alone and take Jones's weight in extra propane tanks.

The inflation went well and I cast off, planning to climb to 15,000 feet and pick up the predicted forty-mile-an-hour wind. Several aircraft carrying press and television crews circled Canada 2, coming at times dangerously close and even spinning the balloon with their propeller washes. I had left behind all radio equipment and carried a critically heavy load of fuel. I would rely on Phillips in the chase plane, who was in radio contact with Sloan at Dublin airport, to give me visual climb and descend signals. Over my shoulder, I could see the great black storm-clouds racing to catch me.

One hour out, the first news plane left, trailing smoke from an engine that had caught fire. Two hours from Ireland, the last news plane turned away from the onslaught of the storm. Freezing rain began to weigh down the balloon, which required more heat to keep it aloft, depleting my fuel supply even faster. Then the chase plane disappeared, and I was alone. I'd flown through many storms in a plane, but in a balloon you cannot steer and must go with the wind, wherever it takes you. If you're lucky, you can manoeuvre up and down. And a balloon's course is never a straight line: it rises and falls in undulating curves as the air in the bag heats and cools, both from the flame and the different air temperatures through which it passes. What might be measured on a map as fifty miles between two points could double in actual flight travel.

I'd been airborne three hours when the storm engulfed us. In minutes, the bag and I were drenched in cold water that turned into ice as I watched. Applying full power we climbed slowly through the wild dark weather. I could hear the wind screaming against the nylon, canting the bag at a crazy angle. I had no idea where I was, but knew that Sloan, in the darkened radar room at Dublin airport, had me fixed as a blip on a cathode tube. He would know when Canada 2 fell out of the sky.

A blast of wind hit so hard it turned the balloon on its side, causing the brilliant flame to stretch out and eat a large hole in the bag. As I turned the flame down, it went out. To relight it, I turned on the gas and ignited the fumes with an open flame. But a strong wind across the burners dissipated the explosive mixture, and no relight would occur. I tried desperately to start the flame. As a last resort, I climbed on the railing of the gondola, heaved my body upwards to lay it across the two burners, let the cylinders fill with fumes, and then rammed a sparker inside one from underneath and triggered it.

I was kicked in the chest and smothered in flame at the same time. The fire-ball swept across my face and damaged my rubber life-jacket, but the burners were alight and they would heat enough air in the bag to maintain my height. I lost track of time after that; the spinning of the balloon disoriented me. Once more a great wind snuffed out the flame, and again I had to lay my chest across the burners and explode them into life. This time the blast of fire rendered my life-jacket useless. Then I reached the point of exhaustion; I didn't care what happened, as long as the storm stopped and I didn't have to fight any more to stay alive.

Suddenly the chase plane was near me. Phillips waggled its wings, circled once, and was lost again in the enveloping vapours. I felt the fear then, deep inside, and moved to block it before it took control and rendered me incapable of responsible thought and action. Fear, I had learned, was something you must control. It was nothing to be ashamed of but something you faced and accepted. I reminded myself again that fear was physiological, the body's normal way of marshalling its resources to meet a danger.

I was almost out of fuel. When it was gone, I would go down, at the speed of an express train, for the last time. I swore great oaths into the wind that I would keep my word to God never to ask for His help and that no terror could break my pledge. If the cold sea was to be my grave, I would meet it with no debt owing.

"Quitter, quitter, quitter." The storm threw my unspoken thoughts back at me, as a pinprick of conscience stabbed through my rage at heaven. The tiny wound enlarged itself into a desperate need to care for my family. That's when I again tied a slim line from my wrist to the gondola. If the balloon was found, so might my body, and the matter would be laid to rest.

Unknown to me, millions of people were listening to the news reports and waiting, and all police, military, and lifeboat crews on Britain's west coast had been alerted and were poised, ready to help if they could. A police inspector patrolling inland from Whitehaven in northern England had been searching the storm-clouds through binoculars. He had seen the flicker of light from the dying flame as

Canada 2 plunged earthwards and slammed into a 1,400-foot-high cliff in the Cumbrian Mountains. He had seen me thrown out of the gondola and hang by the rope tied to my wrist. I was found later, some distance away from the gondola, face down in a soggy marsh. Together we had flown a flight path of 300 miles and stayed aloft four hours and fifty-five minutes, farther and longer than any hot-air balloon in history. The Irish Sea had been conquered, by Canada, and the twenty-eight world records I had challenged were won.

EPILOGUE

My relationship with Thora had become increasingly strained over my airborne activities, which she felt were extremely dangerous, even though I had withheld from her many of those adventures I considered hazardous. In an effort to restore in her some feeling for me, I decided to give up all endeavours that could possibly cause her concern.

Joanne had married and was raising a family, and Rob had concluded his education with a master's degree in business administration. He had joined Air Canada, fallen in love with a delightful Italian girl, and purchased a new home in Montreal in anticipation of his forthcoming marriage. We saw each other every few weeks, and while he had earned his private pilot's licence, I was continually concerned about his inexperience. I was particularly worried that his aircraft might be flipped on its back in a huge jet's wake turbulence during his landings at Montreal airport, so I spent some time teaching him to recover in flight at very low level from an upside-down position.

I sold the aerobatic airplane I used in air shows, the prototype of the Munro Microplane I had designed and built, my three famous balloons, and my parachuting equipment. Then I disposed of our real-estate holdings and moved to Calgary to begin a new career with Thora and our children, who now numbered three. Rob and I parted, as close friends should, with a touch of sadness and a hoped-for early reunion.

In Calgary I enrolled in university for a year, to broaden my understanding of human nature through philosophy and psychology. I tried to settle down to a sedentary existence, but my relationship with Thora remained stalled at an almost uncommunicative level. Thinking that perhaps Edmonton would be a more vibrant place in which to live, we moved there. The children seemed content, and I took the position of managing director of a national institution and spent my free time with the family. Thora, however, finally decided we should separate.

While I was pondering a course of action, I answered the door to a young man, who introduced himself as a member of the RCMP. Before he could tell me, I knew that Rob was dead. And he was, by his own hand. He had died in a fume-filled car in the garage of the new home in which he would never live with the girl to whom he had given his heart, and who had, at the last moment, rejected it. I flew immediately to Montreal in a state of shock. My final goodbye was to a coffin in a stark room of a crematorium, after which his earthly remains were placed in a square cannister, then borne aloft with great respect and reverence by four of this nation's greatest aviators to the flank of a special mountain on Vancouver's north shore, where we had spent our happiest time. His childhood wish had been granted: he was with the mother he never knew.

I moved into a bachelor apartment and left behind all but my personal possessions.

Roy, Grace, and Rob, whom I had loved, and who had loved me, were gone for all time. Joanne was estranged, while Donald, Janet, and John were in their mother's keeping. I no longer saw any reason for living.

I needed time and space to review my life before I could face the future, so I headed north once again, to the solitude of the taiga. There, I considered the events and influences on my life. I realized I could forgive my father for his wandering ways, for his searches for rainbows that eluded his grasp, and for the rootlessness that was his only legacy to me.

I saw also that my sometimes distorted view of human behaviour was caused partly by the troubles I faced during my early years. It was then warmed by the violence of war and reheated by the dangers I faced daily for over thirty years. My anger came to a full boil when I saw myself being tossed aside by a family I had fought hard to protect and nurture.

As those feelings subsided, I recognized that I had marched to the beat of a different drummer. It wasn't that I wanted to set myself apart from others, but rather that they chose to match their stride to a cadence fit for the spectators of life. I, on the other hand, chose to be a participant. This book is a partial account of that participation.

INDEX